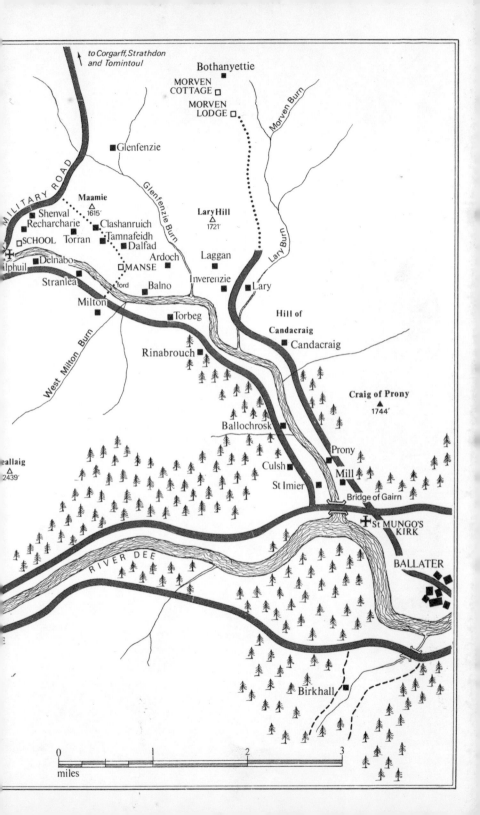

IN MEMORY
LONG

BY THE SAME AUTHOR

THE HILLS OF HOME
DAE YE MIN' LANGSYNE

IN MEMORY LONG

Amy Stewart Fraser

Routledge & Kegan Paul

London, Henley and Boston

First published in 1977
by Routledge & Kegan Paul Ltd
39 Store Street,
London WC1E 7DD,
Broadway House,
Newtown Road,
Henley-on-Thames,
Oxon RG9 1EN and
9 Park Street,
Boston, Mass. 02108, USA
Set in 11 on 13 point Scotch Roman
and printed in Great Britain by
Morrison & Gibb Ltd,
London and Edinburgh

British Library Cataloguing in Publication Data

Fraser, Amy Stewart

In memory long.

1. Fraser, Amy Stewart
I. Title
941.1082′092′4   CT828.F65

ISBN 0-7100-8586-9

Forty years on, growing older and older,
Shorter in wind but in memory long.
                  John Farmer

As one grows older the memory becomes more
vivid and selective, and the images
more jewel-like.
                  Walter de la Mare

CONTENTS

PREFACE

When one has lived a full and active life with home and family and voluntary public service, one looks forward to retirement with mixed feelings, predominantly relief at the prospect of shedding a load of responsibility, of enjoying a measure of relaxation, and having *time* for at least some of the things there has never been time for before. Somewhere I read, 'When you finish with a job, make the break complete; cut off the old life, clean and sharp. If your mind is tired that is the only way, if your mind is still lively, you'll soon find other interests.'

I've often thought I must be a Hobbit. Hobbits, you remember, are fond of music and fireworks; they are inclined to stoutness and the drawing up of genealogies—all true of me and to complete the picture, I spent a couple of rewarding years rustling among the branches of my family tree; then I turned to writing.

I felt it would be a good thing to tell my grandchildren, and all who come after them, what life was like in a remote Highland glen in those far-off days before radio and television, the days of oil lamps and candles, as necessities, not, as in these days, mainly for decorative purposes; when we *walked* everywhere, on heather tracks and unmade roads, when a

motor-car was a rarity, a gramophone a novelty, and when we, as children, got enormous pleasure from a painted rubber ball, a hoop, or a skipping-rope. I began jotting things down as I recalled them; memories came flooding back, and at last the subject matter was arranged in chapters to my satisfaction. I called the book *The Hills of Home*, from those nostalgic lines of Robert Louis Stevenson,

'Be it granted to me to behold you again,
Hills of Home!'

When it was about to be published, my good friends, my publishers, warmly approved my wish that a copy should be sent to the Queen, and I wrote to ask her if she would graciously accept it. It may not be generally known that every one of the many letters she receives is given the personal attention of the Queen, who either makes notes on it or tells her Private Secretary what to do about it; so, when a letter arrives saying, 'I am commanded by the Queen to say . . .' it is quite literally true. The reply to my letter stated, 'I am commanded by the Queen to say that it will give her great pleasure to accept a copy of your book, *The Hills of Home*, which is about a part of the world she knows and loves so well', and, 'to enhance the value of the book', she requested me to inscribe on it a simple message and my signature.

The project was immediately put in hand, and the result was a handsome volume beautifully bound in royal blue leather, on the title page of which I proudly inscribed my signature and my message . . . 'To remind Your Majesty of Glen Gairn and your Highland hills, With my loyal greetings, Amy Stewart Fraser.'

This book is for my many friends who read *The Hills of Home* and asked for more.

'All this still legible in memory's page
And still to be so to my latest age.'
William Cowper

I am indebted to Malcolm Muggeridge for permission to quote him on page 131; to Ella Fletcher for the privilege of consulting her kinsman's *Tales and Memories of Cromar*; to

Walter Duncan, Colin Gibson, Rosalind Messenger, and Douglas Sutherland for kind permission to quote from their books, and to the *Aberdeen Journal* (now incorporated within *The Press and Journal*) for liberal use of 'Notes and Queries'.

In spite of careful enquiry I have been unable to trace the owners of certain copyrights and beg forgiveness from anyone whose rights have been overlooked.

CHAPTER I

A MAN O' THE MEARNS

My father, born in 1863, was a Lowe of Laurencekirk, the parish anciently called Conveth in that district of old Kincardineshire known as the Howe o' the Mearns. The derivation of its name since then is obvious, the kirk having been dedicated to St Laurence. The Mearns, lying between the North Esk and Aberdeenshire, guarded the great highways to the North in days long past; the Men o' the Mearns were then of some consequence and to be one of them was to feel the heartening warmth of local pride.

My father attended the village school, and in due course became a pupil-teacher under the scheme inaugurated in 1846 to cope with the problem of mass education in towns and villages which had arisen from industrialisation. It was a route to higher education for able scholars. With his younger brother, Tom, for company he often climbed the Garvock Hill, refreshed by the caller air and the sight of the broad fertile plain below. There was Halkerton Wood which took its name from the hawks that falconers carried on their wrists; nearby, he could picture the King's Castle and Royal hunting-ground, and probably a marsh with many kinds of water-fowl for the King's sport. The name of the Royal huntsmen, the falconers,

is kept alive in the family name of Lord Kintore whose seat is not far away. My father spent happy years as a student at St Andrews University, first at St Salvator's College, and then at St Mary's, founded in 1537, which has been a theological college since the time of the Reformation. He loved its quad, that green and quiet place, its fantails, and the holm oak with its massive branches. I like to go there sometimes and walk where he once walked.

In those days, the university's comparatively small numbers enabled every man to know all his fellows, and every professor to know each of his students. Distinctions between teacher and student were kept to the lecture-room; the common meeting-ground was the professor's house for tea, or the links for golf, described by one student as 'a great leveller' . . . not that studious men had much time for golf . . . it was not of them that was written

> Gowfin', gowfin' a' the day,
> Daein' nae work ava,
> Rinnin' aboot wi' a bag o' sticks
> Aifter a wee bit ba'!

Two years before my father went to College, the Rev. M. B. Reid, a pioneer of the movement to provide Scots students with a collection of fine songs for singing, published a small book of songs for St Andrews men. My father possessed a copy of that book in crimson hard covers with gold lettering which I remember well. It often brought to mind his favourite songs of student days, 'The Yang-tsi-kiang' and 'Upidee-i-da'. Thomas Davidson wrote the words of the first song; his story, told by Dr James Brown, became a Scots classic. The song was composed after a train-journey in the company of a douce old body who proudly told him that her son was a soldier 'far away on the banks of the Yang-tsi-kiang'. (My father, too, loved to enter into conversation with his travelling companions and to entertain their wee nickums, as he called them. He would take littlins on his knee and amuse them, disregarding sticky fingers and biscuit-crumbs.)

[2]

Various versions of 'Upidee' were sung at student gatherings, all of them parodies of Longfellow's 'Excelsior'.

A great friend of my father's student days was Millar Patrick, who was the main inspiration and indefatigable instigator of the production of *The Scottish Students Song Book*, of which my mother had an early copy. Lois Millar Patrick, his daughter, told me that she and her brother were brought up on tales of the sing-songs at St Andrews University, and on *The Students Song Book* and its eventual production, for which mammoth work their father was awarded his doctorate. Dr Millar Patrick went on from Student Songs to the Revisal of the Church Hymnary; after he retired he visited the United States on behalf of the Hymn Society, and later published an important work on Four Centuries of Scottish Psalmody.

During the Long Vacation between April and October, my father tutored young men in such subjects as Mathematics and Greek History, in preparation for their entry to a university. He also did a vast amount of study, setting himself a fixed amount of daily reading. His great joy was to explore the countryside. One day he made a pilgrimage to Edzell Castle, signing his name in the Visitors' Book, in which, sixty years later I sought in vain to find it, as early volumes had been removed to a place of safety. That day he spent long hours in the Pleasance and Tower House, wandering alone among the ruins. It was for him a day's outing from Laurencekirk, trains being infrequent and slow, and at either end of his trip he had a considerable distance to walk. He recorded his impressions at some length in his diary, which all his life he kept with meticulous care, noting as well every ha'penny of his income and expenditure. He 'put himself through College' from 1881 to 1888, that is, he paid his way entirely by his own efforts, and when he graduated Bachelor of Divinity he placed on record his total expenditure for that period, viz ... £244.17.1½.

When in 1973 I met Douglas C. Mason, the writer and authority on St Andrews, he was eager to read my father's diaries of which he had heard, and was disappointed to learn

that, owing to deterioration through damp, they had been destroyed, I being unaware of the excellent modern methods of restoring old documents. An earlier student, Duncan Dewar of Acharn on Loch Tay, also kept an accurate account of his expenditure during his years (1819–27) at the University. The manuscript was handed down to his nephew, the Rev. John Dewar of Kilmartin, Argyll, who gave it to Professor Scott Lang. In 1926, when the manuscript was a hundred years old, it was published, and remains a valuable chronicle of the life of a student in the first quarter of the nineteenth century.

In 1884 my father spent the summer months in the Orkney Islands, his eldest brother, William, being minister of Hoy, the second largest island among the Orkneys. To get there must have been a tedious journey to his sister, Jessie, who was keeping house for William, but probably not to my father who enjoyed every new experience . . . first, there was the long train journey from Laurencekirk to Aberdeen and Inverness, back to Fort George, and by boat to Fortrose where he was engaged to preach next day. He then went to Cromarty over the Black Isle and by ferry across the Beauly Firth. With his brother he visited crofts in the scattered parish. Everywhere they were warmly welcomed and, in turn, the crofters received hospitality at the Manse of Hoy. My father preached again on the Black Isle, at the quiet Royal Burgh of Fortrose, and several times in the little kirk at Hoy. He worked very hard in the garden which had been sadly neglected. Walking on the cliffs at Rackwick Bay, a place of wild beauty on the Atlantic shore, and visiting Cromarty from time to time he delighted in exploring the region, and in collecting oak-ferns which he found high up on the Sholty Burn, climbing Ward Hill which is noted for its rare plants, and gazing at the Old Man of Hoy, that impressive rock-stack which can be seen from far-away Caithness across the Pentland Firth. He paid one visit to the coloured cliffs of Berry Head, and sailed to the North Souters Caves, covering the ground along the fulmar-haunted cliffs at Rosemarkie, and the fossil-bearing beds at Eathie Burn made famous by the geologist, Hugh Miller, who was born in a

thatched cottage at Cromarty. At Rackwick he found the Dwarfie Stone, associated with Scott's novel *The Pirate,* and on which Hugh Miller carved his initials. At the end of his visit my father 'boated' from Hoy across to Stromness, staying overnight, and leaving next morning by the *St Clair* for Aberdeen. It was a stormy passage and he was very seasick. From Aberdeen he returned by train to Laurencekirk and at once began to prepare for the opening of a new session at St Mary's College. Years later, as a girl in my teens, I learned from some of his contemporaries, who were surprised to find him ministering in a remote parish, that he had been a distinguished student of Greek Theology and Philosophy, and had gained many of the highest prizes. When he was twenty he delivered lectures on the Messianic Prophecies and on Diogenes of Apollonia, and remained a keen student of the Athenian Empire. In 1917 he was still being called upon to examine, in New Testament Greek, young men who were not yet licensed ministers. 'His command of the English language', wrote one eminent cleric, 'enables him to express his ideas with great facility. Rarely does one meet a man so well acquainted with every department of theological study.'

In 1891, after a period as an assistant minister in Stirling, he was ordained to the Quoad Sacra parish of Glen Gairn, known affectionately to my sister and me, as we grew up, simply as The Glen. (Quoad Sacra literally means 'as far as concerns sacred matters' of a parish disjoined for ecclesiastical purposes only.)

At one time the three parishes of Glenmuick, Tullich, and Glen Gairn were distinct, each with its own separate kirk, the ruins of which are still to be seen at Tullich and Fit o' Gairn, and a portion of the old Glenmuick kirk still stands as part of the wall of the kirkyard. Historically, the Tullich ruins are the most interesting. Some sculptured stones leaning against the north wall indicate that there must have been a place of worship on that spot for 1,500 years.

The names of two saints of the sixth and seventh centuries

are associated with the district. St Kentigern, or St Mungo, was a missionary in Glen Gairn; Tullich was dedicated to St Nathalan who, according to legend, commanded his flock, after a winter of famine, to sow sand, and was rewarded for his faith by a bountiful harvest. Sluievannochie, 'the moor of blessing', got its name from this miracle, and, in my childhood, the coach-driver, who lived there, was known as Auld Sluie.

It can never be correct to write the name Glen Gairn in one word as is sometimes done. Gairn relates to the river and the valley alone; Glen is an appellative, common to a class. It is no more correct to join them in one word than it would be to write in that way Ben Nevis, Glen Nevis, Loch Muick or the Larig Ghru.

Before there was a kirk in Glen Gairn the parishioners used to attend a cramped mission chapel at Rinloan, and on Communion Sundays joined the congregation in the village church at Ballater. On these occasions it was uncomfortably crowded, we are told, though it had been built to hold 800 persons. In these days of partly-filled churches, it is astounding to read of a congregation of over 800 souls, many of whom had travelled many miles on foot, by pony-trap, and on farm-carts to be present at the Sacrament. A new church was built in Ballater in 1801, a year after the little kirk was erected in the Glen and dedicated to St Mungo. My father conducted a Centenary Service there in 1900. Intended originally to seat a hundred, like other old Scots churches it has windows on one side only, and two at the west end where the bell still hangs within its stone belfry, and the rope runs right down the outside of the gable. At the east end is a blocked-up window which dates back to the days when this was done in dwellings and kirks to avoid payment of window-tax. For many years, there was a wooden stable in the grounds for the accommodation of the horses of visiting preachers.

The pulpit in my father's time was said to have come either from the pre-Reformation kirk of St Mungo's at Fit o' Gairn, or from the old kirk at Tullich. There is no pulpit in the kirk now. I have always hoped to discover that what I still think

of as my father's kirk is one of those designed by Thomas
Telford, better known for his bridges, in the 1820s and earlier,
but can find no information on this point. It certainly belongs
to Telford's period, and resembles kirks known to have been
designed by him in his capacity as architect and engineer to
various Parliamentary Commissions.

The Church of Scotland, happily, is aware of the need to
preserve its older kirks, and I am content to know that this
small sanctuary, beautifully cared for, in its peaceful setting
among the hills, has been designated a building of historical
and architectural interest, and that every effort will be made
to preserve it. The parish in my father's time was in the
Presbytery of Kincardine o' Neil; he regularly attended meetings there, the oldest village on Deeside, which was a flourishing community in the twelfth century. He quickly made himself familiar with the history of his new environment, especially
in Church matters. He was particularly impressed by the fact
that the Rev. James Robertson, who was minister of the
combined parishes from 1699 to 1747 had passed unscathed
through the troublous times of both Jacobite Risings. He
learned that, at one time, ministers had to be able to preach
in the Gaelic, and the settlement of one minister had been
disputed on account of his lack of that language. The matter
was referred to the General Assembly in Edinburgh, and there
the 'fathers and brethren' decided that a knowledge of the
Gaelic was no longer essential for a minister in that part of
the country. It appeared that Gaelic-speaking folk in Glen
Gardyne, the old name for Glen Gairn, were in the habit of
attending public worship in the old kirk at Crathie, where a
gallery had been specially built to accommodate them. My
father's parish extended far beyond the valley of Gairn, over
to Micras in Crathie, down to the Braes o' Cromar under the
shadow of Morven and Culblean, and up to Loch Builg (pronounced Boolig) between the Broon Coo and Ben A'an, which
is one of the giants of the Cairngorms, easily recognisable by
the granite tors on its skyline. By its geographical position,
Cromar should have been in the parish of Coldstone, and

Micras was situated geographically in Crathie, but for some reason these places had long ago been attached to Glenmuick, and so became part of the new Quoad Sacra parish of Glen Gairn. In the Howe o' Cromar, on what was once a lonely stretch of moor, now stands a thirteen-foot-high chunk of granite, which serves to remind passing travellers who pause to inspect its stark simplicity, that here, under Byron's 'Morven of snow', was fought the Battle of Culblean, which long after Bannockburn, finally consolidated the independence of Scots as a nation.

The first letter my father received as a parish minister was from James Abercrombie, his wife, Isabella, and five of their sons, all full communicants and signatories, obviously a family of some consequence and fully aware of their rights of representation in the parish. In the letter they jointly nominated their neighbour, Charles Rattray of Wester Micras, as an elder of Micras district. There have been Abercrombies in Crathie for generations; one James, I remember, was head gamekeeper to King George V at Balmoral.

Soon after his ordination in July 1891, my father held a class for young communicants and prepared twelve lads and lasses for their First Communion. They attended the Fast Day Service of Preparation on the Thursday prior to Communion Sunday, when they received the right hand of fellowship from ministers and elders, and were then said to have 'jined', that is, to have been admitted to church membership. Seventy communicants gathered round the Lord's Table on the Communion Sunday, a striking thought in view of today's woeful depopulation of the Glen. No unnecessary work was done on Sundays in those days, but, before my father's time, there was an occasion in Cromar, related by Donald Farquharson, when, after a very wet week when stooks were standing sodden with rain, Sunday dawned bright and sunny; the minister declared from the pulpit that Providence had at last bestowed an opportunity of saving the crops, and it was their plain duty to seize that opportunity. He then pronounced the benediction and sent the congregation home to their waiting fields. One

[8]

small boy, who saw the day apparently being observed as an ordinary day of the week, began to whistle and was reproved by his father, who said that though the minister had given advice to save the crops, that did not make it right to break the Sabbath Day. Whistling was only permitted if the tune was a psalm. The Fast Day used to be known as 'Whistling Sunday', but, there again, there was dispensation only for psalm-tunes. The wisdom of the minister's well-intentioned advice on that Sunday in question was not justified, according to Donald, for Monday dawned bright and fair, and work in fields went merrily on. Those who had refrained from labour the previous day secured their crops in prime condition while many who had yielded to the minister's law of necessity were compelled to turn over their heated stacks, or worse still, to haul the stuff out again to the fields to dry. In Cromar my father visited a clachan of thatched houses which, like most of the dwellings in the neighbourhood, had large open fireplaces with pots and kettles hanging from crooks and chains on a swey. At both the but and the ben end there was a recessed bed called a box-bed. The door which enclosed it in daytime swung outwards and remained open at night . . . even so, light and ventilation were imperfect, yet occupants lived to a good age. Within living memory, a centenarian died in the box-bed in which as an invalid she had spent the greater part of her life.

The old Scots dish known as Fastyn Cock, made with oatmeal and suet and shaped like a fowl, was boiled in a cloth and eaten on Fastern's Eve, the night before Lent began. Cock fights were held to celebrate the festival, and were common in the eighteenth century, as a means of raising school funds. They had long ceased to be held in Cromar, but Donald Farquharson's mother, born in 1815, told her family how, for big fights, every bairn was required to take a fighting cock to school, and hold it in his or her oxter till it was its turn to fight. There were no lessons in school that day. As many as thirty cocks were pitted against each other in the presence of

a large gathering which included local gentry. The best fighting cock was called the King, the second best the Queen, the next best the Knave; any which refused to fight were called 'fougie'. Those that were killed became the property of the school 'maister' who feasted his family on well-boiled fowl for days on end . . . a pleasant change from their normal diet of porridge. Cock fighting over, the scholars were regaled with home-brewed ale. Donald's mother remembered an occasion when there was no suitable bird for her to take to school, and one of good fighting quality was borrowed from a neighbour who, anxious for it to put up a good show, fed it for the fight on a mixture of oatmeal and whisky, components of the renowned Athole Brose. The little girl marched away proudly to put her champion in the lists and to her delight and the great satisfaction of the owner, it 'came off the field in glorious triumph'.

A story is told in Edinburgh that when the Duchess of Kent visited the city she wanted to sample some specially fine biscuits and there were none in the hotel. A waiter hurried round to the baker's house behind his shop, but it was Sunday and the baker declined to do business on the Sabbath Day. Far from being annoyed, the Duchess expressed admiration for a man who stuck to his Christian principles. Next day she not only placed a weekly order, but she told the Queen and she, too, became a customer. (The Queen was Victoria, and the Duchess her mother.)

Donald remembers a day when his father driving his family in a horse and cart near Abergeldie stood aside to allow the carriage of the Duchess of Kent to cross the narrow bridge, and the Duchess sent her footman to see the little family safely across. That bridge must have given way at a later date for, when I was a child, it was well known that before the Queen had the suspension bridge erected the crossing of Dee had to be made in a kind of cradle. The sad day was often recalled when a young gamekeeper, Peter Franklin, and Babbie Broon, 'the Floo'er o' Deeside', his bride of a few hours, were swinging

across when the rope broke, both were thrown into the river and drowned. Years later, Crathie was again plunged in sadness when two small Rattray brothers were drowned in a spate in Monaltrie Burn. Sandy, the three year old, was found the same day; Jimmy his ten-year-old brother, two days later, on an islet in Dee opposite Cambus o' May. The Queen was much distressed at the tragedy, and on the day of the boys' funeral, drove to the West Lodge of the Castle to watch in silent sympathy the pathetic procession wend its way to God's Acre behind the Manse with its single window looking on to the kirkyard. In years to come she was to have that window fitted with opaque glass so that her visits to the grave of John Brown would not be overlooked. It was said in Crathie that on at least one occasion two other queens knelt there with her.

I was nine years old when May Ritchie, a bonny lass in her twenties, was drowned in Torran Burn, which, like Monaltrie Burn, was normally very small but a torrent when in spate. William Duguid of Tannafeidh saw her body tossed like that of a child over the waterfall into swollen Gairn. He ran to the bank to try to grasp her, and actually touched her before she was borne swiftly away. Weeks passed; it was feared she had been carried out to sea, but her body was recovered from an islet in Dee, not far from the place where little Jimmy Rattray had been found so many years ago. Such tragedies cast a gloom over the entire neighbourhood; sincere sympathy was felt in every home for the sorrowing families.

Seeking information on the occupied homesteads in his parish, my father learned that as far back as 1676, at a Baron Baillie Court, Calum Macgregor of Ardoch was brought before the Court for wounding Alastair Coutts at Stranreich in Glen Gardyne, which he read as Stranlea. Calum had drawn his sword and cut the other man twice in the head, in the left eye, and in the left arm. Even in those days this was too much, and he was fined £50 Scots money, and ordered to present himself before the Court upon twenty days' warning should his victim die of his wounds. In 1634 Recharcharie and Torran

were reckoned to be part of the property of Malcolm Macgregor of Dalfad, and Sleoch, Auchentoul, Tamnafeidh, and Inverenzie were all mentioned in documents dated 1726, when the Glen was still called the Parochin of Glen Gardyne. Dalnabo and Glenfenzie appeared in the same document, as did the now forgotten place-names of Renovocatin, Rhinochat, Dubh Chlais (pronounced Doo Clash), Pitfiantach, and Rinabrouch, with its haugh land once again cultivated after an untold number of years, and the larach still visible from the road. Renatton, 'the shieling among the etnach', once belonged to the Macdonalds of St Martin's in Perthshire, and in their private burying-ground there are inscriptions on two of the stones, one to the memory of Christina Farquharson, wife of James Macdonald who died in 1781, the other to John Macdonald who died in 1776, and Helen, a Grant of Tullichmacarrick, his wife.

My father crossed the Hill of Lary from Mullach to Bothanyettie, to visit George Coutts, a shepherd who lived with his wife and family at the foot of Morven on Gairn side. There were numerous larachs nearby, fast disappearing under juniper and heather, where there had been a thriving community, a clachan which Meggie Mitchell, over ninety years of age, remembered well. There had been several meal-mills in the Glen at one time; the Mill O' Prony still operated, but those at Stranlea, Laggan, Easter Tullichmacarrick, and Kirkstile had ceased to function. Above Gairnshiel a drystane dyke still winds up the hill. These dykes to this day form some of the boundaries between one hill-farm and another, but the old skill in building them with no mortar as a binding agent has largely been lost. (It is now carefully fostered in the Stewartry of Kirkcudbright.) The art lay in choosing stones of suitable size, packing them without much regard for regularity, filling in the spaces between the big stones with smaller ones, and keeping the dyke in an approximate straight line. Built of locally gathered stones, they may still be seen, clinging, as at Gairnshiel, to the side of some steep hill whose contours they follow with incredible exactitude. They have

withstood the elements for long years, giving shelter to flocks during winter gales and reducing the risk of them straying to be lost on the hills. Like drystane dyking, thatching is a dying craft in the north, more's the pity. The sight of a craftsman renewing the thatch on some old stone but-an'-ben has not been seen in the Glen for eighty years or longer.

On the near side of the brig at Gairnshiel, where the road climbs along the lower rocky slopes of Craig o' Tullich, stood Kirkstile, a tiny cottage guarding the approach to the kirk, its tarred roof secured from winter's gales by strong ropes or fencing-wire laid over it and weighted with large stones. The Coutts boys, who all wore the kilt for everyday, with celluloid collars and bow ties on Sunday, lived there with their sister, Maggie, who from her early teens had devotedly looked after her father and brothers after the death of their mother. Of the old mill on the hillside behind their cottage much could still be seen. The walls still stood, and the lade which drew its supply of water from the dam, now overgrown with reeds, was visible at the roadside near Recharcharie. The immense granite mill-stones lay within the crumbling walls; powered by the mill-race, they had ground oats and barley into meal for the 'daily-bread' of oatcake and barley bannocks and porridge for many a family.

From his upbringing in the Howe o' the Mearns my father knew all about feeing-markets to which farm-servants went to renew their half-yearly contracts, or to make new ones with other farmers. 'Are ye fee't, or are ye bidin'?' was the general greeting, and when agreement was reached there was the Fair for their entertainment, with swing-boats, shooting-galleries, and 'Hairy Marys' to be knocked back at three for a penny, with a coconut or a woolly monkey as the prize. There were trays of gey cheuch gundy, ging'bread horses, and dollops of sticky dates for sale, and all the cheap knick-knacks that were hawked round the country fairs. He was knowledgeable on such matters as the rotation of crops, and could intelligently discuss seasonal work with his farmer-parishioners. He was familiar with the setting of any ferm-toun, which in Scotland

means not a village or a town but a farm-steading and adjacent buildings. He often sought out the menfolk at work in the byres where the nowt were ranged two to a stall, separated from each other by a yard or two of space, each set of two separated from the next two by the traviss. Their necks were encircled with chains which gave them room to move their heads up to the hakes, or down to the trochs when the orra loon came in with a barrow-load of neeps, halved and quartered, and tipped them into the trochs on the prongs of a graip.

In olden times, when the only winter food for stock was the hay that had been harvested in early summer, most of the cattle and sheep had to be killed in the autumn, for only a bare minimum of beasts could be kept alive, and the meat was salted and eaten during the winter months. Then along came Lord Townshend, who became familiarly known as Turnip Townshend, for he cultivated turnips in fields as he had seen them grown in Holland.

Scotland took up the idea . . . England followed. Turnips provided good feeding for beasts when other feed was scarce; it was no longer necessary to kill off beasts in the back-end. Crofting was to all intents and purposes a communal way of life. Many tasks were shared, such as peat-cutting, sheep-clipping and dipping, turnip-singling, and, of course, the hairst. As bairns grew up the croft could not support them all, and they had to leave home to seek their fortunes, or at least to 'better themselves'. Professor Douglas Young, one of the great Scots of his generation, once remarked to me, 'the best of the lads became policemen, and the lassies became nurses . . . they all did well and I never heard of one who turned back.' My father spoke of his boyhood and the occasional ploughing-match which was a social event, in preparation for which kitchen deems set about trimming last year's Sunday hat, and farmers' wives aimed at acquiring something new from the village store which stocked 'a' thin' fae a preen tae a braw new goon'. The clash was all of the coming event, with recollections of matches langsyne, and when the day came

round it was observed as a general holiday. Ploughs shone with fresh paint, harness was brightly polished, horses' hides were gleaming, and ribbons and brasses much in evidence. Not even the torture of a hard collar could quench the high spirits of the loons in their Sunday jaikets. The judges from another district looked as important as they felt; competitors took a preliminary stroll over the ground, removing the odd stone that might spoil a furrow, then the match started. All eyes were on the contestants, audible comments freely made. The men ploughed steadily on, grasping the stilts, each trusting in his ability to keep a straight course, the older men striding on boldly, the younger placing their feet with care and trying to give the impression that this was no new experience. Solemnly the judges examined the finished furrows, gave their decision and departed before adverse opinions on their ability, or the lack of it, to judge, reached their ears. The winner and runner-up were given three hearty cheers, their prizes were admired, and at the end of the day there was the usual dance in the barn, with fiddles, moothies, and melodeons to provide the music.

Spring was a busy time for all on the land, all the work being done with horses, and every pair of hands employed. The dung-heap in the farmyard dwindled as carts were loaded. One man filled a cart using a large four-pronged fork called a graip, another took the load to the ploughed field, moving down each drill, throwing off dung in forkfuls. Sometimes the bairns followed with smaller forks, spreading the dung along the drills.

Corn was sown by a man with a canvas creel slung round his neck and shoulders. The rhythmic swing of the arms, in and out of the creel in a sweeping movement, in a steady methodical stride up and down till the whole field was covered was fascinating to watch. Then came the harrowing and when the heavy stone-roller was taken over a field the horses' hooves made an attractive pattern on the smooth surface of the soil. Then followed a period of anxious watching for the breer . . . the first green shoots to appear. The whole agricultural year

led up to the hairst in September or October after the grouse-driving season was over, and loons got new boots for school, and new suits for Sunday with the money they had earned on the hill.

In 1810, the scythe was introduced by William Anderson, a farmer in Hutton o' Fintry, but for many years the old shearing-hook was not superseded. The value of a day's work at the hairst used to be calculated by the number of thraives cut. A thraive consisted of two stooks of twelve sheaves each. After the introduction of the scythe the most experienced men did the cutting, women made the bands and bound the sheaves, then the younger men stooked the sheaves. A stooker, they said, was entitled to claim a kiss from the gatherer if the band slipped; when the gatherer was a bonny lass such forfeits occurred with amazing frequency.

It was a Scots minister, the Rev. Patrick Bell of Carmyllie who, in 1826, invented the first reaping-machine with a sheer-action cutter. I can remember when the harvest-field was a busy scene, with teams of workers following the horse-drawn reaper, gathering the sheaves, tying them firmly and setting up the stooks. The Sunday when every field was dotted with neatly-spaced stooks ready for 'leading', was known as Stookie Sunday. No matter what year is claimed as the Year of the Short Corn, 1826, 1868, 1872, 1881, or 1911, each a disastrous hairst, the story is always revived that the craws had to get doon on their knees to peck it. (The K in knees was often pronounced, which somehow emphasised the wry humour and drawing of the long bow.) Rumours have acquired authenticity with repetition down the years; some declare the corn was too short to be cut and had to be pulled by hand, others that it was less than a foot high, and many assert that soil appeared in the meal after milling the short grain. My father always referred to 1826 as The Year of The Short Corn, and spoke of the 'anxious thirties and hungry forties' that followed. After a bad hairst in the Glen in 1892, the laird, Alexander Haldane Farquharson of Invercauld, in the following Spring sent to every farming tenant on his estate a gift of seed-corn, and my

father wrote a letter of grateful thanks on behalf of them all. The following lines, by J. M. Caie, express the bewilderment of a heart-sore small farmer in Aberdeenshire, who, unable to afford machinery and to keep up with the times has, after close on forty years, to give up his farm:

> I've vrocht the fermie, man an' loon,
> For twa nineteens an' a bittock mair;
> I've ploo'ed the lan' an' keepit the toon,
> Bit noo I maun gang, an' it's sair, sair.
> They tell me I'm ahin the times,
> Jist splatterin' aboot here,
> Like a stirk lair't i' the moss,
> Makin' naethin' ava bit a foul soss.
> Me a fermer! Tyach!
> That fairly gars them lauch.
> It's a' my ain wyte, they say,
> Aye stickin' tae the aul' wey;
> (The peer aul' doiter gomeril, warkin' wi' horse
> He fairly maun be fey!)
> Frae hame an' ferm I be't tae gang,
> Altho', wae's me, I'm terrible laith;
> Bit here's the en' o' a richt aul' sang,
> Sae ferm an' hame, gweedbye tae ye baith.

Winters in the Cairngorms can be the worst in Britain. People who have never been on the hills in winter have no idea how severe conditions can be, even in the lower ranges. Shepherds in the Glen may still have many weary nights on the hills, when sudden blizzards rage round the homesteads, and snow drifts with the wind and effaces well-known landmarks. Snowstorms may come unexpectedly, as in April 1975, when the lambing season was at its height and the loss of yowes and lambs was very heavy. Shepherds floundered in snow-drifts up to their necks, and with the aid of their crooks, floundered out again; battling against blinding snow, the dreaded 'blin'drift'; gasping for breath they continued to stumble forward with no other thought than the welfare of the

sheep and lambs. These men live by the shepherds' calendar, the normal seasons of lambing, clipping, breeding. Yowes and lambs are brought down from the hills for clipping, usually done in the warm days of July and August so that the sheep, divested of their heavy fleeces, will not be liable to catch cold. In my childhood this was done by hand-shears in the open air for the best light. The air filled with their bleating, the struggling sheep resigned themselves to the indignity of being fleeced, and looking surprised and rather ludicrous, ran off to join the others. Dipping took place a few weeks later, when neighbours helped, and an interested policeman watched the procedure, as the law then demanded.

Seeing a shepherd like Charlie Anderson sitting on the hill-side at Rinabrouch on the Torbeg Brae, with his collies Toss, Glen, Tweed, or Spark stretched out at his side, a stranger might have been forgiven for thinking, 'Some folks have an easy life.' There he sat, his hands clasped over the crook of his cromach and his chin resting on them, while sheep cropped the short grass around him. In actual fact he had every sheep under close observation. Jock Murison once told my father that in order to make a complete survey of his flock he might 'traivel' twenty miles or more over the steep slopes of Morven, out at dawn in the lambing season, climbing to the top, moving sheep down as he descended, his object being to spot a yowe on its back which could not right itself, or one needing help to give birth, or a lamb in difficulties; later in the day he would move them all up the hill again. Jock never felt lonely; he might have said with Walter de la Mare

> Marvellous happy it was to be
> Alone, and yet not solitary.

All around him were familiar sounds, the bleating of yowes and their lambs, the chatter of hill burns, the wind in the trees, and the wild crying of curlew and plover. To unobservant folk one sheep is very like another but the true shepherd, like Charlie and Jock, can tell each one apart. Times have changed since their day when wages were low and a shepherd had only

500 sheep to look after. Nowadays a man must manage up to 900 hill-sheep for it to be an economic proposition, and stock must be hardy enough to live out on the hill with the minimum of management. The best lambs are kept for breeding when they are a year and a half old. In September sheep are 'gathered' in order to pick out the old yowes which are too old for the hills but can be kept for breeding on low ground, but before that there is the July clipping and dosing and then the big gathering for the August lamb sales. Shepherds are weather-wise; they know that stormy weather is at hand when sea-birds fly inland, when swallows fly low, and sheep huddle under bushes and in the lee of drystane dykes. Fair weather is heralded by a grey sky in the morning and a heavy dew. They expect windy weather when clouds are ragged with a hard edge, and the sky at sunset is bright yellow. In my father's flock were a number of gamekeepers.

There were at Renatton Harry Michie, his son Sandy, and grandson, Young Harry, all dressed alike in tweeds made by a local tailor from a roll specially woven for the Laird of Invercauld and kept for the exclusive use of Invercauld keepers on both sides of the hill. They had fore-an'-aft hats, knickerbockers, Norfolk jackets and spats. Young Harry was responsible for rearing pheasants in early summer, going round farms in search of clockin' hens, paying half-a-crown for each. Clockers were returned to their owners when the pheasant chicks had been successfully reared. Old Harry lived to the venerable age of ninety-five. During his long service he met many distinguished men. He had attended on the moors every one of the Prime Ministers of Britain since the passing of the Reform Bill, and had also attended the Prince of Wales, later King Edward VII, with whom he was a great favourite, and from whom he received many marks of kindness. He twice visited Sandringham at the Prince's invitation. His daughter was housekeeper to Queen Victoria at Osborne. His son, Sandy, was a gentle-voiced 'leading elder' of the kirk, with the manners of a courtier and a quiet smile. It was he who accompanied my father on parochial visits when he first arrived in

his parish. The keeper at Corndavon (Old Lundy), Macpherson at Loch Builg, and Donald Fraser at Gairnshiel were also employed by the Laird of Invercauld.

Mrs Cargill, now well over eighty, remembers that when she was a girl living with her parents at Crathienaird, she used to traivel three days a week carrying letters and 'messages' to outlying glens. Every Saturday she went to the lonely lodge on the shore of Loch Builg to take Macpherson his weekly bottle of whisky and half a dozen 'butteries'. He was a dour man and seldom made contact with his neighbours, but now and again, with his dog for company, he went down to Crathie to post a parcel of stones to an Aberdeen jeweller who paid him well for his find. The Cairngorm stones were of an unusual bluish tint and, when cut and polished, were very beautiful. Macpherson never divulged the location of the lode he had discovered among the high hills, and it has not been found to this day.

Heather-burning in spring is still part of a keeper's duties, requiring strict control at all times for a change of wind can suddenly rise and sweep the fire swiftly uphill over a large area, or blow the fire horizontally along the moor in great gusts, so there must always be a band of competent men to watch it and keep it from spreading. I recall seeing Donald come staggering home one afternoon, sweat-stained, exhausted from coping with such a blaze, in agony from cramp, too weak to remove his singed and blackened clothing. Our childish chatter was silenced while, awe-stricken, we heard his groans in the adjoining bedroom where his wife ministered to him with hot soothing cloths on his pain-wracked limbs, and probably rubbed them with embrocation or horse-liniment which was a great standby. Muir-burning is done systematically. Once I gave Davidson, a keeper at Rinloan, a colour photograph of the Glen hills and he could tell me exactly when the picture had been taken by looking at the patchwork colours on the moors. 'We burned that bit that year', he observed, pointing to a faded patch. Burning must normally be completed by

April, for by then grouse and other hill-birds are beginning to nest; there are exceptions, when there have been late winter storms as in April 1975.

In August the shooting season opens with grouse. The dogs used in walking up the grouse are usually pointers or setters, trained from the age of eight weeks to find game by scent, worked against the wind and a joy to watch at work. Grouse are sensitive to changes in the weather, sheltering from wind on the leeside of the hill, and in bracken on sunny days, so a keeper must note the direction of the wind and plan beats accordingly. To bring down a grouse when the birds are whirring over the moors with their startled cry of 'Go back! Go back!' as the beaters waving white flags send them rocketing over the butts at over 60 miles an hour, takes good shooting and a lot of practice, as well as unspoken approbation, or otherwise, from a silent loader.

Installed in his first charge in July my father received no money till November, and he was thankful to have a little 'put by' on which to live for the first six months of his ministry, and to be able to accede to the blunt request to 'head the list with a guinea' when farmers came collecting cash to provide a worthy wedding-gift for their much-respected laird. He joined in the general rejoicing when Colonel Alexander Haldane Farquharson, grandfather of the present laird, married the beautiful Zoe Musgrave, whose family has owned for centuries the fabulous Luck of Eden Hall, a precious goblet fashioned by some Eastern glass-blower. Legend says it was stolen from the fairies by a butler who surprised them dancing round a well in the garden. Enraged, they warned him

> If e'er this cup should break or fall
> Farewell the Luck of Eden Hall!

Eden Hall, near Penrith, has gone, but the Luck of Eden Hall has survived; the 700-years-old goblet is safe in the Victoria and Albert Museum in South Kensington.

My father discovered that the Marquis of Huntley had

earlier engaged a mining expert to survey the district above
the Bridge of Gairn where there were said to be lead and silver
mines near the ruins of the Castle of Gairn. Later he employed
Cornish miners to begin operations behind the steading at
Abergairn. The project was abandoned as neither mine justified
the expense. My father liked to point out the deserted silver
mine to visitors, and to tell them how it was said to have
produced only enough silver to provide the Marquis with silver
buttons for his doublet.

One of his elders told him of a Crathie fiddler who was seen
lying in a ditch by the minister who was on his way to catch
an early morning train at Ballater. He drew up, got down from
his gig, and approached the man, murmuring sadly, 'O Willie,
Willie, I peety your case!' But Willie was concerned only for
the safety of his fiddle. 'Gin the fiddle be a' richt', he assured
the minister, 'I'm no' carin' aboot the case.' There was another
old man in Crathie who used to preface many of his utterances
with a solemn declaration, 'Min' noo, this is no' a lee A'm
tellin' ye', and everybody knew they were about to hear a very
tall story indeed.

In his researches my father unearthed an article on an old
custom kept by Catholic folk in the Glen; on Candlemas Day
they brought to chapel hand-dipped candles which were considered superior to moulded ones. They made them by fastening five or six wicks round a stick; the stick was dipped in
melted tallow, then withdrawn, the process being repeated till
the candles were the right thickness, then a thumb and fore-
finger were passed over them to give them a nice smooth finish.
At this time the crusie, that primitive form of iron lamp, was
in common use. They said it gave a grand light! The best wick
to use in the crusie was the dry pith of an ordinary rash, and
two or three were often plaited together. Train oil was most
commonly used in the crusie; this was whale oil extracted from
the blubber by boiling.

In those days the cutting of the priest's peats was an

important occasion. The people gathered on an agreed date at his house, which was probably then at Ardoch, and the guid-wives in the congregation vied with each other in sending contributions to the evening feast such as dressed chickens, home-baked scones, and plenty of milk. Off they all went to the hills, the lads and lasses skylarking and heaving divots at each other, and by a united effort the peats were cut and stacked. They then returned to the priest's house where the older women had prepared the feast. Afterwards the barn was cleared, and the day ended with a dance.

Eventually it became known that the peats were dry, and this was announced in fine style by old Willie Ritchie the Clerk, who was almost as venerable as the priest himself. On the Sunday, as soon as the chapel had skailed, it was Willie's custom to hurry after the congregation shouting in Gaelic, 'Hearken ye, hearken ye, the priest's peats are fine an' dry this day!' which was his way of intimating that they were all expected to turn up next day without fail to bring home the peats; and so, towards evening of the following day when cart-loads of peats were creaking along the roads there was another gathering at the priest's house. The final load was always brought home to the skirl of the pipes, refreshments were served, and again there was 'a wee bit o' a dance'. On a good day as many as fifty loads would be brought home, for various households as well as for the priest.

In preparation for a feast after a wedding, or any other celebration, the barn was always swept, sheaves were piled against the wall at one end, and stable-lanterns swung from the rafters to lighten the interior gloom. After the feast came the dancing. The fiddler found a perch on a kist covered with straw; as the night wore on perspiring dancers rested on the piled-up sheaves, sometimes some of them fell asleep and were still there in the early hours when the dancers broke up and went home to get ready for the day's work.

There were times when a dance could not be held . . . during Lent, for example. Once, a gathering of young folks, clamour-ing for a dance, sent a lad home to fetch his father's bagpipes,

but his mother removed the reeds before handing them over, to prevent any desecration of Lent. The most religious woman in the Glen at the turn of the century was Maggie Macgregor who lived alone in a hut beside Laggan Burn. She was well educated and possessed many books. She employed her time carding and spinning, and on a small loom wove garters so strong that no amount of wear and tear damaged them. She also spun from scraps of raw wool strong ropes for shepherds who used them for tethering sheep at clipping time. All day long she worked and prayed aloud in the Gaelic, and her piety was the admiration of all her neighbours. Her diet consisted mainly of boiled neeps, mashed, with a sprinkling of oatmeal on top. Her home-made shoes looked like carpet-slippers with thick rag-soles sewn with string. She seldom left home except to go to Mass. Over her blue homespun dress she wore a gray hooded cloak, and thus clad, in her clootie sheen, she could be seen tramping over the hill the nine miles that lay between her hut and the chapel at Corgarff. At a later date there was a chapel at Clashanruich ('the hollow of the heather'); later still one was built at Candacraig, which would have been very convenient for Maggie. As the Catholic population dwindled this was pulled down and a new chapel erected in Ballater and dedicated to St Nathalan. When my father arrived at Ballater for the first time, Father Meany of Candacraig was a member of the welcoming party that met him at the station, and they remained good friends till the kindly Father left the Glen to become Monsignor Meany of the Roman Catholic Cathedral in Aberdeen, when they lost touch. In after years the Monsignor described to friends how he was invited to dine at Balmoral Castle, and how, in place of flowers, the Queen had on the table silver statuettes of her gillies.

Old records show that Invercauld tenants had to pay their rents mostly in coin of the realm but a small portion was permitted to be paid in kind . . . so many bolls of meal in winter, or a small quantity of coal in summer. The Mill of Stranlea, about 1798, had to pay the laird 'one poultry fowl and five loads of peats'; Torbeg and Rinloan also paid part

rent in poultry and peats. Payment in kind was not confined to tenants; at one time Farquharsons of Invercauld held their lands on condition that they presented the King of Scotland with a bucketful of snow any time on request. This they contrived to do from the Laird's Tablecloth, a snowfield on Bheinn-a-Bhuird, where snow lies all the year round. My father studied, whenever possible, Glen history, its associations with clan warfare and its connections with freebooters. From a study of the Ordnance Survey Map dated 1869, which I treasure, he knew all the larachs; the story of their former inhabitants he learned from old men and women who had heard it, from their fathers; like many in the lean agricultural 1880s, some had gone to America to seek security, if not a fortune.

They spoke mournfully of the Clearances of 1814 and 1820, as if within living memory their forefathers had been driven from their homes. It was, in fact, farther north, from 1792 onwards, that cottars were evicted, their houses and property burned, to make way for large flocks of Cheviot sheep, which had become more important than people because of the greater income they provided. The homeless were sent to the coast, there to make a miserable living from fishing, an occupation to which they were unaccustomed. Many died from starvation and exposure, thousands emigrated to Canada and Australia in circumstances of great hardship. All this was related to my father as if of recent date, and as if he could not have previously heard of this black chapter in Highland history. It brought to mind what he had read as a youth, that in the Highlands it was still believed that Thomas the Rhymer, True Thomas, who flourished in the thirteenth century, had foretold the Highland Clearances in his prophecy, 'The teeth of the sheep shall lay the plough on the shelf.'

The making of whisky was an almost essential side-line in olden days when the glens were inhabited by far more people than crofting alone could support. There were dozens of little stills on the hill-burns. The name 'whisky' means in the

Gaelic 'water of life'; actually it meant a living for many crofters . . . often they depended for their rents on what they could make by this means, perhaps a profit of £3 15s. on the cost of the barley. All the equipment they needed were a few large copper cauldrons, now greatly prized by collectors, a condensing pipe, peat for the fire, and a steady supply of clear spring water. With scouts keeping watch for the excisemen, the long strings of ponies came over the hills by night; in the daytime the whisky was hidden, often in the cellars of friendly lairds and ministers. I have been told of a day when crofters were sitting round the fire in a house when they were warned of the approach of gaugers. They had small casks of whisky in the house which were impossible to hide, so they emptied the casks into a large pot and hung it over the side of the fire on the swey. When the gaugers entered, the house reeked of whisky; they searched high and low, sniffed the air, swore and left. The women at times did more than their men-folk for the concealment of liquor, and in contriving schemes to outwit the gaugers. One wife, being alone and in desperate straits, hastily arranged a bed of bottles in the cradle under the baby. When the gaugers arrived she was busy at her spinning-wheel, giving the cradle a rock at intervals to keep it moving and present a picture of innocent domesticity.

I have had the privilege of studying the manuscript of a journal now in the Scottish National Library in Edinburgh, written by a man who was born in the middle of the nineteenth century, and who travelled all over the world. The paper is brittle with age, spelling and grammar elementary, punctuation ignored; the style is flamboyant and repetitive, yet it has a quaint strength and vigour. The writer was evidently of a restless nature and never stayed long in one place; his wanderings and adventures make enthralling reading. In his boyhood on Donside there were whisky stills among the hills, although the preparation of the 'braich' or malt was illegal. When gaugers were in the neighbourhood little time was needed to hide away incriminating evidence but inevitably some were caught. Alexander Shaw, father of William Shaw of Inverenzie,

one of my father's much-respected elders, and grandfather of
Robert Shaw and Margaret Fraser, when a lad, was assisting
at a broust when he was taken unawares at the still with all
the evidence about him. Two excisemen marched him over the
hills to Aberdeen, taking a couple of days on the road, and he
was charged and sentenced to a fine of £30 or three months'
imprisonment, with hard labour. Not having any money to
pay the fine, he was compelled to go to gaol, and languished
in the West Prison for three miserable months. For lack of
fresh air and exercise, and with inadequate feeding, he lost
weight, and when liberated he was weak, listless, and light-
headed. He set off to walk home, a matter of fifty-six miles,
and arrived in the evening of the second day with 'a light and
cheerful heart, but bruised and bleeding feet'.

When whisky-distilling was finally stopped, the hill-roads
were still used by drovers taking their cattle to the Lowland
trysts; and women, too, used them when they came barefoot
over the hills at the time of the hairst with their hose and sheen
slung round their necks. Every year they came, from clachans
like Piperhole, with their reaping-hooks inside their bundles
on their backs to reap the Lowland crops before returning to
attend to their own later hairst on Deeside and in the Glen.
Eventually the scythe and the reaping-machine put an end
to these journeys, just as auction marts ended the journeys of
the drovers.

While still a youth, Alexander Shaw and his worthy father
went on foot from Corgarff through Glen Bulg to Braemar,
over the Cairnwell to the Spittal of Glenshee, where they
stayed the night; then on to Blairgowrie, and thence to Forfar,
the object of their journey being to escort home his two young
sisters who had been in service at Scotstoun for over a year,
and could not have made the journey alone. After a day's rest,
they all set off for home, the sisters carrying their few possessions in bundles on their backs. They travelled by Newtyle
and Alyth, where they stopped to choose a warm shawl or
plaid for each of the girls, choosing gray plaid with white

stripes, probably woven on the famous looms at Kirriemuir, and paying for them out of their year's wages. They trudged along the banks of Isla to Glenshee, and fair forfochen they arrived home on the third day's march, having completed a long, long traivel, over 140 miles.

Before this young man achieved his ambition to join the police force he served a number of years in a variety of occupations in places far from home . . . as a halflin on farms, as a shepherd lad warmly wrapped in a good gray plaid woven specially by his mother; as a navvy, as a hairst man, and as assistant to a Scotch Packman. Determined to join the police force he went to London by train with all his baggage, which comprised his bed and carpet-bag and all his clothing sewn up in a piece of packsheet. He went to a police station near Scotland Yard, to volunteer, and was told to come back next day. In the Strand he was nearly run over by a fast-moving carriage and pair. One of the horses seized him by the shoulder, tearing his fine black coat, the shaft struck him a severe blow in his side, and he would have fallen under the horses' feet had not the vicious horse's teeth held him upright. As soon as he was free he made off as quickly as possible, in great pain where the carriage-pole had struck him, and with the shoulder of his Sunday coat nearly torn off. He found a little shop where he bought needles and thread and proceeded to mend his good coat, and with no thought of returning to Scotland Yard, boarded the *City of London* at the Aberdeen Steam Wharf to sail back to Aberdeen. He vividly describes how they sailed down the river in company with another steamer bound for Calais, passing the 'monster ship', the *Great Eastern* lying on the blocks, still in course of construction. (The fabulous and ill-fated monster ship, launched in 1858, was designed to carry 4,000 passengers, nearly twice as many as the *Queen Mary*, launched seventy-seven years later.) On board he encountered a serious and thoughtful man, and discovered that he was Captain McLinton, on his way to take command of the *Fox* at Aberdeen, bound for the Arctic regions, with the expedition in search of Sir John Franklin. After a

stormy passage, the *City of London* dropped anchor in the harbour at Aberdeen on Monday 15 June 1857.

The symbol of the Church of Scotland is the Burning Bush. My father was one of a number who sought to discover if an unconsumed burning bush was compatible with the facts of nature. It had always been difficult to show how a plant could burn and not be consumed, a spectacle that so struck Moses that he called it a great sight. One theory was that the bush was one of the stunted trees known as the Chaparro, which resists fire for a long time. Its branches burn very slowly, and its trunk is practically fire-proof, and flourishes in the midst of great prairie fires. If a long period elapses without a con-flagration, the Chaparros pine away and even die, but the moment that flames burst out and roar and hiss among the vegetation, the incombustible bushes begin to recover, and shoot up on the devastated waste land . . . a subject which my father used in an early sermon.

The beginnings of Ballater he found made interesting reading . . . how an old woman who suffered from scrofula perceived herself cured when she had bathed in a spring at Pannanich. News of the miracle spread, and a bath-house and houses had to be built to accommodate the ever-increasing crowds of people who arrived hopeful of cures. 'For the most part, those who came were really in need of the waters', said the *Deeside Guide* in 1852, 'but a great many came whom nothing ailed, and who came merely for diversion because it was a fashion-able resort.'

Dr John Ogilvie, Editor of the *Imperial Dictionary*, for many years spent a holiday in Pannanich, and in one of his dialect poems, which my father found diverting, sang the praises of 'blithesome, healthful Pannanich', and declared, with some poetic licence,

> I've seen the sick to health return,
> I've seen the sad forget to mourn,
> I've seen the lame their crutches burn
> And loup and fling at Pannanich.

When the popularity of Pannanich Wells as a spa eventually waned, crowds continued to flock to Ballater to enjoy the scenery and fine air, and to hope for a glimpse of the Queen and the Royal Family . . . and so it is today.

The history of Inchmarnoch and Glen Tanar were also of absorbing interest. Inchmarnoch means 'the island of St Marnoch', for the chapel was situated on an islet in Dee, and the saint's burial place was there. The graveyard was badly damaged in the great floods of 1829, and nothing can be seen of the chapel now. Inchmarnoch disappeared in what became the united parishes of Tullich, Glenmuick, and Glen Gairn.

In the early part of the eighteenth century Glen Tanar was one great forest of tall firs, and Tanar folk were engaged in timber-floating; Tanar fir was even more famous in Aberdeen than the fir woods of Ballochbuie and Invercauld. In the second half of the century Glen Tanar became noted for the breeding of goats, and sufferers from consumption came to the glen, as others did to Pannanich for the curative waters, to drink goats' milk as a remedy.

In 1761, an advertisement appeared in the *Aberdeen Journal* intimating that Arthur Copland had fitted up his house for the reception of those who intended to drink goats' milk that season. His charge was 5s. per week for each room. Goats' milk was 4d. a pint, and the goats were milked within a hundred yards of his front door.

My father became very friendly with Sir William Cunliffe Brooks of Glen Tanar, whose daughter married the Marquis of Huntly; he found him a kind and generous man, a well-loved laird, eccentricities and all, with a passion for building and road-making. He erected deer-fences, new farmhouses and steadings, and houses for his employees, a remarkable series of improvements that made Glen Tanar unique in the north.

During my father's ministry, an elderly man in Coldstone was in the habit of bragging that he had three accomplishments . . . 'girdin' a cogie, ca'in' oxen in the pleugh, an' singin'

the psalms o' Dauvit'. A cogie, often seen in Victorian pictures tucked under the oxter, or resting on the hip, of a pretty milk-maid, was made of wooden staves girded by iron bands. One stave projected above the others to form a handle. Carried twice daily to the byre at milking-time, a well-made cogie lasted a lifetime, and when it was eventually discarded the bairns fell upon it with whoops of glee, claiming the iron bands for girds.

It is a very long time since farmers in the Glen ploughed with oxen. The last was John Fleming who, I remember, used an ox and a horse in double harness on his meagre croft at Shenval, where the last wolf in Scotland is believed to have been slain in the eighteenth century. He was the last of the Flemings, but there had been a John Fleming on the neigh-bouring farm of Recharcharie as far back as 1757, according to parish records.

Up to the time of the Disruption in 1843, the minister in the Glen acted also as schoolmaster, and was known as the Dominie or the Maister. He lived and taught at Dalphuil, which for long was called the Old Schoolhouse. The last dominie was James Coutts who continued to live there after his retirement, and after a school and schoolhouse were built across the moor, beside the church. To the end of his long life he was called The Dominie, and survived many of his former pupils. The Queen Mother acquired the old house in 1950 and saved it from becoming derelict. (Sixteen years later, Helen Cathcart in her biography of the Queen Mother referred to a happy day at the Queen's two-room cottage, an old school-house on the moors 'one room used as a dining-room with a little table in the centre, and an open fireplace opposite the door; the other a large room, evidently the kitchen, which also had a large open fireplace with equipment for cooking' as an earlier guest, Mr Mackenzie King, described it.) I treasure a letter in which she thanks me for telling her its long history. It is the oldest building in the Glen and, because of its great age and associations, deserves to be remembered by its ancient name, Dalphuil, which means 'the field of the pool', a reference

to a salmon pool in the river nearby, no longer to be found, presumably lost in winter spates and shifting channels.

Following the Rising of 1745 three bridges were built to link up the military roads that were necessary for the movement of troops; these were Fraser's Brig in Glen Clunie, built in 1750 and still carrying some traffic to Braemar; the Invercauld Brig, whose graceful arches have stood since 1752, still within sight and sound of the main road seething with traffic; and Gairnshiel Brig, sometimes erroneously called the Bridge of Gairn, and even Wade's Bridge. It was built in 1751, three years after the death of General Wade, and spans Gairn within sight of Dalphuil. There is a legend, known to few, that the bridge is haunted by the piteous sound of weeping children, but whose bairns and what the cause of their grief the story does not say. It would not be unseemly to link the legend with the desolate wailing of Glen bairns whose fathers did not return from the carnage of Culloden.

The true Bridge of Gairn spans the river near its junction with Dee, the place which older folk still call Fit o' Gairn, where a typical village store and a smiddy have been established since 1806.

Most people know that Lord Byron, when a boy, spent holidays with the Robertson family at Ballaterach, in 1796 and some years after that. When Mary Robertson used to visit her uncle, Captain Macdonald, the Laird of Renatton, Byron sometimes accompanied her as far as Gairnshiel where he stayed, and enjoyed fishing in Gairn. His love of Deeside, his poems on Morven and Lochnagar, the legend of his stumble and narrow escape at the Linn of Dee, are kept alive in song and story, but his association with Glen Gairn is almost forgotten.

Glen Gairn became a Quoad Sacra parish in January 1863. Prior to that date the Manse was at Tullichmacarrick. When a new Manse was required the Marquis of Huntly granted a site where once had stood the dwelling of the Laird of Dalfad whose name was Macgregor. It was here that twenty-four Macgregors mustered, and marched away over the Glas-

choille to join other clans and fight at Culloden in 1746. It is said that the Manse was built on the remains of an old thatched house, which would account for the uneven floors and low ceilings of some of the original rooms, which were later reconstructed. Thus it would appear that when Dalfad is mentioned in early records the reference is to the Manse of Dalfad, my birthplace, which has long been in ruins. In a birch-wood nearby, on the road to Balno, a Roman Catholic chapel had been partially built, and a piece of ground enclosed to form a burying-ground. In it may be seen several flat stones, one marking the grave of John Grierson, who died on 2 May 1757; another with the initials, C.McG. carved in the stone. Both these stones have a cross roughly carved at the top, and other stones set in the ruined walls bear symbols which led to a theory that the spot had been used for worship in pre-Christian times. Somewhere in the tangle of overgrown birches there is said to be a Culloden Stone bearing the names of six Macgregors who fell in that slaughter, but its position is uncertain. After the defeat of the Jacobites the chapel was left unfinished, but the place where the altar would have been raised is still visible, though some suppose it to be a headstone marking the resting-place of the priest. A mound close by was known as the Laird's Seat, for there he lingered day after day, gazing across the fields to his house and considerable lands, mourning the Macgregors slain on Culloden Moor, and doubtless turning his melancholy gaze at times to the uncompleted chapel and the consecrated ground where one day his bones would lie. There was a muddy little well at the roadside called the Laird's Well, which was the only source of water for use in the Manse, except when it was laboriously carted in barrels from Gairn, till there came a day in 1893, or thereabouts, when money was raised to have piped water brought from a spring on Maamie.

The Manse was on Morven Estate, the church on Invercauld, so there were two heritors; the Marquis of Huntly, who contributed approximately £8 to my father's stipend, and Colonel Farquharson who contributed £11. The rest of the

stipend came from the Endowment Committee of the Church of Scotland, bringing it to the annual figure of £100. Lady Grace Gordon, who married Hugh Lowther, 'The Yellow Earl', fifth Earl of Lonsdale, was a sister of that Marquis of Huntly who sold his Morven estate to James Keillor. Their Scottish home was Aboyne Castle, and he, as the premier Marquis in Scotland, bore the proud title of Cock O' the North.

In course of time, my father established a happy relationship with the minister of Glenbuchat on Donside, whose name was Spark, and they regularly arranged in the summer months an exchange of pulpits. Mr Spark drove over the hill in his gig and stabled his horse at the kirk; my father pushed his bicycle over the Glas-choille and went spinning down the other side, and down the long Strathdon road. The history of Glenbuchat as a parish dates from 1475; previously it formed part of the mediaeval parish of Logie-in-Mar. This meant that the parishioners had to cross Don to attend public worship in Logie kirk. One Easter, some were drowned in attempting to cross the river; after this tragedy Glenbuchat was made a parish, and the kirk was dedicated to Saint Peter. No longer in use, the old kirk is carefully preserved, and keeps intact, to a degree unique in Scotland, the internal arrangements of the eighteenth century. The floor is in natural stone, and the pine pews are arranged on three sides of the pulpit which, with its sounding board and precentor's desk in front, is lit by two skylight panes in the roof. In common with other ancient Scots kirks there are no windows or doors on the north side. Facing the pulpit are box pews known as 'pumphels', a corruption of pen-folds, containing narrow tables. It was the custom on Communion Sundays to remove the partitions between the pews, and set the tables end to end so that they became one long Communion Table running the whole length of the church. Many generations of Glenbuchat folk sat stiffly but reverently at this table, as the elements were dispensed.

The Laird's Loft, erected in 1828, is made of pinewood from

[34]

Mar Lodge, and displays in faded heraldic colours the arms of the Earl of Fife.

There was at one time a minister who travelled all over Aberdeenshire, and farther afield, and, wherever he went he preached the same sermon, on the prophets Elijah and Elisha, who, we read in the Book of Kings, both encountered a widow with a miraculous cruse of oil. My father purchased, when it was first published in 1915, *The Nor' East*, a book of reminiscences by the Rev. W. S. Bruce, D.D., who was minister of Banff for many years.

The following lines, telling of the travels of a contemporary minister appear in the book; was he, as some believe, the Rev. George Cowie, who lived at the Cabrach a long time ago?

> Up by Tough and down by Towie
> He preached the wifie an' her bowie;
> In Forbes, Keig, an' Tullynessle
> 'Twas aye the wifie an' her vessel;
> Up by Rhynie, down Strathbogie,
> 'Twas aye the wifie an' her cogie;
> A' the folk roun' Craigievar
> Kent the wifie an' her jar;
> E'en ower by Skene an' Peterculter
> Appeared the wifie an' her pewter;
> At Turra, Meldrum, an' Fingask
> Again it was the only cask;
> At Peterhead an' Mintlaw Station
> 'Twas aye the same auld lubrication;
> But now, they say, for verra shame,
> He's locked the wifie up at hame.

The following lament for conventional behaviour was written, tongue in cheek, by Royston J. Milne, then a student at Aberdeen University, for the University Magazine many years ago. It gives in its few lines a fair sample of the common speech of Deeside. 'Up the Ninety Twa' refers to the Ninety Second Gordon Highlanders raised in 1794.

Faither, aye, an' Tam the Grieve,
Dichts their noses on their sleeve,
Roarin' oot, 'ye prood wee monkey!'
Jist because I tak' ma hankie!
Whiles I canna sup ma tea,
The wey they sit an' glower at me,
O, the peety,
O, the shame,
Naebody's genteel at hame!

Bedded oot among the barley,
Lies ma mither's Uncle Charlie,
Ninety-fower an' blin' an' slow,
Sleepin' aff the Fintry Show;
Doon his nose he puffs an' whistles
Pure Drambuie roun' the thistles.
O, the burden
Hard an' heavy,
A'm that coorse aul' carlin's nevvy!

Granpa's bocht a penny-fairden,
Jist tae cycle roun' the gairden,
Shooin' pigeons aff the peas,
While he steers it wi' his knees;
Even noo he starts tae fa',
Skirlin', 'Up the Ninety-Twa!'
O, the sorrow,
O, the dolour,
An' he hisna on his collar!

In an age when anecdotes of Scottish character and humour
were popular at social gatherings my father was in great
demand as a raconteur for he had a fund of stories on which
he could draw at great length. At Church Socials all over the
Presbytery oft-told tales of ministers, beadles, ministers' men,
and precentors delighted the audience. One of my father's
favourites was of a minister who had arranged to marry a

young couple, when the bride called off the wedding, explaining 'I've ta'en a scunner at'm.' Later she changed her mind and a date was again fixed. A few days before the marriage was to take place the bridegroom called at the Manse and told the minister it was all off because he said 'I've ta'en a scunner at'er.' The quarrel was patched up and the now happy pair together approached the minister, but he had had enough. 'Awa' wi' ye!' he raged, sending them packing, 'I've ta'en a scunner at ye baith!'

William Soutar, who died in 1943, wrote of a contented man

Wi' meal in the girnal an' milk in the bowl
A man will haud thegither baith body an' soul;
An' wi' a hert that's ready tae thole the rochest days
A man will hairst contentment frae a gey puir place.

The meal girnal, lined with zinc to keep out mice, is a thing of the past, but in my grandmother's day it was an essential piece of kitchen equipment. Meal in those days was the mainstay of country fare. Porridge made in the traditional manner, with meal sifted through the fingers, stirred with a theevil and salted to taste, was always referred to in the plural . . . 'they' were served with a sprinkling of meal on top of each portion, each person was provided with a small bowl of milk and when 'they' were eaten each spoonful was dipped in the milk. Neither sugar nor syrup was added for that would have spoiled the flavour. Bairns found that the occasional overlooked 'knot' of uncooked meal had a deliciously nutty taste. Very correct Highland 'chentlemen' were known to sup 'them' standing, as their forebears had done in the days of bloody clan warfare, when it was expedient to be constantly on the alert, ready to launch a counter-attack. Oatmeal bannocks were known as bread; bakers' loaves were called loaf-bread, made in batches, separated only on the counter when necessary. There is still nothing to beat the flavour of a hand-made Scotch 'plain loaf' fresh from the oven, with its fine floury crust . . . well worth queueing for! Oatcakes were made

at home on a Cooriss (Culross) girdle hung from a swey over a hot peat-fire. Meal was sprinkled on the baking-board, the mealy dough kneaded and rolled on it several times before it was quartered and slipped on to the greased girdle. There the pieces were turned over with a flat, spade-shaped metal implement, and the cakes, when cooked, were placed on a rack in front of the glowing fire to get their final toasting. When they began to curl inwards they were ready to eat. There was nothing my father enjoyed more than 'a bit cake' which he broke with his fingers and ate, standing, while it was still hot and crisp. There was no National Health Service in those days; old folks were inclined to boast that their health had been so good they had 'niver socht a doctor' in their lives. Only when there was serious illness was the doctor sent for.

Old home remedies were considered infallible . . . sulphur and treacle for cleansing the blood, blackcurrant tea for sore throats, cloves for toothache, bread poultices for drawing out the painful hairst thistles from swollen fingers, sowans for a winter tonic, and a cobweb wrapped round a child's cut finger to stop the bleeding. Sowans, made from the sids of meal after milling, were sourish to taste and on that account were often supped with golden syrup.

Brought up as I was to eat what was put before me, I ate without comment or enjoyment the dish of sowans served as a treat by May Leys of Sleach in her home in Ballater which she and her shepherd-brother, Charlie, built with their life-savings and called it Ben A'an. My grandmother kept house for my father until his marriage, and afterwards came from Laurencekirk on frequent visits to the Manse. She, as a child, had been brought up

> Where the old red cliffs are bird-enchanted
> And the low green meadows bright with sward.

near the lovely Bay of Lunan with its sand-dunes where Lunan Water, flowing gently through lush pastures of Lunan valley, the rich farm-lands of Angus, met the North Sea half-way between Arbroath and Montrose. Her forebears had lived

in Lunan for generations; her parents and grandparents were held in high esteem. She and her four brothers played round the ruins of Red Castle poised like a sentinel guarding Lunan Bay as it had done ever since it was built by William the Lion at the end of the twelfth century. The bairns fished for trout in the placid reaches of the quiet river, and romped on the fine stretch of sandy shore. My grandmother in her long life had known much heartbreak, having lost eight of her fourteen children in diphtheria epidemics, and in spite of a hard life which had largely been

> Labour by day, and scant rest in the gloaming,
> With Want an attendant not lightly outpaced

she had a fine uncomplaining spirit. Her brothers had gone into the ministry of the church, and she was proud that, of her surviving sons, three became parish ministers and one a lawyer. I remember some of her quaint sayings, such as 'It's no' the hen that cackles loodest that lays the bonniest eggs'; her compassion for the bride of an unfortunate marriage, 'She'll no' hae her sorrows to seek'; her country toast, 'May your joys be as deep as the snaw in the glen, an' your sorrows as few as the teeth o' a hen!'; her terse description of a scold and a scandalmonger, 'She has a tongue that wad clip cloots', and of a restless bairn, 'hoppin' aboot like a hen on a het girdle'. She was given to quoting 'there's a slippery stane at every door' which I never clearly understood, but assume now that it means that even within the family one may slip up if careless in behaviour.

She could not see a cut of worsted without wanting to knit it up into something useful; I recall that she made me a pair of scarlet bedsocks of which I was inordinately proud, and while her busy needles clicked and flashed she, who had inherited the art of story-telling, regaled us with tales of Laurencekirk where she had spent the whole of her married life. Next to Aberdonians who manufacture jokes against themselves, Angus folk, with their rich dry type of humour,

probably come a close second for story-telling. At one time, when diddling competitions were common, and in some places are still held, part of the programme was devoted to the recital of traditional tales which were much enjoyed by audiences in Angus villages. One of my grandmother's anecdotes concerned an eccentric laird who had a pet piglet that followed him about like a dog. Every night he carried it upstairs to his own bed where it cooried down beside him under the blankets. When it grew too big to share his bed he provided it with a cot in a corner of the room, and every night when he undressed he covered the pig with his breeks to keep it warm.

My father's devotion to his 'good old mother', as he called her, never flagged. She was constantly in his thoughts, and he showed his concern in a number of practical ways. To the end of her life, when the twice-yearly groceries order went from the Manse to Cooper's of Glasgow, a similar order was directed to Laurencekirk. Scorning the mileage he bicycled over the Cairn o' Mounth to visit her. Sometimes my mother accompanied him and enjoyed the fine free sensation of a spin downhill though brakes were none too dependable, but having to push a cumbersome bicycle up the steep Mounth on the homeward journey was a wearisome business. Two hundred years ago the Cairn o' Mounth was the hill-pass used by cattle drovers, and the inn that once stood near the summit was a welcome halt for thirsty men.

My cycling parents on their Mounth occasions passed through the fertile valley of the Feugh (pronounced Feuch) but always called first on their blind friend, John Moir, musician and poet, who published two volumes of Feugh Spray, poems in praise of the valley, including the oft-quoted lines on the Brig o' Feugh . . .

> Fowk cam' frae far tae thrang the Brig
> Fan kelpie spates wad dance an' jig,
> Tae see the Feugh gang roarin' by,
>   An' watch the salmon loupin' high.

Folks still come to see the loupin' fish, and safely stand on the footbridge which has been erected alongside the stone bridge. Motor traffic can now cross the old bridge without the former hazard of encountering spectators too engrossed in salmon-watching to keep to the wider places on the parapet.

My mother read with amusement in the *Girls' Home Companion* for 1891 some serious advice to women cyclists:

Before starting for a ride, look to your nuts, lamp, tyres and brake. Sound your gong before passing crossroads or turnings. Never travel without sufficient cash in your pocket to take you and your mount home by rail in an emergency.
Do not ride unaccompanied by a male relative or friend.
Do not accompany club runs unless small and select.
Always ride in correct cycling costume. The ideal costume consists of a vest, bodice, and knickerbockers, a cloth skirt and short jacket with a waistcoat, wool stockings, and well-cut boots of tan leather. A yachting cap is the most serviceable headgear.

My mother, in fact, wore when cycling a small felt hat, a tweed skirt and jacket, with a shirt blouse, and lacing boots. She laughed aloud at the following awful warning—'The lady cyclist should be on her guard against the acquirement of that terrible malady "The Bicycle Face". It attacks nervous riders and, if not corrected in time, the face gradually settles into a hunted, drawn look.'

A high-class London tailor offered to make a 'capital trotteur skirt of excellent quality' for 10s. 9d., with wide pleats which hung down neatly on either side of the back wheel and, with a jacket to match, cost 29s. 6d. A valentine in 1891 caricatured women cyclists in a drawing of a jolly lady in knickerbockers and knee boots, a jacket with leg o' mutton sleeves, and a large unsuitable hat. The caption addressed a Lady Scorcher:

Scorching along at a terrible rate,
Always resolved to be quite up-to-date,
Pray take my advice and don't think me unkind,
You had best ride more slowly, or perhaps you'll be fined.

A DAUGHTER OF
THE ROCK

When my father and mother arrived at Ballater after their March honeymoon on the wind-blown Angus coast, and their kirkin' at Arbroath, they drove up the Glen in a wagonette hired from Auld Sluie's stables at the foot of the Darrach. It deposited them at Milton Brig and went on to cross the ford with the luggage. They walked down the path by the burn-side, grassy and springy underfoot, crossed Gairn by the foot-bridge and climbed the Manse brae, little more than a cart-track that wound upwards and eventually merged with the road to Donside. At the first bend they took a breather and looked up at the Manse perched on a height, the house that was to be their home for twenty-five years, facing the sombre bulk of Geallaig, within a sound of Gairn, the 'noisy little river'. Its contours somewhat resembled the house a child of that day would draw at his first attempt . . . four walls, a slanting roof with chimneys at the four corners and smoke drifting skywards. (The child of today, I am told, draws television aerials where chimneys used to be.) There were three windows above, two below, with a door between complete with knocker and big brass door-knob.

Neat, square, stone-built, it was roofed with blue slate that reflected light when rain fell. Trained up the harled walls were twining hops, now comparatively rare in Scotland. The Manse was approached by a leafy avenue and surrounded by a broad pathway. On that early spring day in 1892 my parents, hand in hand, strolled round the sunken garden and, to their delight, found one or two timid snowdrops peeping through. A few days later, my mother's furniture arrived on five farm-carts which rocked through the ford and toiled up the brae. The load included a complete bedroom suite hand-made by my grandfather, a couple of blanket-kists which contained not only blankets but the contents of my mother's bottom drawer (a dozen of everything as befitted a well-endowed bride) and a bountiful assortment of household linen. In another Scots parish, about the same time, the kist of a country bridegroom is remembered as having contained no household linen (that was the bride's province) but it held a handsome supply of hand-woven blankets from the looms of Kirriemuir, as well as dozens and half-dozens of personal wear, shirts of linen and wool, hand-knitted socks, and stockings of varying weights to be worn with breeches.

My mother was born in Edinburgh but the family moved to Stirling while she was still a babe-in-arms and she was brought up there; she considered, therefore, that she was entitled to be known as a Daughter of the Rock, the name given to those raised in the protective shade of Stirling Castle, haunt of Scotland's kings.

She had a profound love of music and, as a girl, had her voice trained by Dr Allum of Stirling. She took leading soprano parts in amateur opera and oratorio from the age of seventeen. Her new neighbours in the Glen approved her gracious personality; they thought her a richt genteel wumman and grew to love and respect her. At first she missed the pleasant bustle of the town. The common sounds she now heard were the melodious comforting 'purring' of cushat doos, the barking of sheep-dogs on distant farms, and the murmuring of Gairn

[44]

which somehow reminded her nostalgically of the passing of railway trains.

She had been photographed in a bustle in 1887, but when she married bustles were no longer in fashion and she wore long full skirts held up by one hand when she walked out-of-doors, showing a little lace on her petticoat, a shirt with leg of mutton sleeves, and a mannish collar and tie. With this ensemble she wore a straw boater with a ribbon round the crown, and a waist-belt to match her hat-ribbon and tie. Of necessity, she had to do much of her buying by post, and her friend for life was John Noble, who advertised Home, Holiday, and Half-Guinea Costumes, and in after years she bought 'strong serge Knockabout Frocks' for Ellie and me for 4s. 6d. Advertisements appeared in the Badminton Magazine which Mr Forder at the Shiel passed on to my father . . . 'Strong boots to stand the wear and tear of the athletic man or woman, with a hundred years' reputation behind every pair.' The top price for men's boots was 21s. a pair, and for ladies', 13s. 6d. A gentleman's gold watch could be bought for £3 15s., and a lady's for £2 15s. 6d. About this time the Laird marked a national event by giving every man on the estate a new sixpence and every woman a new shilling (or possibly the other way round). My mother had both my father's coin and her own mounted on silver pins and wore them as brooches.

Her insight into social work in the Baker Street Mission in Stirling was not forgotten; she was in her element in parish work, interested in people as individuals, and naturally kind. She loved to accompany my father on long walks across the moors with some parochial object in view; he was an unwearying visitor of the sick and aged, and they both had an abundant reserve of energy and the will to expend it. Well aware that they were incomers and would be so regarded for many a long day, they resolved from the outset to gang warily, and secretly amused, took to heart the experience of a guidwife in a neighbouring parish. She had lived there all her married life, sixty years or more, and one day was on the point of answering a visitor's query on some local topic when her man interrupted

with a brusque, 'Haud yer tongue, wumman! Fit div *ye* ken aboot it? Ye're jist an incomer yersel!'

They kept open house, and many of the women-folk were glad to drop in, if they had traivelled far, to rest their legs and to enjoy a fly cup. It was a grand way of 'getting to know you', on both sides, and the kettle was seldom off the boil. My mother was a good listener and gave unstintedly of her help and friendship. The women rallied round her, offering the advice of experience on the rearing of her first child. When she was preparing for my arrival she had a little book to guide her on a baby's first outfit. 'An overlarge stock is a frequent fault', said the writer, 'for, after all, the period when a baby wears his first clothes is very short. The following outfit will be quite sufficient' . . . then came the list.

Two robes
Four day-gowns
Four long white petticoats
Six nightgowns
Six shirts of fine bishop's lawn, trimmed with valenciennes
   lace, the only lace that remains soft after washing.
Six pilches or barracoats
Three dozen diapers and three dozen Turkish diapers
Three pairs woollen bootees
A large woollen shawl
A fine wool head-shawl

There was a theory that an infant back needed support, so a yard of fine soft flannel about eight inches wide had also to be provided for wrapping round the naked baby.

'Fegs!' exclaimed canny Jean Farquharson, when she saw the layette my mother had provided, '*This* bairn'll nae want for happin'!'

When I arrived at Christmas (a honeymoon baby, as the saying goes) there was deep snow on the ground and a storm was raging. Dr Gordon-Mitchell had to leave his gig and make his way to the Manse on foot, met by my father halfway. A nurse from Aberdeen was already installed, an innovation in

the Glen, for in those days every parish had a handy wifie
willing to help, who usually became skilful with much practice.
I recently read of one such midwife on Deeside at the turn of
the century who died in her eighty-fifth year. During her fifty
years as an untrained handywoman she brought into the world
upwards of 1,500 babies, and what was remarkable in her day,
she never lost a mother. Had I been a boy my father intended
me to be educated at Robert Gordon's College in Aberdeen.
Gordon was an Aberdonian who in the early 1700s accumu-
lated a fortune which he bequeathed to found a school for
boys. In every generation there have been distinguished
Gordonians.

When I was two months old, Miss Gatt, school-teacher and
precentor, left to take up another appointment, and I was
carried to the kirk and put to sleep in the vestry while my
mother led the praise. This happened on several Sundays till
a new teacher was appointed precentor, and after a time an
American organ was installed.

I have been told of an old body, long since gathered to her
fathers, who could recall when she first attended Divine
Service there was only one bonnet in the kirk and that was on
the head of the minister's wife. What a picture it must have
been, as the kirk skailed, to see all the women in their snow-
white mutches with goffered frills! It was then their custom to
walk barfit to the kirk, carrying their shoes and hose; before
putting them on they washed their feet in the burn and
demurely entered church.

One of my mother's favourite psalm-tunes was Crimond
which, though not specially composed to the words of the
twenty-third psalm, has been wedded to them for many years
and has been sung with deep feeling on a great many occasions.
It was originally set to the words of a hymn by George
Washington Dand who died in 1859, and my mother had it in
her cherished *Northern Psalter* published in 1877. The tune
takes its name from the village in Aberdeenshire. It was
composed by Jessie Irvine, daughter of the parish minister,
but is sometimes attributed to David Grant who was intensely

interested in Scots psalmody. Sir Hugh Roberton and the Glasgow Orpheus Choir by their beautiful rendering gave the tune to the world, and in 1947 it was sung at the Marriage Ceremony of Her Majesty the Queen with Prince Philip.

In the spring, when much of the snow had disappeared, my parents took me, and my feeding-bottle and a supply of scalded milk for three days, on my first railway-journey, to Stirling, and there, in Graham and Morton's sedate establishment, they bought a go-cart with a hood, high wheels and long handles, a high chair, and a cot with a brass knob at each corner to replace the wooden cradle which had been my father's and from which the rockers had been removed because my mother disapproved of the custom of rocking babies.

My grandfather, George Smart, who was one of the pioneers in photography, photographed me in his studio in Viewfield Place. Fortunately he was not in favour of the vogue for exposing a naked baby on a white bearskin rug to its perpetual embarrassment in after years. He was an admirer of the work of David Octavius Hill and Robert Adamson, and of George Washington Wilson, who was Scotland's pioneer photographer and was summoned to Balmoral in 1855 to take the 'likenesses' of the Queen and the Royal Family, the first time they had ever been photographed. He must have pleased the Queen and the Prince Consort for he was made Photographer Royal in 1860. My grandfather was a pioneer in another field, for he and a few fellow-workers founded St Cuthbert's Co-operative Association in Edinburgh in 1859. A fascinating history might have been written of the inception period, of the hopes and fears of those earnest advocates of social reform, and of the ridicule with which their ideals were received; unfortunately, little remains to make an authentic record of their early struggles. It would be interesting to know how they selected the name for their Association. It is possible that the pioneers who gave it the name it bears today knew the tradition that surrounds St Cuthbert, 'that his body never changed its appearance; it seemed to defy time and decay'. The Association

has had much of that quality; it had many imitators in Edinburgh but none survived their infancy. St Cuthbert's was the first, and the only one to 'defy time and decay'. A small extract from the fragmentary early records is of interest in these days when women have to campaign for equal pay for the job. 'In 1885 a small shop was opened in the Dumbiedykes District, and a woman was put in charge of it instead of a man, *so that expenses might be kept down*. Miss Frier carried it on most successfully till she died of smallpox contracted from a customer in discharge of her duties. *She was one of the most successful branch managers in our service.*' (The italics are mine.) The Association of which my grandfather was a co-founder and latterly a director, has the unique distinction of holding a Royal Warrant as Coach Painters to Her Majesty the Queen, with the task of maintaining all of the many Royal Coaches. The unobtrusive buildings at Fountainbridge are in fact the workshops of the Royal Mews at Buckingham Palace, the maintenance side of an institution that reaches back over centuries of our monarchy. The main reason why St Cuthbert's was originally entrusted with the care of the Royal coaches is because they have the practical experience that is vital. In addition to the art of the coach-painters who renew the outsides, they have skilled upholsterers who rejuvenate the luxurious interiors; they have men skilled in the ancient craft of saddlery, wheelwrights to build the man-sized wheels, replacing metal tyres with rubber ones; they have specialised body-builders, joiners, engineers, even artists to repaint accurately the intricate coats-of-arms on the doors. There are times when scarcely a day goes by that there is not a coach either on its way north to Edinburgh, or on its way south after renewal or repair. It is a steady two-way traffic. The coaches have frequently to be stripped down to the bare bones. Every scrap of the old upholstery must be removed, the wooden wheels dismembered and the last particle of paint scraped off, all to be meticulously put together again, a dozen coats of paint applied, and finally the coach turned out better than new. One of the coaches to receive this treatment was the

Glass Coach in which Princess Anne and her bridegroom rode on their wedding-day.

A walk round St Cuthbert's stables, tucked away in one of Edinburgh's less fashionable streets, is a fascinating experience. Here one may see sixty beautiful horses . . . great white Percherons, Frieslands, Irish carriage-horses, and other breeds. Horses are supplied for all occasions, the Military Tattoo, for example. Police horses come from here, so do horses for Common Ridings, and they are exercised and kept contented by part-time occupation, such as pulling milk-floats which glide on rubber-tyred wheels to every part of the city. There is more to see than well-groomed horses. There is a private collection of horse-drawn vehicles ranging from a tiny pony-cart like the one Queen Victoria used for trotting round the grounds at Balmoral, to a magnificent four-in-hand stage-coach, the like of which rumbled over our highways in more gracious days. There are broughams, barouches, hansom cabs, and elegant open carriages, all in perfect condition and ready for the road. Carriages from the collection may be seen from time to time bowling along the city streets, for they may be hired, complete with horses, for a special occasion. It is not surprising that many a bride longs to ride from the church with her bridegroom in a carriage drawn by two fine horses, and feel like a princess on her wedding day.

My parents conscientiously attended church functions throughout the Presbytery, bicycling everywhere, to support the organisers. A Deeside personality, Dr Robert Farquharson of Finzean (pronounced Fing-in) opened a bazaar at Lumphanan at which they were present. Making a round of the stalls with the opener they came upon an old body who was admiring a picture by Joseph Farquharson, the distinguished Royal Academician. The old woman turned round, observed Robert and exclaimed, 'Eh, sir, yer brither's an awfae bonny penter o' sheep!' (adding without pause) 'His he iver pentit *you*?'

A rare visit was to Glen Fearder, one time haunt of cat-

terans, which lies close to the valley of Dee, but cut off from it by pine-clad heights. Near the head of the glen is the secluded shiel of Achtavan, beloved of the Queen Mother. An ancient hill-road leads to Loch Builg, so does another from Invercauld, and also the military road to Glen Gairn which branches off near the head of the Stranyarroch. The three roads meet at the Loch and continue as a bridle-path to Inchrory and Tomintoul.

My parents approached it from its lower end near the old Inver Inn, once called Inverfearder, leading to the valley now known as Aberarder, at one time the property of the feudal earls of Mar. For hundreds of years their tenants were the Farquharsons of Invercauld and their kinsmen, the Shaws of Rothiemurchus, whose family records date from the year 1124. There were also a number of bonnet lairds, in a state of perpetual warfare with each other or with some common enemy. Weary of this unhappy state of affairs, the Farquharsons invited all the bonnet lairds to a meeting in the great barn of Aberarder, and hanged eighteen of them from the roof-tree. Since the Rising of 1745 Aberarder has been owned by the Farquharsons.

Crofts may still be seen, including Belmore and Ratlich which were tenanted by Shaws as far back as the sixteenth century. A sheep farmer now stores hay in the ruined kirk where services were held within living memory. Betty Barr's grandfather, who became a successful architect, was born in Aberarder in 1844. He attended the one-room school at Dalchork which was packed to the door with some forty scholars . . . the bairns in the front row learning to read and write, the loons at the back studying Greek and Latin. She treasures a book of mathematical exercises done in his fine copperplate handwriting. Margaret John, too, has memories of that Symon family, for generations rooted in Crathie. The school in Glen Gairn was also a one-teacher school which my father, as Chairman of the School Board, visited at regular intervals. He derived genuine pleasure from the progress of the scholars, and regretted that they had to leave school at

too early an age. He lent text-books to the school-leavers and encouraged them to continue their studies whenever possible, as he himself had done as a youth. George Rettie remembers to this day how my father gave him a copybook so that he might continue to practise good handwriting.

All through the summer months a succession of family friends came to spend a holiday and the Manse pew was full every Sunday. They were always in the forefront of the cheering crowds that lined the Station Square to greet the Queen, and later, King Edward VII, on their arrival at Ballater by the Royal Train. A walk they always enjoyed from the Manse was to the shepherd's cottage at Glenfenzie (pronounced Fing-ie) where Mrs Gillanders welcomed them with scones and honey and a pot of very strong tea. The date when the cottage was built (1820) may still be seen engraved high on the stone walls which, with a skeleton roof, are all that now remain. There had been an earlier homestead for the name appears in a document dated 24 December 1740.

One summer we briefly entertained Roger Quin, 'The Galloway Coaster', who was on a walking tour from Spey to Dee. When he was a child of seven he was allowed to hold in his hands the temporarily unearthed skull of Robert Burns, and in later years in a shop served Thomas Carlyle, and claimed that these unlikely events set his mind on literature. Poet and journalist, he took to tramping the Border Country with a flute and a concertina. He declared that he had the blood of a tramp in his veins and wished to be known as The Tramp Poet. Among other verses, some in Lallans, he published *The Borderland* and *Midnight in Yarrow*.

Percy Tarrant, the painter, with his wife and daughter, Marjorie, came to Torbeg one June, and my mother was delighted to meet the artist whose pictures she knew well. Marjorie, as Margaret Tarrant, became famous for her delicate paintings for the Medici Society, and for her enchanting illustrations of children's books.

When Sir Henry Campbell-Bannerman was Liberal MP for Stirlingshire, my uncle, James Drummond Valentine, who was proud of his Drummond ancestry, was one of C.B.'s staunch supporters, and I learned a good deal about him from conversation at the breakfast-table. (The history of the Drummond clan is recorded before Bannockburn. It takes its name from the lands of Drummond, or Drymen, in Stirlingshire.) In the roll of his old school, Glasgow High, the name of Campbell-Bannerman does not appear, for it was not till he was over thirty that he acquired Bannerman under the will of an uncle. He disliked what he termed the 'hyphenated mouthful', and by his own wish came to be known as C.B.

My mother had no vote till she was sixty, over thirty years after her marriage. In spite of her Liberal upbringing, she, in spirit, supported the Unionist candidate for whom my father voted. In the Glen, national politics were rarely mentioned except at the time of a General Election when they were apt to assume a personal flavour. My father and several farmers used to share a hired wagonette to take them to the polling station in Ballater. The old dominie regularly refused to reveal his political views, and it was suspected that his vote was given to the opposite party from the chosen candidate of the other voters. They felt a mite resentful that he had the nerve to share their transport, but my father declared, as he often did, 'It's a free country!'

My mother considered it in poor taste to discuss money matters; never did she allude in company to the cost of food, clothing, or household furnishings. All her married life she had to practise great economy which she did without rancour or resentment, laughingly referring to the day 'when our ship comes home'. Only in adult life, from her carefully kept accounts, did I learn what care had to be exercised to show a respectable front on £100 a year. She was excessively reserved in her choice of subjects in conversation, and almost puritanical in her rating of what is seemly. I recall her being scandalised when a caller happened to mention in mixed company an idea that had come to her in her bath. Bathing

was a very private matter, not to be mentioned in public, in her view. She would not discuss pregnancy, even when the situation was legitimate. Illegitimacy was, of course, as a subject, taboo. It was not she who told me of the new baby who was being admired by neighbours. Mrs Spence, a canny soul, who had a good idea who the father was though his name was being kept a close secret, exclaimed without thinking, 'O sic a bonny bairn, an' sae like's his faither!' then realising what she had said, added in haste, 'Fa' iver he may be!'

James Rogie wrote to me from Kenmay recently to tell me that he, as a boy, attended his uncle's wedding in the Glen. My father performed the marriage ceremony, and afterwards my mother sang, unaccompanied, to entertain the guests. He even remembers the songs she sang . . . 'Kitty of Coleraine', and 'The Scottish Bluebells'. She was often invited to sing at concerts in neighbouring parishes, such as Corgarff, Tomintoul, Lumphanan, and Crathie. One of her favourite songs was 'The Bonnie Banks o' Loch Lomond' of which she knew the legend. There is an old Celtic belief that when a man dies in a foreign land his spirit returns to the place of his birth by a fairy route called the Low Road. In 1745, during the retreat of the Scots army following its brief invasion of England, several of them had to be left behind in Carlisle as they had not the strength to go farther. Many were flung into gaol. The song that my mother sang with such feeling, written about the time of the retreat, tells of two Scots prisoners; one was to be released and would take the High Road home, while the other, who was to be executed, would take the fairy Low Road. As the release of the one and the death of the other were timed for the same hour, the man on the Low Road, travelling with the speed of a spirit, would be in Scotland long before the living man had tramped the weary miles on the High Road across the Border.

Scots had songs for every occasion, occupation, and sentiment . . . songs of joy and hatred, love, courtship and marriage; songs to commemorate every battle won or lost. There were songs of ploughing matches, feeing markets, poaching,

fishing, drinking, and begging, cradle songs and lullabies, and long-winded bothy ballads which incorporated shearing, hairst and milking songs. Some were only of local interest, like 'The Hairst o' Rettie' which is a tribute to Willie Rae, an honest gaffer, from his workmates; but 'The Band o' Sheavers', for example, oldest and best of its kind, was known in every county in Scotland. Many fell into disuse as ways of life changed, and some handed down by word of mouth were never seen in print, maybe because they were too boisterous and down-to-earth. As a small girl I was taken by my parents to a soirée, and halfway through the evening a young plough-man from Crathie perched himself on a table, corn-kister fashion, and with arms folded across his chest and an impassive face, sang a very long bothy ballad which I was too young to understand. At one point in the narrative, I recall, the bride-of-an-hour thus informed her brand new husband,

> This ae nicht I will lie wi' him,
> Syne every nicht I'll lie wi' you.

Puzzlement fixed the words on my brain for all time, but I have yet to see the ballad in which they appear.

Other ballads, like 'The Wark o' the Weavers', have been successfully revived. This was a popular bothy song towards the middle of last century in Forfar and in other centres of the weaving industry. It has a most compelling rhythm; young people have rediscovered it and are singing it with gusto. The author of the song was a Forfar weaver, David Shaw, who published two small collections of poems, the best of which is reckoned to be 'Tammie, Treadlefeet', a sly reference to the weaver's loom. Ballad style has been copied in the modern 'Sair wark's nae easy', which begins 'Doon at Nether Dallachy there's nayther watch nor nock', 'The Skyscraper Wean', who moans that 'ye cannae throw pieces frae a twenty storey flat', and the story of Wee Annie and her lost Yo Yo. Like folk songs of the past, they are all sung in simple unaffected fashion, and have nothing in common with current pop numbers with their restless extravagant gestures.

My mother sang simple ballads like 'Auld Robin Gray,' 'The Laird o' Cockpen', and 'Jennie's Bawbee', flicking her finger and thumb in the final line to indicate how Jennie birled her bawbee, a figure of speech in this case for shelving her fortune. In some quarters it has been asserted that the word bawbee came into use as a coin in the childhood of Mary, Queen of Scots, thus baby became bawbee, but I prefer the theory that it is derived from the French 'basbillon'.

CHAPTER III

BAIRNS AT THE MANSE

On the night of Queen Victoria's Jubilee in 1887 a party of men climbed Ben Macdhui to set off fireworks, and bonfires like twinkling points of fire were seen on many peaks in the Cairngorms. There were plans to repeat the bonfires on the Queen's Diamond Jubilee night in 1897 but these were defeated by drenching Scotch Mist . . . but not in Glen Gairn. There they danced all night in the open, they had fireworks, the flag my mother had run up on her treadle sewing-machine flew bravely from the cairn that Jock Kilgour, Duncan Davidson, and other young men had built on Maamie, and there was not a drop of rain. My sister had joined us at the Manse a month before, and in no time at all, so it seemed, I found myself helping Mary Mackenzie to push the baby in the long-handled go-cart along the moorland road to Belnaan to have tea with her mother and Flora, an ethereal child who died at a tender age. Some years later I recall my small sister affronted me (I was easily affrontit) by shouting 'Eggie! Eggie!' before we were well inside the house. Having been there before she knew what to expect. Mrs Mackenzie welcomed us, as always with a kindly 'Come inbye', and put a small pan on the peat-fire, saying in soothing tones, 'Wheesht,

bairn! Ye'll be gettin' an egg tae yer tea!' By this time I was a scholar at the school, and I clearly remember my first singing-lesson there, learning by ear, for there was no piano, Tanna-hill's 'Bonnie Wood o' Craigielea', and a ditty which began

> Delia walked abroad alone
> On a morning early.

The chorus ran

> Delia, Delia, Delia far,
> Delia walking early.

I have not heard it since nor seen it in print, but I remember the melody. We also learned a duet for a boy and girl which we sang in unison. It went like this . . .

> O pretty pretty Polly Hopkins, how do you do-o? How do you do?
> I'm none the better, Mr Topkins, for seeing you-oo, for seeing you!

Lessons were preceded by The Lord's Prayer from which recital Roman Catholic bairns were excused; they, by arrange-ment, remained seated while we others stood to chant the prayer. Every child in those days wore thick hand-knitted stockings and laced-up boots, except in summer when the loons went barfit. Queyns wore pinafores and our long hair tied back with a bow of ribbon. Ribbons were greatly prized and to lose one was a misfortune, as I recall . . . when I lost a new white bow at a soirée in the school on a Friday night I was sent to look for it early on Saturday morning. Every inch of the riverside path I searched, all the way back to the school. Luckily I found it in the playground and ran home in triumph.

I once had a tiny pewter tea-set, perfectly proportioned, of which I was very fond. My mother gave it to a sick child, and when next I saw it, it was being distributed, piece by piece, among the other girls at school, and so was scattered and lost. I have since seen an identical set in a Museum of

Childhood. There must be a lesson here; was I selfish? Somehow I did not grudge the gift, it was the throwing away of a
tiny cup here, a plate there, the wee cream-jug elsewhere, that
I minded. Maybe Lizzie, who had so little, was the generous
one, sharing her few possessions with others, but at the time
I could not think that way. I felt that she had not appreciated
the beauty of the tiny teapot as I had done, and I secretly
grieved for many a day . . . after all, I was only five-and-a-bit!

As soon as we were able to write legibly on a slate we were
issued with copybooks and lead pencils; later, promoted to
ink and steel-pointed pens which we dipped in the ink-wells
in the desks, practising thin upstrokes and thicker down-
strokes with the pen pointing over the right shoulder. Left-
handed bairns had a miserable time for they were obliged to
conform. Writing was twice as hard for them as for the rest
of us, and if they were caught using the left hand they were
punished. Reading came easily to me, and I loved new words,
rolling them round, tasting them, liking the feel of them on
my tongue though their meaning might be obscure.

There had long ago been a Sunday School Library and the
musty volumes, with not a picture among them, were moulder-
ing in their sombre bindings in a damp press in the vestry.
My mother allowed me to take a book in to the Manse pew to
while away the time of waiting between Sunday School and
Church Service. Thus I discovered among the dusty Victorian
stories for children such treasures as 'Christy's Old Organ'
and 'Jessica's First Prayer'.

My sister, who was christened Ethel but called herself
'Little Ellie', was barely five when she accompanied me on the
mile-long road to school, for at home the days were long for
her without a playmate. Wearing her new canvas school-bag
with a horse's head pictured on it, she first took my hand on a
Monday morning when all the farm-house and cottage
gardens along our route were decked with gay splashes of
coloured washing, waving like bunting all a-flutter. We
trotted contentedly along, carrying our small enamel milk-
pails, which we left in the porch on arrival, along with our

buttered pieces, hard-boiled eggs, and prunes and an apple each in a paper-bag.

On one of Ellie's first days at school a small girl called Katie had been at Mrs Davidson's wee shoppie at Rinloan in the dinner-hour to buy black sugar and on her return had amused us by smearing it over her face till she looked like a Christy Minstrel. We all thought it very funny and helped her to wash it off before Miss Arkle, the teacher, saw the state she was in. Little Ellie, sitting alone at her desk with nothing much to occupy her, thought it would be quite in order to copy Katie's antics. She had no black sugar but that did not deter her; she simply dipped her hankie in the inkwell and applied it liberally to her face. When she was observed I was permitted to take her out of school and clean her as best I could, so I took her for a walk across the moor to the school-well, where we splashed about where the cotton grass grew, and stopped to pick the sweet marsh orchis which we loved. Cotton grass, with its flower-heads resembling cotton-wool, is really a sedge found in boggy places, plentiful at the base of Geallaig near Stranlea, and we have since seen great bowlfuls of it in Dunrobin Castle, where it is a clan symbol. Shetland bairns call it 'lukkie's 'oo'.

Making allowance for Memory's rose-coloured spectacles, our childhood was a happy time. We were never bored . . . there was always something interesting to see or do.

One of our pleasures in the dinner-hour was to watch Donald Grant of Recharcharie at work in the thatched smiddy near the school. Every crofter took his horse there to be shod. Donald heated the iron in his roaring fire till red hot, then held it in an enormous pair of pincers and hammered it into shape. If the shoe did not fit the hoof at the first attempt it was reheated and hammered again to the right size, the horse meantime standing patiently by. Holes for the nails were made, and the hoof burned a little to make it smooth, so that the shoe when hammered into place was a perfect fit. The hoof was hard and horny and felt no pain. Nearby, at the Poolocks, we gathered 'shakky trummelies' and took them home to put

in a vase. They have now disappeared, like the smiddy, the school, and school-children, and so have the 'carle doddies' with which we played a game in which decapitation of our own or our opponents' doddies decided the issue of the contest. Carle stood for Charles (Prince Charles Edward Stuart) and Doddie, a diminutive of Dod or George, referred to George of Hanover (the 'wee German Lairdie'). The game of Jacobites v. Hanoverians survived long long after the historical interest faded. There was a long narrative poem of local interest, written by W. S. Daniel, called 'The Bonfire on Craig Gowan' which appeared in all the School Readers of the day, and we had to learn it by heart . . . no easy task!

An old lady on Deeside, as a child, knew the horseman who rode at the dead of night to carry the news of the Fall of Sebastopol to Queen Victoria at Balmoral Castle. Many a time she heard him tell how he was 'terrible feart' as he rode along mile after mile in the darkness. He was then an eighteen-year-old youth called David Smith who lived at Banchory. Later he was coachmen to the Burnetts.

Skipping ropes and singing games were the prerogative of the queyns at school; bools were the prized possessions of the loons. The small ones were called pizzies, a word that comes from the Gaelic and may be applied to anything small. They searched the Manse woods for forked hazel-sticks for their catapults, and made slings and bows and arrows. The Jews' Harp, or Tromp, that simple instrument beloved of loons and orra loons, was often heard in the playground. It made a peculiar twanging noise. There were various models, but in the Glen it was the Steenhive Tromp that was favoured. It had one or two stangs, or tongues, and cost a penny or tuppence. Steenhive was famous also for the making of pipes for smokers. William Ritchie of The Torran always smoked his Steenhive pipe with its shining metal cap on the bowl.

Even before we were old enough to take an active part in the work that was so important a part of the life of our

parents Ellie and I were accustomed to accompany them, out of school hours, on their travels to remote corners of the Glen, my mother usually carrying something in a covered basket. We were used to seeing one or the other at the bedside of a sick man, or at the fireside of a lonely old woman, when we would be sent to play ootbye. At the Torran there was a big stone where we liked to sit crushing broken crockery into crumbs to throw to the free-ranging hens for grit. Never were hens so well supplied . . . we chipped away, stone upon stone, and the waiting time soon passed. There were hens at the Manse, and I can still hear my mother's call of 'Took, took, took!' to summon them for their ration of grain, but I cannot recall that Ellie or I ever bothered to supply *them* with grit.

We often walked to a cottage at Candacraig with bottle-glass windows and a wide doorstep, and would be shown the cow-creamer which the bedridden old body intended to bequeath to the Laird because he had liked to play with it as a boy.

As we climbed towards Lary we passed the spot where the bank shelves gently and Gairn widens into Pool Mary, hidden under a low ceiling of spreading branches. It was there that Henry Gray and his wife on their honeymoon camped in the birk wood below Torbeg. They swam in the deep pool below the Lary farmlands and one day were visited by a shepherd who sat on the bank and newsed and newsed while the bride was obliged to remain partly submerged, getting colder and colder.

Pool Mary was a place where in the season salmon lay, and young poachers were skilled at taking them by night by the use of paraffin flares. Farther along, in the open, where the road and river run parallel, is the Cock Pool where we used to swim.

We often saw a solitary deer in the woods, and in the early morning a herd in the haugh at Invercauld, and I remember one evening when we saw a large herd on both sides of the road in Glenmuick. They were all over the moor, lying down or quietly grazing. Careful not to disturb them by sudden

noise or movement we watched for about half an hour, and
all that time, high on the skyline, a stag stood motionless as
if on guard, alert and ready to give the herd a signal at the
first sign of danger. When we returned that way some time
later the deer had disappeared . . . not a single one was to be
seen though we had left them fearlessly grazing a few feet
from the roadside. Something had disturbed them, the signal
had been given, and we had missed the splendid sight of the
whole herd galloping up the hill to join the watching stag on
the horizon. We often saw mountain hares; one I met on the
road, sitting up on his hindlegs with his forepaws crossed in
front, looking round him, indifferent to my approach. The
driver of a car coming behind him slowed down in order not
to disturb him. Suddenly he became aware of an admiring
group of spectators and casually loped away towards the
hillside.

We loved springtime when the silver birches came into leaf,
and the leaves danced like fragile green butterflies on the
slender twigs. Here and there we would find a weeping birch,
slender and graceful, its delicate leaves hanging down like a
wood-nymph's hair. There was a profusion of anemones in the
woods and cowslips on the braes; I have never forgotten their
haunting scent. When snow was still to be seen in the corries
of Ben A'an in the middle of May the old folk spoke of 'the
gab o' May'.

When Ellie and I led our guests through the wood on the
way to kirk on Sundays the trees with their varying shades of
green combined with the gold of broom made a picture not
easily forgotten. In the heart of the wood the trees were so
crowded and overhanging that we penetrated a tunnel of
green, eerie and mysterious in our eyes. Small wonder that on
our way home from school on week-days we raced through
that part of the wood as if ghosties an' ghoulies an' long leggit
beasties were after us! Tripping to school on summer mornings,
when spiders' webs hung on the juniper bushes trembling
with dew-crystals, it was a different story; we loved the gentle
wood-noises, a soft whispering under the birches.

There were summer days when we hurried home from school to help to carry the big black kettle and the picnic basket for tea beside the Milton Burn. We gathered sticks and fir-cones to make a fire, and after tea under our favourite tree, played in and out of the burn till midges drove us home. There were stretches of bog-myrtle along the road, with that elusive fragrance that one would wish to capture and bottle for use in months of exile to remind one of the Glen's scents and sounds. I love Isobel Lillie's evocative lines which, like bog myrtle, have a fragrance all their own . . .

> from their bed of sphagnum moss bog asphodels leapt as
> if they had stolen the reds and yellows and soft greens
> of the moss, their beauty a torment to children who had
> no words to express; and above the grey hill-lichens the
> little tormentil spread out its neat mat of pointed leaves
> and yellow flowers in a pattern so precise and pretty that
> it haunts me forever.

There were hot days when we helped at the hairst and had tea and home-baked scones among the stooks . . . I remember no rain in those days, but it must have come later, for a jingle comes to mind which says

> Rain the day an' rain the morn,
> Fan will we get in wir corn?
> Mebbe noo an' mebbe never,
> Michty me, fat awfu' weather!

The hills in the morning sunshine after rain were a soft blue (that blue so delicately depicted in the paintings of W. Heaton Cooper) with the shadowy line of the Cairngorms behind them. The gentle greens of spring gave way to more vivid colours, there was a rustling of tough grasses, rowan berries were turning red, bracken golden and brittle. Fallen leaves whispered round our feet, partridges called to each other across the stubble fields; there was a nip of frost in the air and we knew that it was autumn. The belief that the Northern Lights foretell stormy weather is possibly an Old Wives' Tale. They

are said to be caused by magnetic storms originating in the sun and can take place at any time of day or night and at any season. They do not necessarily mean that bad weather is in the offing, but the fact remains that we in the Nor'East usually see them dancing in all their amazing colours in the night skies of the backend, a natural time of the year for storms. Late in the season we see them when the sky is reasonably clear, and clear northern skies usually mean that colder weather is on the way.

A climber on Geallaig one early morning had an eerie experience. He was on the hill above Stranlea, looking straight across to Maamie, when he noticed a great bank of mist lying over the face of the opposite hill, and on this delicate background was thrown the gigantic figure of a man. Surrounding it was a wide ring of bright rainbow colours. The startling spectacle remained visible for several minutes, the figure apparently copying the gestures of the climber, and disappearing only when clouds obscured the sun. This was his first sighting of a Brocken Spectre, a dramatic phenomenon which climbers on Ben Nevis and other high mountains have seen when weather conditions have been favourable . . . always an unforgettable experience. The rainbow-coloured rings are known as the glories.

Thunderstorms in the Glen were often frightening in their intensity . . . lightning crackling across the sky in blinding spasms, the menacing rumbles of thunder, then the cloudburst when trickling streams became torrents that rushed foaming down the hill-sides. When Mary Essen's shining tin milk-pail was struck from her hand by lightning she had a miraculous escape; in that same storm I cycled through the Delnabo wood, drenched to the skin, riding in fear not of pneumonia but that my unprotected chromium-plated handle-bars might attract lightning. Night storms were also alarming; peals of thunder grew louder and louder, eventually crashing as it were directly overhead while lightning flashes stabbed the darkness; then came the rain as if the heavens had opened.

I remember the hush that falls upon a house when snow is

falling in the world outside. There was intense silence made more so by the soft hush of the river far below; then my mother would hap us up at bedtime and beg us to coorie down. Margaret Hudson's lines beautifully describe the enchantment of first snow on Scottish hills and in the glens:

> The hills are dazzling white; shadows of blue,
> Soft amethyst and green, stain their pure depths
> Where early morning sun's keen rays have touched
> Familiar Whitrigg, and have lit the tops
> With fingers of clear light, transmuting thus
> Her whiteness to one moment's heavenly grace,
> Young fir-trees stand, all softly streaked with white,
> Feathered their spreading boughs with sparkling frost,
> The virgin meadows, soft, untouched and pure
> Stretch to the river's steely darkness . . . all but dumb
> A tiny current through its midst still moves.
> O new-born winter world, so fair, remote and still,
> Have you forgotten summer's gladness now?
> Enamelled flowerets, clamouring birds, soft winds?
> Have you forgotten all that once was yours
> In your cold Paradise of dazzling white?

On winter evenings Ellie and I amused ourselves in a number of ways. My father gave us all the used stamps from his correspondence, and when we had collected enough we threaded them on a long string to make a snake, or covered plates with them for wall-decoration. We outlined in wool or silk perforated pictures, did cross-stitch designs on net, knitted and painted and did crochet work and played paper games. We played draughts and dominoes, Happy Families, ludo, and snakes and ladders, and with an old pack of cards played whist, Snap, and Old Maid.

Looking back, I fear we were inclined throughout the year to take for granted the wild life and wild beauty around us. Skylarks dipped and wheeled in the sunshine; capercailzies nested in the Delnabo wood and over at Dalphuil. Once I found a baby 'caper' in the long grass but did not see the parents

who can be very aggressive and defend their offspring and their territory against all-comers, even humans. On the way to school we were often amused by the sandpipers with their tails going up and down rocking on stones at the edge of Gairn. They went skimming along the water uttering their peculiar repetitive cry which sounded like 'Will-ee, need-ee'. The cuckoo used to fill the air with his shouting from late April to the end of July, and we knew the rhyme concerning him . . .

> In April, come he will,
> In flowery May he sings all day,
> In leafy June he changes tune,
> In bright July he's ready to fly,
> In August, go he must.

The birds that nested under the eaves of the steading we called swifts, but they may have been house-martins and are supposed to bring good luck. We never saw the swifts drinking . . . not many people do, but at Loch Builg they were seen dipping down as they came over the moors, taking a few sips of water as they skimmed the surface of the lochan. Once, on Geallaig, I was followed up the hill by a bevy of swifts which remained with me while I sat on my favourite boulder which resembles a crouching elephant and at its base the turf is worn away by the feet of sheltering sheep. It seemed to me there were a hundred birds or more, darting and circling, never colliding but swiftly criss-crossing; ever getting closer and wheeling past my head with a whisk of their wings, they were fascinating but disturbing, and I retraced my steps leaving the birds still swooping round the Big Stone.

Only once did we see tree-creepers and that was in the woods at the Linn o' Quoich. We saw many of the tiny birds, brown and white, about four and a half inches long, more like mice in their movements than birds. They had a noticeable habit of flying to the base of a tree, then working their way up it in spiral fashion, hunting for insects and spiders. The Glen was, and still is, full of chaffinches, usually rather timid birds, but in Glen Feshie they became very tame and actually took

crumbs of bread and chocolate from the fingers of hill-walkers.

My father's friend, the Rev. W. C. Fraser, wrote a book which he called *The Whaups o' Durley*, whaups being a local name for curlews, with their wild wistful cry. He was a frequent visitor to the Manse and told us the various names of birds . . . lapwings, for example, were also called plovers, peeweets, peesweeps, and teuchats, and the yellowhammer was variously known as yellow bunting, yellow yorling, and yellow yite. At one time this bonnie wee bird was known in all country places; nowadays it is quite an event to hear its song which traditionally sounds like 'a little bit of bread and no cheese!' John Clare, the eighteenth century poet, wrote of it

> The yellow hammer trailing grass will come
> To fix a place and choose an early home,
> With yellow breast and head of solid gold.

Ellie and I in summer came to know where wild rasps grew, and the secluded places where there were clusters of tiny wild strawberries, and blaeberries that stained fingers, lips, and pinafores and were juicy and delicious to eat, but when fruit hung in profusion from the bushes in the garden all hands were required to help with the picking, and cottage bairns came with tinnies to fill for their mothers. Part of every day had to be devoted to picking currants and rasps and the hairy little red gooseberries with their marvellous flavour, and I can still hear the blackbirds squawking as we disturbed them at their feasting and greedily resumed our own.

My mother made jam every day in the busy season, ten pounds of fruit at a time with an equal amount of sugar, stirring it with a long spoon in a large pan hung from a swey over an open wood-fire. It was a warm job and my mother was a crack hand at it. Before the end of the season she had a gratifying show of labelled two-pound pots on the larder shelves . . . blackcurrant jam and jelly, redcurrant jelly, rasp jam, rhubarb and ginger (my father's favourite) and later there was rowan jelly. The rowans had to be red and stripped of stalks. They

were simmered in water till it was red and the berries soft, then strained through a jelly-bag overnight, and a pound of sugar added to every pint of juice. Potted in small containers it was delicious to eat with venison and grouse, both of which came our way occasionally. Sometimes my mother mixed apples and rowans, boiling the berries and sliced apples slowly for a couple of hours and straining them as usual. She did not stint the sugar and this made a lovely jelly for the tea-table. Jelly-making at any time was a long-drawn-out job requiring meticulous attention but the end product more than compensated for the effort. Geans are wild cherries; they grew in the Manse garden and were bitter to eat but they made an unusual jam. My mother believed in wasting nothing, so we picked them when they were turning red, before the birds got them, stoned and weighed them, covered them with water and boiled them to pulp, to which my mother added sugar . . . about a pound to what had started as six pounds of fruit. She added either a pint of redcurrant juice or gooseberry juice, whichever was plentiful, to every pound of fruit and sugar.

She did not make marmalade; oranges were not readily available, and Keiller's excellent marmalade was bought in seven-pound jars from Cooper's in Glasgow. It made a talking-point at the breakfast-table when guests were present and were interested to learn that descendants of the famous Mrs Keiller, who started making marmalade in her own kitchen, now owned Morven estate in my father's parish, and lived near Ballater in what some folk described as a marmalade-coloured house.

James Coutts Duffus of Balclaverhouse told me how his aunt, Mrs Montgomery, bought Morven Lodge (that marmalade-coloured house, now beautifully mellowed) and incurred some local displeasure by renaming it Craigendarroch House. With it she inherited the Laird's Pew in Crathie Kirk and fondly hoped that Queen Mary would call on her. To her acute disappointment, the Queen did not call! James is a devout member of St Columba's Church in Pont Street, that much-

loved Scots kirk in the heart of London, but he still misses the
homely smell of the oil-lamps in Maine Parish Church near
Dundee, where he used to live.

When my mother was asked to contribute a recipe to a
cookery book (not till 1927 demeaned as cook-books) in aid of
some worthy cause (it was, as now, a popular way of raising
money) she invariably contributed one of three favourites . . .
White Egyptian Soup, which was based on lentils; Black Cap
Pudding, using plenty of currants at the bottom of the basin;
and a very old recipe for Bible Cake which required research
to obtain the ingredients. (I have done the home-work.)

Four and a half cups of I Kings IV, 22 (fine flour)
Half pound of Judges V, 26   (butter)
Two cups of Jeremiah VI, 20   (sugar)
Two cups of Nahum III, 12   (figs)
Two cups of I Samuel XXX, 12   (raisins)
Two cups of Numbers XVIII, 8   (almonds)
Two teaspoonfuls of Amos IV, 5   (leaven) (baking
                                      powder permissible)
To taste, II Chronicles IX, 9   (spice)
Six of Jeremiah XVII, 11   (eggs)
One and a half cupfuls of Judges IV, 19 (milk)
A pinch of Leviticus II, 13   (salt)
Directions: Proverbs XXIII, 14   (beat)
Bake for one and a half to two hours

Ellie and I learned early to lay the table, to wipe crockery
and stack it in the press; to polish silver with Goddard's Plate
Powder and keep knives bright by brisk rubbing on a special
board sprinkled with gritty bathbrick. This certainly removed
stains but left scratches on the steel. I was reminded recently
that Watson's Matchless Cleanser, a bar of soap in a tissue
wrapper, was extolled in those days in these words (after
Tennyson),

Half a pound, half a pound, half a pound only,
Into the weekly wash goes a pound only.

The wrappers had to be collected and sent in if free gifts were wanted.

By fording Gairn the distance between Ballater and Donside was considerably shortened for the Corgarff carriers who made the journey at frequent intervals in spring and summer, their tired horses panting up the Manse Brae between the shafts of clumsy farm-carts, laden with goods of every description for farm and cottage, and Miss McHardy's shoppie at Greenbank. James Rogie spent most of his early years at the farm at Cockbridge. His father was one of the carriers who went four or five times a week in the Season with game and luggage, and the butter and cheese which Jim's mother made, hopeful of a better price in Ballater than she could get in Corgarff. On the return journey he brought provisions for the Big Hoose, which was Delnadamph. The carriers rested their horses for a spell at the head of the Manse Brae. One man was called Kellas. At some period of his life he had lost an ear, and was an object of wonder to us bairns. It was said he had been bitten by an angry horse. He and the other carriers lightened their homeward journey with raucous song and imbibed, as they travelled, the supply of whisky they had bought for the road. The need for carriers ceased when a good road carried motor-vehicles speedily from Cockbridge to Strathdon, Alford, and on to Aberdeen. Holiday-makers on the genteel walking tours which were then the rage had to plod uphill for many a mile. In the 1930s they became known as hikers, and wore hiking garb. Dare one suppose that Christina Rossetti knew the trials, as well as the pleasure of hill-walking? Could she otherwise have written with such feeling:

> Does the road wind uphill all the way?
> Yes, to the very end.
> Will the day's journey take the whole day?
> From morn to night, my friend.

Margaret Moubray Fraser of Garve in mid-Cromarty remem-

bers the wonderful summer holidays she and her brothers and sisters had at Delnadamph when they were children. They drove from Ballater in a wagonette, and it was a thrill to ford Gairn, rocking over its stony bed. Briggie Morrison once drove them across when the river was in spate. They went over a boulder and the wagonette nearly capsized. Safely on the far side, Briggie turned round and said to the little Moubrays, with a grin, 'We were nearly over Jordan then!' They all ran up the brae to save the horses, picking harebells and ladies' bedstraw, and all the other Highland wild flowers they were so happy to see again.

My mother held a singing-class at the Manse every Saturday afternoon which all the bairns in the Glen attended. Nellie Douglas recalls how she crossed Gairn from Torbeg on stepping stones and never missed a session. . . . Primarily, the class was formed to practise hymns to swell the praise on Sundays, and it became an institution. From hymn-singing it progressed to songs and ballads such as 'The Birks o' Aberfeldy' to a seventeenth-century air which when played briskly made an excellent tune for reels. She also taught us to sing 'Be it ever so humble, there's no place like home' giving poignancy to the words by telling us the life story in brief of John Howard Payne, who was by turns an actor, editor, poet, and homeless wanderer. The song made his name immortal, and Clara Butt made the song famous by singing it all over the world in her unforgettable contralto to Henry Bishop's melody. Year after year my mother trained a succession of young voices, encouraging them to sing alone and in chorus at the concert she gave in her drawing-room at the end of the season, when all the mothers came to hear their bairns sing, and then had tea and cake. In her own childhood she had been taught to perform on the pianoforte (perform was the appropriate word) 'The Maiden's Prayer' and similar compositions in which the fingers ran up and down the keyboard and called for occasional crossing of the left hand over the right to strike a high note while the right was fully occupied in maintaining

the melody. When she and I played duets at the drawing-room concerts she, with a twinkle in her eye, and with exaggerated flourishes of her long-fingered hands, would sometimes cross one over the other when not strictly necessary, because she knew it amused us and impressed the bairns.

Having grounded us thoroughly she sent us to Ballater to have pianoforte lessons from Mr Whiteley, a genial Yorkshireman who was organist in the parish church. I had my early lessons from Hemy's Tutor of the Rudiments of Music, that great standby of my generation. Ellie, when it came to her turn, had Smallwood's, which considered itself 'the Best of all Tutors'. It was a long trail for bairns to follow on Saturday afternoons in summer, and I also remember winter nights when with my mother we walked home after attending a concert in Ballater . . . nights so dark and still with hardly a breath of wind to stir the trees, the only sounds being the night-birds chuckling and the distant murmur of Gairn; sometimes our road was lighted by a brilliant moon and a myriad of stars.

Maggie Cumming, who for years was housekeeper at Corndavon Lodge and was devoted to Mrs Inge, the wife of the shooting tenant, in my childhood had retired to her own cottage, one of three known as Tullichandurich, where yellow Scotch roses still cling to the rubble. We visited her frequently and she would beg my mother to sing to her, which she did while knitting at the peat fireside. She knitted our stockings and her own, and my father's socks, and was continually knitting for parish sales of work and for the troops . . . it was the South African War at that time. She always had something on her 'wires', and took her knitting everywhere she went. I recall that one lady in whose house we were staying, appeared to consider my mother's busy needles an affront to her hostess. No affront was visualised . . . she was simply unable to sit with idle hands.

Like William Burnes, the father of Robert Burns, Maggie's father had built the cottage with his own hands, stone by stone, toiling from dawn to dusk to make a home in the midst of

stony ground and heather. In those early cottages the roof-tree was laid along the top of masonry walls, superseding the earlier drystane walls, with a chimney built into the gable at either end. The roof was made of poles with a layer of sods neatly pegged together above them, and then thatch. Maggie's but-an'-ben was wind and weather-proof, the walls inside and out were whitewashed, the wooden ceiling was black with peat-reek, and the floor was of roughly hewn stone.

When Ellie and I spent a happy day watching the activity on the farm when the thrashin' mill came to Balno, Maggie told us how very important that day was in her childhood, for that was the day when all the caff beds were renewed. Early in the morning all the old chaff was emptied into the pig-sty; the bed-ticks were washed and dried in the sun . . . even the bolster-shaped mattress from the cradle was emptied and washed. That night, after a long day in the sun, the ticks were filled by hand with clean chaff left by the thrashin' mill, and every member of the family who could ply a needle and thread sat down and worked till all were sewn up. Not until this was done could anybody go to bed! The newly-filled caff beds were now so high that the bairns had to climb into bed, and, said Maggie, the littlins were tossed up and thought it great fun; in fact, the tossing was repeated as often as her father was willing to do the tossing, and until her mother cried, 'That'll dae noo, bairns! Coorie doon, yer faither an' me maun rise at scraich o' day!'

Strict economy was practised, of necessity, in every part of Scotland. Maggie told us of many ways in which her parents economised, but did not mention an ingenious practice of which Mary Little told me. Her mother, left a widow, with a young family to bring up alone, used to cut her laddies' breeks above the knee when they showed signs of wearing thin. She then sewed the leg back in place, but this time the worn place was *behind* the knee. So, with the weak part now at the back the breeks had every chance of giving longer wear, and no need for a disfiguring patch. Bed valances, Mary told me, were on every bed and were of excellent quality in cotton fabric.

When valances were no longer used, the fabric was made into pillow-cases which washed and wore forever.

On the small farms in winter there was little that could be done apart from attending to the cattle and horses. This involved daily threshing of straw which was the only winter feed in those days. The thrashing was done with a flail in the early morning. It was a tiring job on a cold January day to wield the long, jointed, wooden flail for an hour or more. Ellie and I watched the orra man flailing in the barn opposite our nursery window. He laid one or two sheaves on the barn floor, and down came the flail with a resounding thud, thud, till all the grain was separated from the straw which was then made up into bundles. The grain was then separated from the chaff and preserved, and the tired and hungry man could then feed the beasts and depart to Balno for his well-earned breakfast of porridge and milk . . . and maybe a sup of home-brewed ale.

The Manse garden was full of old-fashioned flowers. Columbines, Solomon's seals, peony roses, scarlet poppies, bachelors' buttons, gardener's garters, monkshood, and the prolific yellow Iceland poppies which today have seeded themselves in isolated clumps on the Manse Brae. My father sowed annuals such as Shirley poppies, blue cornflowers and small-flowered sweet peas which had a much sweeter scent than the large-flowered varieties of today, so enthusiastically extolled for size and colour in seedsmen's catalogues.

My father worked very hard tilling and planting the vegetable garden. He exchanged seed potatoes with neighbouring farmers, but mostly used seed from the best of his own crop, which he prepared, setting them out in rows with the eyes facing upwards. We had midday dinner when we were children, but it was 'lunch' when we had it with Mrs Crewdson and her daughters at the Shiel, with Whittaker handing the vegetables. (Surnames only were used then in big houses.) Whittaker had been head tablemaid at Alderley Edge for many years and came with the family to Gairnshiel every

year. One year she did not return with them; Miss Whittaker had quietly married a local man and was now Mrs Coutts, exchanging life in a Cheshire mansion for that in her own but-an'-ben.

One day when Ellie and I were having tea at Torbeg with the Douglas family, Bella, to demonstrate she alone knew what, took her best wax doll which was out of its box for the occasion, and chopped off its head. As soon as the Manse bairns had gone home she received a thorough skelpin' for that exhibition of her prowess with an axe. I once behaved in a similar way; I remember sitting up in my cot with the brass knobs, clutching my best doll which had been a Christmas present from Mrs Forder of the Shiel. I was for the time being a sick child and doubtless bored, but that does not explain why I should have ploughed through the waxen cheeks with an open safety-pin, scoring them repeatedly till the doll was completely disfigured. I was about four at the time and did not get the punishment I so richly deserved.

Ellie and I were rather shy of Meggie Bremner and the bees she kept in straw skeps on the back-green at Stranlea, but Nellie Douglas liked to run messages for her and afterwards was given a biscuit from the tin pail which swung from a hook in the rafters. We heard how Nellie's grandfather, known to us as Old Mr Thow, had killed and skinned his fattened pig and placed the jointed carcase in brine in a large tub in preparation for the prolonged process of curing it for winter fare. During the night the entire contents of the tub were stolen. Only a few people knew about the pig-killing so the thief was obviously a local man. Mr Thow declared that he had a good idea who he was but for lack of evidence took no steps to recover his stolen pig. When marauding deer on winter nights were destroying his turnip crop, he sat up one cold evening with a rifle and managed to shoot a young stag. When he reached the spot where it fell he could find no wound on it; the shot had entered the base of the horns and had merely stunned it. When

it recovered he took it by the horns and led it back to Torbeg and there he killed it. Mr Thow in his younger days had been an outrider in the service of the Queen and had many tales to tell of life in the precincts of Balmoral. Now his days were filled with more mundane tasks. He used to take us and our friends to Braemar and the Linn o' Dee in his pony phaeton and delighted us with his racy stories.

Queen Victoria's arrival in Ballater was always most impressive. After inspecting her Guard of Honour, which ever since her day has been selected from a Highland Regiment, and is housed in Ballater Barracks, she drove off in an open carriage to which were harnessed the famous Windsor Greys. We used to go to Fit o' Gairn to see her pass by, a little old lady, very serious-looking, in a black bonnet with wide satin ribbons, and a dolman . . . a sort of fitted jacket with a shoulder-cape, very elaborate with beaded fringes. I believe, when she was young, when paying calls in the neighbourhood, she wore a Paisley shawl, for my grandmother told me that she, on her wedding-day, wore a shawl exactly like the one the Queen had approved and made high fashion.

The Windsor Greys were ridden by postillions accompanied by smart outriders, all in white breeches, coloured jackets, and black jockey caps. On the box, beside the top-hatted coachman, sat a liveried footman, and two kilted attendants stood on a ledge directly behind the Queen. She was always glad to come back to Balmoral where she could relax and enjoy simple things, away from the formality of Court life. She may have stated on one occasion 'We are not amused', but she did not make a habit of it as some chroniclers would have us believe. Actually she was amused by a number of things. My father delighted in telling of a day when a certain worthy minister had been invited to preach in Crathie Kirk. The Queen had been warned that he had a rather affected way of speaking and also that he would probably choose his favourite psalm, 'O clap your hands'. Sure enough the minister announced from the pulpit the forty-seventh psalm and introduced it in these

words, 'All people clip your hens', and the Queen was seen to have a smile hovering on her lips.

She enjoyed a good play and used to invite theatrical companies to perform before her at Windsor and Balmoral. She was particularly fond of Gilbert and Sullivan operas, and on one occasion, at least, invited the D'Oyly Carte Company to visit Balmoral.

Many years after, a member of the Company, sitting at my own fireside, recalled his first Royal Performance of *The Mikado*. He remembered the slow train journey from London, the cold drive up Deeside in wagonettes, and a long day spent at the Castle. They were hospitably, even lavishly, entertained throughout the day while they prepared to do their own form of entertainment in a rather crowded improvised theatre. There is a great deal of ceremonial bowing and scraping in *The Mikado*, and when the hour came to present the opera it was a somewhat shaky performance, for the men's chorus, prostrated practically at the feet of their Sovereign, had some difficulty in regaining their feet. My father was present when the Queen laid the foundation stone of Crathie Kirk in 1893, and also at its dedication for public worship in 1895. The Queen first attended a Service of the Church of Scotland when she and the Prince Consort were the guests of the Duke and Duchess of Atholl at Blair Atholl; she was present in 1871 at a Service of Holy Communion and thereafter regularly took Communion in Scotland. When she was in residence at Balmoral her Ministers were obliged to make the long journey from London to discuss affairs of state. Trains were not comfortable, there was the drive in a brake from Ballater to Balmoral, and the Castle was draughty. In the memoirs of Court ladies, one and all remark on Balmoral's chilly environment; the Queen did not seem to feel the cold. She went out in all weathers. A story handed down in Crathie tells of a day when there was an outbreak of fire in the Castle. It must have been in the Queen's appartments, for she did not encourage general lighting of fires in bedrooms or sitting-rooms. The fire, fortunately, was quickly extinguished, but the incident upset the Queen who was grate-

ful for the kindly concern and ready sympathy of one of the
maids, a young Crathie girl, who looked after her while more
responsible servants were engaged in putting out the fire. Next
morning, the Queen apparently regretted her temporary loss
of dignity; the young girl was summoned to her presence and
admonished for having presumed to address the Queen as
'Dearie'.

John Brown was allowed freedom of speech and manner
that was not permitted any other Royal servant, or, indeed,
ladies and gentlemen of the Court. He had been the trusted
and faithful attendant of the Prince Consort, and therefore, in
the eyes of the Queen, he could do no wrong. His relatives at
Loinahaun in the Glen, who were visited by the Queen,
encouraged him in his own estimation of himself as a very
important man, 'in charge o' the affairs o' the nation'.
Ministers of State found his familiarity insufferable, and there
is the well-known story of the day he was sent by the Queen to
find her lady-in-waiting. He discovered her in the garden and
exclaimed 'Ye're the verra wumman A'm lookin' for'! She
resented his manner and reported it to the Queen who merely
said, mildly, 'Well, you *are* a woman!'

John never attempted to acquire the polished manners of
the Court, but he was natural and gentle in his approach to the
Queen, and would never have done anything to dim her bright
image, and her unswerving devotion was ever to the memory of
her beloved Albert. When John's father, Donald Brown, died
at Micras in 1875, the Queen attended the funeral service in the
house, watched the sad procession leave for the kirkyard down
by the river, then went back indoors 'to comfort dear old Mrs
Brown', who was Jessie Shaw before her marriage. It was
Lauchlan Shaw who married Agnes Fraser, a daughter of Lord
Lovat in 1407. David Fraser of Balno, who was brought up at
Tullichmacarrick, today claims descent from the Lovat Frasers,
and in support of his claim has a portrait of his father which
shows an amazing family likeness to that of Simon Lovat who
was beheaded after Culloden.

The marriage of the Princess Louise, fourth daughter of

Queen Victoria, to the Marquess of Lorne, eldest son of the Duke of Argyll, in March 1871, was regarded in the Campbell country as an alliance of equals . . . well, almost equals, the Campbell chieftain being thought the superior of Royalty. My father took pleasure in relating the story of the aged Campbell adherent who, on the wedding morning, declared, 'The Queen maun be a prood wumman the day! Her dochter's gettin' the son o' the Duke!' a nice lesson in social values.

In 1899, when I was seven years old, Britons all over the world celebrated the Queen's eightieth birthday. As one journalist put it, 'From the goldfields of Africa, the snowfields of Canada, from the Australian bush and the Indian jungle, a paean of joy wafted across the seas to Royal Windsor.' He went on to say, 'from hitherto silent quarters (Republican America and foreign courts) come tokens of respect and love'. The weight of her power on the side of peace and progress, her sympathy and concern for the humblest of her subjects, and her influence for good were all stressed, and the article ends, 'One cannot think of the age of the Queen, and the ceremonials of which she is the centre, without expressing the opinion that it is time she were spared the excitement which cannot be divorced from such proceedings. Her Majesty has earned a long rest . . . that she may for many years yet reign over us is the wish of millions of loyal men and women today.' (I found the newspaper cutting among my father's papers dated 1 May 1899.)

Undoubtedly many of the thousands of people who eagerly line the road to Crathie Kirk on summer Sundays hoping to glimpse the Royal Family on their way to and from church, firmly believe they have had a special smile from the Queen. Her gift of conveying in a smile a personal greeting promotes in her subjects the affection felt by the woman who ninety-five years ago had a bow and a smile from Queen Victoria. The pleasure it gave her was expressed in verses which were published in an Aberdeen newspaper in 1880. The Queen read them and liked them so much that she enquired the name of the author, who was Dewar Willock, a young journalist.

I'm jist an aul' body leevin' up on Deeside
In a twa-roomed bit hoosie wi' a twa-fa' beside,
Wi' ma coo an' ma grumphie I'm as happy's a bee
Bit I'm far prooder noo sin' *she* noddit tae me.

I'm nae sae far past wi't, I'm gey trig an' hale,
Can plant twa-three tatties an' look efter ma kail,
An' fan oor Queen passes I rin oot tae see
Gin by hap she micht notice an' nod oot tae me.

Bit I've aye been at faut an' the blin's were aye doon,
Till last week the time o' her veesit cam roon,
I waved ma bit apron as brisk's I could dee,
An' the Queen lauched fu' kindly an' noddit tae me.

Ma son sleeps in Egypt, it's nae eese tae freit,
An' yet, fan I think on't, I'm sair like tae greet,
She may feel for ma sorrow, she's a mither, ye see,
An' mebbe she kent o't fan she noddit tae me.

I remember when there was a clachan of thatched cottages at Piperhole on the Crathie side of the Stranyarroch. The people in the clachan had a hard struggle; winters were long and harvests poor. Wild life supplied much of their daily food; few had travelled far from their native hills, so they knew little of what was going on in the outside world, but they were hardy, independent people, living largely a communal life and working hard for subsistence. For a short time my mother had a little maid called Lizzie Lamond from Piperhole who could not settle in strange surroundings, and with her first wages clutched in her hand trekked all the way home over the steep Stranyarroch.

At haytime and the hairst, at turnip-hoeing, sheep-shearing, and peat-casting both men and women in Piperhole found employment on neighbouring farms, The Bush, Crathie-naird, Lawsie, The Lebhal, and the Newton. If work was hard to come by, the able-bodied men and women went over the hills

to The Mearns to give a hand at the hairst for a few weeks, this enabled them to bring back meal which the minister doled out with a careful hand to keep the members of the little community alive till better times came round. The older women-folk were left behind to look after the hens and the soo, and to put their few sheep and cattle to the hills for pasture. Queen Victoria was a frequent visitor to the thackit clay biggins which the original occupants had built with their own hands. She sat at their firesides and brought them presents which they valued . . . tea, a shawl, perhaps a red flannel petticoat, or tobacco . . . in those days many of the cailleachs as well as the bodachs liked to smoke a clay pipe. In country byways as summer passed into autumn the Queen was constantly seen driving quietly in her pony carriage; we were so accustomed to seeing her on her quiet outings, we never realised how much her Court and her Capital missed her. From the year 1848 up to the last year of her life she had formed the habit of coming early to Balmoral and staying late. She built Glas-allt-shiel in a wild spot at the head of Loch Muick. She was a lover of nature and made a point of spending a night or two at that Sheil, preferably when the first light fall of snow lay on the hills. 'Only the snow fleggit her awa', is the legend. Actually, she loved it and found it hard to leave Balmoral. In the year 1897, my father recorded in his diary that the Queen did not leave for Windsor till 12 November. A few days before she was due to leave her Highland home for the last time she drove round the Crathie cottages to say Goodbye. She was too frail to descend from her carriage so she was driven right up to the doors. The women who had enjoyed her visits since both she and they were young, and younger women who had known her since they were children, came out to greet her and wish her Godspeed. I doubt if any of them had the heart to add the timeless 'Haste ye back'. They must have known it was their last sight of her. She died the following spring. In many a home to this day is treasured a red and gold tin box that once contained chocolates. It has Queen Victoria's head embossed

on the lid, and the dates 1900–2. It was presented by the Queen to every man who gave his services in the South African War. My own recollections of that war are mainly of my father's 'Black and White', and other periodicals devoted to war news, of wearing lapel buttons showing the picture of favourite generals, of victory celebration dumplings, and of hearing Winston Churchill's marvellous escape from being a prisoner of war; but Leah Neal remembers the day that Queen Victoria died. She and her little brother were indulging in a noisy game of 'Liberals and Tories' and were suddenly told, 'Hush! The Queen is dead!' A picture by S. Begg, familiar to me since childhood, shows the Queen leaning from her carriage to speak to an old woman in a mutch and spotless apron. The coachman has the Windsor Greys under control and a mounted groom, who preceded the Queen's carriage at all times, is in attendance. I have always supposed the scene to be Piperhole. The picture was reproduced as an almanac in October 1900, and a copy hung in every cottage and farmhouse, and in the Manse kitchen long after 1901 had expired.

Year after year we attended the Lonach Gathering, where John Philip of Garchory invariably won the prize for the Best Dressed Highlander . . . a fine figure in Highland dress, with a family of sturdy boys, each the image of his father.

In August, on the day of the Gathering, old Scottish traditions come to life among the wooded hills when clansmen follow again in the footsteps of their forefathers. Early in the morning, when mist is wreathing the hills, there is bustle and an air of expectancy as men don kilts, doublets, plaids and buckled shoon, and in their Glengarry bonnets place the sprig of broom that is the badge of the Forbes clan, as their forebears have done for over a hundred and fifty years. They congregate at Bellabeg where pikes and Lochaber axes are distributed and, led by their chieftain and standard-bearers, with pipers playing 'Blue Bonnets', they set off across the hump-backed briggie and away over the brow of the hill, a stirring sight with morning sunshine glinting on halberds.

[83]

More than three miles up the strath they march, with a number of stops on the way where traditional hospitality is shown, and at Candacraig they are joined by a contingent in the colourful Wallace tartan, with heather in their bonnets. The horse and cairtie is a long-established feature of the Clansmen's March. Any Highlander who fell by the wayside was given a hurll in the cairtie, which is a freshly-painted farm-cart to which a handsome cart-horse with polished harness and shining brasses is harnessed and led by a brawny young Highlander. In the years between 1850 and 1861 it was the Lonach custom to take part in the Braemar Games. Through the valleys of Don, Gairn, and Dee they marched, arriving in Braemar at nightfall. Next day they took part in the Games, danced at the Ball, and rested in their camp by Dee for a whole day, gathering strength for the long trek home. They were often visited by the Queen who loved old customs, and in her Journal of her Life in the Highlands she describes how the Balmoral gillies gave the Lonach men lifts on their backs across the Dee.

In 1854 she presented them with the Colours they still proudly carry. Nowadays, after the Clansmen's March, they feast in the oak-beamed banqueting-hall, then make their triumphal afternoon March of Honour round the arena. As in former times the contestants compete in feats of strength, fleetness of foot and nimble dancing to the skirl of the pipes in the lovely setting of the hills at Colquhonnie. As in most places the Games are followed by a Ball when the people of Strathdon, lords and ladies and farming folk forget their worries in the sheer enjoyment of the splendour and colour of the dance. Another democratic occasion is the Aboyne Highland Gathering when lairds and farmers, ploughmen and shepherds, employers and employees, meet on a common ground, intent on enjoying all that the day holds for them in the old Scottish tradition; the same applies to Ballater where Highland Games have been held for over a hundred years. Highland Games can be traced back to the ninth century when Kenneth MacAlpine became King of the Picts and Scots

but for centuries they were small informal affairs. After the
'45 Rising it looked as if these meetings of clansmen were gone
for ever. The rights of the chieftains were abolished, the
bearing of arms and the wearing of tartan forbidden, and
bagpipes declared an instrument of war, so Highland gatherings were not held for nearly a hundred years. In 1832 a Royal
Highland Society was formed in Braemar, a gathering was
held, and proved a popular revival. Sixteen years later Queen
Victoria attended the gathering at Braemar and by this
gracious act not only set the seal of success on the Deeside
venture, but restored Highland Games to their place of honour
in Scottish tradition . . . a field of contest for kilted stalwarts
who practise ancient Highland sports . . . caber tossing,
hammer throwing, wrestling, jumping, racing. To others it is
a pipe-music festival, and to others again it means an
exhibition of the most accomplished Highland dancers. I
remember some of the athletes who competed when I was a
child. There was 'Lawsie' . . . Sandy Macintosh of the farm of
Lawsie in Crathie, who could toss the caber when he was over
seventy years of age. He was standard-bearer to the
Farquharson clan in the annual March of the Clans, competed
with great success at the Braemar Gathering for over fifty
years, and on his seventy-fourth birthday kicked the lintel of
a doorway six-and-a-half feet high. None of the young men
looking on could attempt such a feat. He was also a popular
singer of ballads in the old castle of Mar, and gillie to King
Edward VII. James Michie of Renatton was a champion
dancer; so was David Rose, known as Dancie Rose, who was
Master of Ceremonies at the annual Gillies Ball at Balmoral
for many years and taught the younger members of the Royal
Family Highland dancing. There was an old man in Braemar
who remembered when ladies climbed Lochnagar in long
trailing skirts, and recalled how William Ewart Gladstone,
who achieved his ambition to climb Lochnagar, did so twice,
and later managed to reach the remote Pools of Dee but
refused to go a step further, so depriving himself and his
gillie of the grand view over the Spey.

At Old Mar Castle lived the Princess Dolgorouki, a very rich woman whose London house was in Portman Square. She had been Miss Fleetwood-Wilson, daughter of a shipping magnate of the Wilson-Ellerman Line, and married Prince Alexis Dolgorouki, the youngest son of the Secretary of State and Privy Seal to the Tsar of Russia. They rented the Old Castle of Mar from the Farquharsons of Invercauld, and entertained there on a lavish scale. When her husband died, the Princess lived very quietly, and her famous jewels were seldom seen. Edward Shirran, whose father was the Bank Manager in Braemar, remembers a day in 1912 when he, ten years old, and his brother aged six, met the Princess in the village and they were invited to have tea with her next day. Their father thought they were romancing. However, in due course, a footman arrived at the Bank House to escort the boys to the Castle. Due to some misunderstanding, they were ushered into the Servants' Hall where they were given a splendid tea, with substantial sandwiches, scones and cakes, to which they did full justice. Presently, a door opened and the major-domo in livery of velvet and gold braid, white stockings and buckled shoon, appeared and demanded if the young Masters Shirran had arrived as they were expected to have tea with the Princess. They were shown up to the drawing-room where the Princess was waiting, and they were given another tea, which luckily consisted of the tiniest daintiest sandwiches and small cakes which they managed to eat, and did not give the show away!

CHAPTER IV

A SCHOOL-GIRL IN EDINBURGH

31 May 1906 is a date I find easy to remember; it marked the end of my school-days in the Glen. It was also the wedding-day of King Alphonso XIII of Spain and our own golden-haired Princess Ena, who was born at Balmoral Castle and spent long holidays there. Her widowed mother, Princess Beatrice, was Grandmama Victoria's constant companion, and a close girl-hood friend was her cousin, Princess Alice, who became the Countess of Athlone. We had often seen them driving in a phaeton along our country roads. I still retain the memory of the widespread horror when news came that a bomb had been thrown by a terrorist, Matteo Morral, at the King and his beautiful bride as their carriage drove through the streets of Madrid. They escaped unhurt, but five soldiers and two horses were killed. What a shock, we exclaimed, for our gentle Ena and her young husband, at the outset of their married life, to hear the crowd outside the Royal Palace screaming for blood throughout that night of terror!

Great preparations were going on in the Manse for my imminent departure to a boarding-school in Edinburgh that

had been founded for the daughters of ministers. Had we lived a century earlier my parents might have read something like this . . . 'Pupils are entitled to have *one* set of underclothing, *one* pair of stockings, and *two* handkerchiefs per month, and complete baths three times a year, in May, June and July. Pupils who are unable to take their bath on the appointed day must wait till the following month.' That extract was from the prospectus of a young ladies' school in 1794. No trousseau could have been more lovingly prepared than was my school outfit; never before had I possessed so many new clothes! My mother took me to Aberdeen on a shopping spree, the first time we had ever done such a thing. We spent the entire day in Pratt and Keith's First Class Emporium in Union Street, long since disappeared, its commanding corner site has changed owners many times since those days. Armed with the school's official clothing list, we went from one department to another, spending long hours and what seemed to me a great deal of money on sheets and shoes and sundries, hats and hose and handkerchiefs. My mother paid cash for everything, as was my parents' habit, and was rewarded, not by generous discount, which she naïvely did not look for, but with a voucher for afternoon tea for two, which we thought was a marvellous gesture.

Somebody must have carried our numerous packages to the station, and at Ballater there must have been a hire to take us home, but such details are now forgotten. The following weeks were busy ones, entailing the stitching of woven name-tapes on everything washable, and involving the use of indelible marking-ink on everything else. Girls carried no hand-bags in those days, but Mrs Ritchie of the Torran made me a Granny Pooch of printed cotton lined with scarlet. It was a Lucy Locket type of pocket. The nursery rhyme says that careless

> Lucy Locket lost her pocket
> Kitty Fisher found it
> But ne'er a penny was there in't
> Except the binding round it.

[88]

I could not have lost mine, for it was made to be tied round my waist and worn under my skirt which had a side fastening. The slit in front of the pocket admitted my hand so my purse would be safe from pickpockets. It was customary to carry one's small pasteboard railway-ticket in the palm of the hand, inside one's buttoned glove.

The summer months passed, then one afternoon in September my parents left a timid, bewildered daughter in the care of an older girl, and with brave encouraging words turned away from the School, which was grandly called a College. Each of us had a catch in the throat which we managed to conceal, aware that the weeks would seem interminable till we met again. Never before had I been away from home without my parents. When it dawned on me that for the next twelve weeks I would not be free to go outside the gate, to read a book or to write a letter without permission, or to take a single step without specific direction, I was appalled.

That first evening at the supper-table I shaded my eyes with my hand as my father had taught me to do when Grace was said, but a titter and a murmur of 'Gosh, how holy!' showed me that in that huge place packed with strangers this was Not Done. Eager to please, credulous, and painfully shy I was easy to fool. 'Word of honour' was supposed to be binding . . . how was a gullible country child to know there were ways of rendering it negative?

At first I seemed to live in a permanent state of perplexed embarrassment, but gradually made friends whose companionship was a comfort; it was the absence of freedom and privacy I found hard to bear.

Not for one minute in the day could a girl be alone, except in the one obvious place, and even there not for long . . . there were only two on each landing. Every minute had its ordained employment. When the rising-bell sounded at 6.30, we fetched warm water from a tap in a housemaid's pantry on the landing to wash in the basin provided in each cubicle. There was no suggestion of fagging, but it was an unwritten rule that the youngest girls in a dormitory carried water for

[89]

the seniors. It was a privilege and a pleasure to fetch and carry and run errands for our chosen idols.

Curtains enclosed our cubicles; we dressed and undressed modestly behind them, and pulled them back only when the cubicle was unoccupied. Roll Call was at 7.30, followed by Prayers, the hymn being accompanied, as at Evening Prayers, by a girl on a wheezy portable harmonium. We then filed out to the dining-hall where long tables spread with spotless white cloths extended almost the length of the hall. Breakfast consisted of oatmeal porridge, tea, bread and butter with golden syrup and marmalade but *never* butter and syrup (or marmalade) on the same piece of bread. (We had a boiled egg for breakfast once a year, on Easter Day.) At 8.30 precisely we trooped upstairs to make our beds, and at 9 o'clock lessons began.

The formrooms had floors of unpolished wood which always looked clean though we never saw them scrubbed. This must have been done in the early hours of the morning, for the rooms were in use every hour of the day till bedtime. Upstairs was out-of-bounds during the day, presumably to allow the domestic staff to work undisturbed.

There were two pepper-pot turrets in the building, which were said to be haunted, a legend that was perpetuated by succeeding generations of girls. The smaller turret, with its locked door directly behind my bed, served as a repository for new brooms and cleaning materials; the larger made a pleasant bedroom for one, when required.

Our school was built in 1863 on land which in olden times formed part of the Burghmuir, where, as told in 'Marmion', the Scots Army mustered under King James IV before they marched to Flodden.

Turner's picture of 'Edinburgh from the Braid Hills' depicts the ground as far as the north side of the Meadows, covered with trees and cultivated fields.

In recent years the school buildings have become the property of the Royal Bank of Scotland, and are used as a residential centre, providing courses for all grades of student-

bankers from beginners to managers. Outside, there is little change apart from new gates; inside, the entrance hall and staircase with the stained glass windows, have been transformed by beautiful carpets and interior decoration. School-rooms are now well-equipped lecture rooms. Upstairs there are suites of rooms where once were dormitories, and from the top floor hangs a large chandelier which lights all these floors. The old 'lab' is now an exact replica of a bank, where students learn procedure, and the 'gym' is a theatre with tip-up seats and audio-visual aids for lectures.

The Principal in my day was an elderly lady with snow-white hair and a sweet, saintly face, who lives in memory as a gently rustling figure who addressed us as gels. She took prayers each morning wearing a tailored skirt and blouse of Macclesfield silk, softly draped in front, with long gold chains disposed about the folds. This standard blouse, in varying tones of blue or grey, had a high neck, a lace jabot, and full sleeves gathered into long close-fitting cuffs with a dozen silk-covered buttons like tiny balls. In the afternoon she wore with quiet elegance sweeping black dresses, and when we occasionally caught a glimpse of her descending the staircase on her way to an evening function, with Jeanie hovering at hand with her cloak, she was beautifully gowned in black velvet, with a silver-mounted reticule on a chain at her waist. She possessed a variety of reticules; even in daylight hours she wore one in which to carry her handkerchief. I never saw her fumbling in a pocket let into a side-seam of her skirt as most ladies had to do in those days.

She took no part in the educational side of school life, except to give us informal Bible lessons with the aid of a faded old map of the Holy Land; but she used to read aloud to us during our afternoon sewing sessions . . . the books I recall her reading were *The Prisoner of Zenda*, and its sequel, *Rupert of Hentzau*, Horace Annesley Vachell's new novel, *The Hill*, Scott's *Kenilworth*, A. E. W. Mason's *The Four Feathers*, Neil Munro's *The Daft Days*, and Wilkie Collins' *The Moonstone* and *The Woman in White*.

[91]

Many years later I read of a visit to Cumberland which Collins and Dickens, who were related, paid in 1852, and learned that their stay in the tiny village of Allonby, along the coast from Silloth, looking across the Solway to the long line of Scottish hills, and an excursion to Ewanrigg Hall, resulted in *The Woman in White*. The hero in that tale had to wait for a couple of hours at Carlisle railway station before proceeding to his destination, an exasperating experience since shared by thousands of travellers.

Miss Robertson read simply and smoothly, without art or affectation, without raising her voice, and with no gestures beyond an occasional lifting of her hand, but she transported us to a new environment and new emotions.

We saw no newspapers and it was years before I acquired the habit of news-reading, but once a week we were fed selected titbits from the *Scotsman* and *The Times*, and in this way learned that Peary had reached the North Pole, and that Bleriot had flown the Channel. Miss Robertson also read us selections from *Punch*, each time announcing that it was a national institution, repeating the name of the Editor, Owen Seaman, and explaining all the topical jokes. I remember two of them to this day: one following a piece of flowery English Prose, descriptive of blue water and palm trees. *Punch's* comment was 'Isn't it bay-utiful?' The other was a problem in etiquette; a young man entering a crowded drawing-room supposedly gets his coat-tails caught in the door . . . what should his hostess do? *Punch's* advice. . . The hostess should at once seize the cake-knife, cut off the coat-tails and introduce the young man to the company as 'My son from Eton'. Where is my sense of humour? I did not think it funny then, nor do I today.

Between novels she read Kipling's *Just So Stories*, the Uncle Remus stories of Gerald Chandler Harris, and Jerrold's Curtain Lectures, so that we came to love Dog Dingo, Brer Rabbit, Brer Fox, the Elephant's Child, and the Tar Baby, and laughed with her at that garrulous lady, Mrs Caudle.

In sewing-class we might have been taught to use a sewing-

machine, but this we learned at home, and my parents gave me a hand-machine for a Christmas present.

There was an idea that persisted well into the twentieth century that ladies' underwear must be hand-sewn, so we hemmed long seams, gathered (and stroked each gather) back-stitched, over-seamed, stitched flounces on petticoats, and hid the joins under bands of insertion through which blue ribbon had to be threaded. We made buttonholes, and tacked on tapes, and at the rate at which all these stages of needle-work were accomplished, it was just possible to finish a garment in a couple of terms.

These garments consisted of long, full-skirted petticoats set in a shaped waist-band, high-necked full-length nightdresses with long sleeves and frilling at wrists and collar, and a little way down the front (exactly like those in my mother's trousseau!), frilled knickers with a shaped waist-band and back-fastening with large linen buttons, a jigsaw of odd shaped pieces which was at times hard to assemble; these masterpieces were all constructed of hard-wearing nainsook, and there were also camisoles of fine cotton, laced round the top with baby-blue ribbon, their main function being to provide a discreet foundation for the semi-transparent silk blouses then in vogue.

Plain Sewing Days were interrupted by a day for Fancy Work, which could be anything from a nightdress-case or a brush-and-comb bag with a stamped design which we outlined in lazy daisy stitch with coloured floss silks, to a tray-cloth in drawn-thread work, using hanks of mercerised cotton or linen thread on huckaback linen. On that day we were also expected to darn our long black woollen stockings unsupervised, the result in many cases being real fancy work. We had no school uniform, only a tie in stripes of blue and gold, and a mono-grammed band on our hard straw hats. As juniors we tethered the hats with elastic under the chin; later, promoted ourselves to long hat-pins which pierced the crown in two places, skewering it to the hair. Shirt-blouses worn with the school tie went with coats and skirts, then called 'costumes'. I have

painful recollections of a blouse which had a stiffly-starched collar fixed with studs like a man's, which rubbed cruelly on my neck.

Our afternoon blouses of rather limp voile or starched muslin had high net collars with supports which had to be removed for washing and laboriously re-stitched into place. Elastic round the waist was necessary to keep the blouse from riding up, which would have been considered slovenly. A special device was a band which fastened with a hook and eye; in the middle-back was a steel bar four inches long with prongs which spiked the blouse and kept it from slipping.

Only in my gym-suit was I really comfortable, and as I was in the Display Team, earmarked for daily rehearsals, I moved freely most week-days in that amazing ensemble, which comprised a long-sleeved, high-necked garment of navy serge, buttoned through from neck to knee, worn with the school tie and baggy serge bloomers. Recently I found this costume pictured in the *Girls' Own Paper*, dated 1884. Physical training for girls was just then beginning to be recommended.

The gymnasium at our school was built in 1883, and marvellously equipped with wall bars, horizontal bars, climbing ropes, a vaulting horse, and a Giant's Stride. The pupils at that time, pioneers of the new freedom, were introduced to physical exercises wearing the newly designed costume, the style of which remained unchanged for close on forty years!

Our gentle Principal belonged to that school of refinement which declared that 'animals and the lower orders sweat, gentlemen perspire, but ladies merely glow'. Sweat was one of the words that must never be uttered. The standard of modesty imposed on us is hard to credit; no girl must be seen outside the gymnasium in her gym-suit without a skirt to cover her knees, not even when crossing the yard between the gym and the main building, which was in no way public or even overlooked. Under the impression, I do believe, that we merely glowed, we were advised that in summer it was unnecessary to change our black stockings once a week . . .

brisk brushing would suffice, but this advice we ignored. It was sufficiently hard to bear that one pair only was permitted in the weekly wash, which each girl sent out in a large bag embroidered with 'Laundry' in flowing letters. There were no facilities for washing and drying stockings.

Once a month we had an orgy of hair-washing. We lined up at the wash-basins, and had a solution of powerful-smelling soft soap poured from a large brown enamel jug over our heads. We lathered well, rinsed out the soap under the tap, then each plunged her head in a bath of cold water, and downstairs we trooped to dry our hair at cheerful coal-fires. We liked going down to the basement best; there we had the company of Cook, fat and good-natured, and the young girls who worked so hard in the service of the school and were, in many cases, no older than ourselves.

Ordinarily, conversation with them was discouraged, but in their subterranean quarters we talked with them while sharing their blazing open fires in kitchen and servants' hall. Hair-drying upstairs was not such a relaxing experience, for whispering was forbidden in the formroom where, under the vigilant eye of a mistress, prep. was going on as usual at the ink-stained tables ranged down the length of the room. The penalty for whispering, for passing notes, or for not being seated when the mistress entered the room was, of course, a Bad Mark. To be really naughty . . . say, to persist in whispering, merited the loss of FIVE GOOD MARKS in one swift action. The result of these deductions was inscribed on the Report of Progress and Conduct which was posted to parents at the end of each term.

There were few diversions to break the monotony of prep.; hair-washing was one, another was the periodic visit of the official clock-winder whose supple wrist movement was a joy to imitate. There were many clock-winders on their regular rounds in cities at that time, but they disappeared at the time of the First World War.

To prepare for sitting the Leaving Certificates Examinations of the Scottish Education Department in due course, we

received an excellent education in a wide range of subjects which included physics, chemistry, and elementary botany, but found no place for the study of natural history, handi-crafts, general knowledge, or current affairs. We learned little history save that of Queen Victoria's Empire, which was then considerable, touching lightly on that of France and the Americas.

There were inkwells in our desks; younger girls wrote first with School nibs, later were promoted to Relief and Waverley nibs. A contemporary advertisement declared

> They come as a boon and a blessing to men,
> The Pickwick, the Owl, and the Waverley pen.

We were issued with a standard set of exercise-books and jotters, a flat music case which slid into a locker in the hall, and a set of brass instruments for maths . . . only the ruler and set square being of thin wood. It was the Done Thing to scrape off the coloured transfer which adorned the lid of a new wooden pencil-case, and, instead, to inscribe one's name in large letters in ink.

We passed half-hourly from one subject to another, but it was the book-laden mistresses who hurried from one class-room to the next. . . . From our desks we produced, as required, English Literature by James Logie Robertson, who was a poet in his time, Nesfield's Grammar, and Hall and Stevens which contained the Pons Asinorum.

We read Daudet's *Tartarin de Tarascon*, and his entrancing *Lettres de mon moulin*; we learned about Molière's pretentious parvenu, *Le Bourgeois Gentilhomme* and the Fables of La Fontaine. *Travels with a Donkey* inspired in me a lifelong devotion to 'R.L.S.' and with *Palgrave's Golden Treasury* ever at hand I became passionately fond of poetry. Soon my ear was attuned to the haunting cadences of Tennyson's 'Prin-cess', enchanted with the discovery of onomatopoeia and the 'murmuring of innumerable bees'.

In Latin we inherited a useful jingle:

Many nouns in -is we find
To the masculine assigned,
   Amnis, axis, caulis, collis,
   Clunis, crinis, fascis, follis,
   Pustis, ignis, orbis, ensis,
   Panis, postis, piscis, mensis.

And another rhyme which ran

   Common are to either sex
   Artifex and opifex,
   Common are sacerdos, dux,
   Vates, parens, et conjux.

As a form of relaxation we learned to sing 'Comin' through the rye' in Latin which was more fun than parsing Ovid. In the Science Laboratory it was a pleasant change from book-work to experiment with crucibles, pipettes, bunsen burners and other pieces of elementary equipment, producing in the process some curious smells and minor explosions.

There was a short morning break for cocoa in winter, milk in summer, with appetising 'door-steps' of bread, fresh and buttery. We paraded the corridors with arms entwined with those of a special friend and, on a cold day, staked a claim to a lean on the hot-water pipes till the bell rang to summon us back to the classroom. Everything was done to the urgent clanging of a town crier's bell, . . . 'to a tintinabulation that so musically swells', except meals, to which we were called by the discordant sounding of an immense gong which hung, immovable, on its massive stand in the entrance hall. Booming away as day followed day, and year succeeded year, how many thousands of girls did it bring flying down the reddened sandstone backstairs? Flying because the penalty for being late for a meal was a Bad Mark to which we (and our parents) attached some importance. Simple mistakes and human errors of judgment on the one hand, wilful breaking of rules on the other . . . all were punished in the same way . . . by the imposition of a Bad Mark. This amounted to the deduction at

[97]

one fell swoop of *three* of the hundred Good Marks with which we were presented at the beginning of each term, and were mainly for unpunctuality and the heinous offence of *Talking*. Looking back, it seems to me that we were forbidden to utter a word anywhere, or at any time, out of class, save for that forenoon break. NO TALKING was the warning in the long passages, on the landings and on the stairs; NO TALKING in the bathroom, in the 'boot-hole', or in the 'dors' after the dor-mistress had extinguished the gas-light at 9 p.m. Few could take it, and though I am aware that the Silence Rule had been faithfully observed for generations at another school, most of us found it hard to see any dignity in perpetual silence or in burdening healthy growing girls with a continual sense of wrong-doing because we were unable to behave like Trappist monks.

Only when showing visitors round the school could we ascend the front staircase with its imposing mahogany banisters, or use the front door and front gate. There were the usual exceptions; we sped our parting guests at the front door, accompanied our parents through the front gate, and on our way to the bathroom on another floor slipped quietly in dressing-gown and slippers up and down the front stairs, which were covered with polished brown linoleum edged with Greek Key pattern. Senior girls who had reached the Olympus of the Sixth Form were created monitors, i.e. prefects, whose duties were to maintain law and order, to see that silence was observed in all the right places, and to discourage whispering in the dors after the ringing of the Silence Bell, except on the privileged occasions set apart as Talking Nights. They also supervised prep. where we sat at long tables after tea, intent on our home-work, standing in for a mistress who wished to keep an evening engagement. Mistresses had their stated hours off duty, and had to find deputies on other occasions.

It was the Rev. W. A. Spooner, Warden of Queen's College, Oxford, who by his unconscious habit of transposing initial letters added a new word to the English language. When he referred to pink stuff as stink puff, assuring those who were

occupewing pies that the Lord was a shoving leopard, and similar transpositions, these became known as spoonerisms. One of the mistresses in my day had a weakness for spoonerisms. 'Now, girls,' she would say, 'band in your hooks', or, before a walk, 'time to put on your hoats and cats.' Once I overheard her say to a girl who had to take a tonic in midforenoon, 'Well, Sophie, have you been suggesting your danatogen?' Never by word or look did we make known her error, lest we hurt her feelings.

Fraulein never let us forget that she was entitled to the aristocratic 'von' in her name, nor that her brother was a high-ranking officer in the Bavarian Army. She assured us that one day he would march through Edinburgh's streets at the head of his men, and put us firmly in our place. 'When he comes', she would say, 'he will carry away two of you, one under each arm.' We laughed at the picture, as we were meant to do, never imagining that already the Kaiser's Germany was dreaming of a conquered Britain. Though very strict in the teaching of music, and prone to rap knuckles when wayward fingers stumbled, she and I became firm friends. She brought me up, musically, on a diet of Chopin, Schubert, and Grieg, encouraging me to pass the examinations of the Royal Academy and the Royal College of Music. For relaxation, she taught me Weber's 'Invitation to the Valse' which was originally a piano piece. It was Berlioz who transcribed it for orchestra, and since has been known as 'Invitation to the Dance'. My happiest hours were spent in the cell-like practice rooms with the metronome tick-tocking away on the top of the piano. In each room there was a relic of the early days of the school, an ottoman covered in brown American cloth, containing a quantity of tattered forgotten sheet-music. It was my delight to dip into a treasure house of old discarded sheets, and the restful change of sight-reading, unauthorised as it was, did me lasting good. It was a much-appreciated privilege to have access to the best piano, in the Large Drawing-Room, a gracious room that reminded one of home, with books and flowers and pictures. It had high French

windows which glanced down to the broad lawns and the tall
trees. Eyes strayed to the garden, for peeping from the case-
ment curtains that hung at classroom and dor windows was
discouraged.

The bathroom on each floor was fitted with a row of basins
on one side, with a long mirror above; on the opposite side,
a row of bath-cubicles where three times a week a girl could
bath in privacy and comfort. Cards on the doors indicated
who had baths in that cublicle each night. First Bath meant
that the water was good and hot; Second Bath, that most of
the hot water had gone; Third Bath was the night when one
was resigned to a tepid wash. Those were the days of small
tins of pink tooth-powder. It was impossible to dip one's
toothbrush in the tin without displacing some powder so, as
the evening progressed, the shelf under the mirror became
decorated with tiny heaps of powder in varying shades of
pink. These had all magically disappeared by morning, so
fairies must have waved their wands about 5.30. Occasionally,
one heard them referred to as skivvies, now, I trust, an
obsolete term. Their dormitory was exactly like ours, furnished
with dressing-table, wardrobe, and washstand in each cur-
tained cubicle.

Jeanie, the Head Tablemaid, was a good-looking woman
with a happy smile and a rosy complexion. She was assisted
by a number of timid young girls who scurried to and fro at
her bidding. She had a kindly way with her underlings, who
were obliged to move always at speed, bustling into the
dining-hall with large ashets of meat, heavy dishes of boiled
potatoes, and milky puddings in trough-like enamel pie-
dishes, which came up from the kitchen regions with a rumble
and a thump in a noisy lift; and, in no time at all, they were
again hustling round 'clearing away'.

They wore morning 'wrappers' of printed cotton, linen aprons
with a bib and broad ties round the waist, and starched caps
folded back from the face. In the afternoons they wore black
dresses and prettier caps and aprons.

Our food was plain, wholesome, and plentiful. We had

ample portions of meat, potatoes, and pudding, but there was a singular inadequacy of green vegetables, possibly due to the difficulty of preparing by hand vegetables to serve approximately 140 people. Puddings were of the filling variety. Suet puddings with lashings of golden syrup, 'spotted dogs', i.e. steamed puddings with currants in plenty, milk puddings, and 'hockey balls', which were whole apples enclosed in pastry . . . these were all good to eat. Not so appetising was chocolate pudding made with cocoa, which somehow emerged a pale purple colour, and sago pudding coloured with plum jam, the result reminding one painfully of frog spawn. A Marie biscuit and a ginger snap were issued in mid-afternoon, and so accustomed did we become to helping ourselves to two biscuits that an Old Girl having coffee in a conventional gathering, not long after leaving school, and being offered biscuits, to her dismay found herself automatically taking two. When a visiting team came to tea after a hockey or cricket match, a wonderful spread of buns and cake was provided, and we enjoyed entertaining our guests. Normally, at tea-time we had bread, butter and jam, with an occasional bun.

We played a Club called the Omnium Gatherum, and most of the girls' schools in Edinburgh, known to us simply as George Square, Queen Street, St George's, and St Hilda's at Liberton. In an age when school colours tended to be sombre navy blue, brown or crimson, and gym tunics were the prevailing mode, St Hilda's struck a new note with neat black pinafore dresses, with their school colour emphasised in artists' bows of orange silk. Throughout the winter months we attended dancing-lessons in the gym, wearing white or champagne-coloured tussore silk dresses, mercerised cotton gloves fastened with two pearl buttons, and French sandals with elastic crossed over the ankles. Artificial silk stockings had made their appearance, with ornamental 'clocks', which were open work seams terminating in an embroidered arrowhead, which ran up the sides of the stocking. Sometimes stockings had an openwork panel in front, stretching from the ankle almost to the knee; skirts being more than knee-

[101]

length it was not deemed necessary to carry the pattern higher.

Dancing class started with a slow march round the room, dresses held out daintily between finger and thumb, sliding forward each foot with ankle stretched and a pointed toe. How attractive and how fortunate were the girls who possessed accordion-pleated dresses which added so much to their grace!

With infinite patience we were taught to walk with perfect simplicity and to curtsy. The Five Positions of the feet were mastered before we progressed to dancing steps combined with graceful arm movements. In the front row were the naturally gifted pupils who received much attention and praise, and were constantly called upon to demonstrate to the rest of the class how the steps should be executed. Admiringly we did our best to copy their featherlight, agile movements. Then we formed into aisles and seized our skipping-ropes. Skipping to music began with simple steps and pressed onward to whimsical variations. One crossed one's rope, twirled it on either side of one's head, polka-ed deftly from side to side, and finally reached the peak of skipping mobility, the double-through.

We also learned the waltz and square dances, some Morris dancing, and Highland reels, when every traditional movement was meticulously observed, and so to the final March Past and a curtsey to the teacher. Cabined and confined as we were, I remember to this day what joy it was to be sent, by way of the front door, to pick for the Art class, one or two sprigs of velvety wallflowers that scented the borders under the windows, and how invigorating it was to inhale great draughts of morning air when, in the Sixth Form, it was my privilege to descend the flight of steps to the lawn to take a daily reading of the rain-gauge, and to record the direction of the wind. Simple pleasures, and always worthy of mention in the weekly letter home.

Prior to returning to Edinburgh after my first school holidays I, with my mother, stayed overnight in Ballater where May Leys gave us a supper of sowans, and wakened us

on a cold grey morning. We dressed by candlelight to consume a sketchy breakfast, for we had little appetite. Bundled up and overclad in heavy garments, and clumsy of movement, I recall how I sat shivering in the unheated compartment of the train, while a whistling porter slung in a flat metal foot-warmer which he had filled with boiling water. In daylight hours on subsequent journeys the prospect seemed less formidable. In that charming book, *Perfume from Provence*, the author at one point writes of her mother, 'She told the story of an English countrywoman seeing off her young daughter at the station. The girl was going to her first place as a scullery-maid in a great house. Her mother kissed her goodbye, and pushing her into a third class carriage, thus admonished her from the platform, "Now remember! Eat as much as yer can, do as little as yer can, and if yer don't like it, come 'ome!" It amazed me to read this, for I actually heard a woman express these sentiments at Ballater station. Her daughter and I were seated in opposite corners of the same compartment; our mothers were seeing us off, I to school, she to work on a farm. My mother and I exchanged startled glances at the other mother's parting words . . . 'Noo min',' she said, 'eat as muckle as ye can, dae as little as ye can, an' gin ye dinna like it, jist come hame!' Is this advice well known in some quarters, I wonder, or was the mother of Lady Fortescue within hearing in that remote Deeside station, and did she adapt the story for English readers?

In old-fashioned trains, when darkness was about to fall, a man used to walk along the roof of a stationary train with a bunch of lighted lanterns, inserting one into each compartment through a hole in the roof. Presently a dim religious light would appear by which we were able to discern our fellow-passengers, but reading was out of the question. Corridors were introduced in 1892 on the Great Western Railway between Paddington and Birkenhead, but by 1906, when I first began my travels, they had not reached the Great North of Scotland Railway between Aberdeen and Ballater . . . at

least, I never saw any. Few compartments on an ordinary train were furnished with lavatories, and in those which were so furnished, the narrow door through which one was expected to squeeze, was placed in a break on one side of the compartment, flush with the upholstery, and was so hatefully public that one was too embarrassed to use it unless alone in the compartment, or to have the good fortune to travel in a 'Ladies Only'. In the 'Smokers', I believe, there were still cavities in the floor which at one time held spitoons.

One associates arrival at Waverley with a bitter wind scything in from the east, and Waverley Steps the notoriously wet and windy exit. On our way to board a tram, Ellie and I used to linger for a last look at the little shops bordering the Steps, to note the souvenirs in improbable tartans, and the gay boxes of Edinburgh Rock and Ferguson's Tablet in rounds the size of a five-shilling piece, flavoured with ginger, peppermint, lemon and rose.

When firemen came to school to instruct us in the use of the fire-escape . . . a canvas tube which was kept rolled up on a window-ledge in the servants' sleeping quarters was hooked on the sill and, unrolled, fell into the courtyard. Two firemen held it at a safe angle from the wall as, one by one, we stepped into the open mouth of the chute and slid rapidly to the ground. As one girl emerged another stepped in; it was a claustrophobic sensation.

We had no organised games in the garden but, in summer time, when the scent of wallflowers and new-mown grass filled the air, grass courts were marked for tennis.

Girls who owned five-shilling Box Brownies, cameras which had made their debut in 1900, augmented their pocket-money by selling prints to camera-less form-mates, doing the printing and developing themselves.

On hot afternoons we were overjoyed when, instead of a walk, it was ordained that we take rugs, books, and floppy sun-hats to the garden, to lie on the grassy slopes over-

looking the lawn, within the sound of the pat of tennis-balls and lady-like calls of 'Vantage in', 'Love all' and 'Game and Set'.

This privilege was granted, we were well aware, every fine day to the girls at the Miss Gossips' School next door. We took forbidden peeps at them from upstairs windows. There they were, relaxing in their garden at all hours, even drying their hair in the sun, and, with more than a flavour of sour grapes, we would wonder aloud when *they* did any work!

For those of us who were not on the day's list to play games, exercise consisted of a prim walk of an hour's duration. In preparation for this, we descended a flight of stone steps to the basement 'boot-hole', from which we presently emerged coated and hatted, and went by the outdoor steps leading to the courtyard, chattering and arranging partners for the 'croc', which was led by two senior girls, the mistress-in-charge, flanked by two smaller girls bringing up the rear. Our accustomed routes excluded shops and avoided roads where we might meet BOYS, possibly on their way to their playing-fields.

Along the quiet avenues and crescents of Grange we walked, by Fountainhall Road, Warrender Park and Whitehouse Loan; every turn of these roads was familiar to us. Blackford Hill was the nearest approach to a country walk, with whins and broom and wild flowers. Discipline was relaxed when we left residential avenues behind. One winter day an understanding mistress allowed us to slide all over Blackford's frozen pond, and on a long-remembered spring day, instead of following our usual path at the base of the hill, we were permitted to roam all over the golden broom-clad slopes, climbing almost to the top of the hill where stands the Royal Observatory. Exalted by unwonted freedom some of the younger girls 'tumbled the cat', and rolled like puppies on the sweet-smelling grass, but I was the unlucky one who burst an essential button and, lacking a safety-pin, was obliged to carry a superfluous garment tucked under my arm all the way back to school. To make matters worse, I dropped it in Kilgraston

Road and with a very red face had to retrace my steps to retrieve it.

Mild excitement arose in the Colinton area when we chanced to meet the man, bearded and shabby, in a deerstalker hat and an ulster down to his heels, to whom we had given the name of 'The Miser'. There was in Napier Road a unique piece of architecture which aroused our perpetual curiosity . . . a house of towering turrets and gables, its walls encrusted with large polished pebbles of every colour. We often wondered aloud what it must be like to live in such an astonishing house. In Oswald Road we used to pass a house with a pair of ornate, gilded lamp-standards at the gate, which denoted the residence of the Lord Provost of Edinburgh, and bore the City's Coat-of-Arms. The convention is traceable to a seventeenth-century custom of erecting two ornamental posts at the gates of the Chief Magistrate in important towns. In later years, when we sought out an old family friend in Montrose we found her living in a house which has associations with Robert Burns, who called on friends there in the Bow Butts in 1787. The Provost's lamp may still be seen above the gateway. On our walks through Newington we always waved to the handicapped children in the Longmore Hospital who smiled and waved from their top floor windows.

A valiant figure in the streets of Edinburgh at that time was Theodore Napier, who was never seen out-of-doors except in full Highland garb, as worn by a chieftain in the time of Bonnie Prince Charlie. His kilt was of Royal Stuart tartan and his plaid was held in place by a silver brooch. He wore a lace collar and frills at his wrists, a sporran of ancient hide, a skean dhu in his tartan hose, and brogues with silver buckles. Two long feathers in his bonnet were held upright by a cairngorm brooch. On special occasions he was said to carry a targe and claymore. Apart from his dress he was an imposing figure, for his white beard and long curls falling to his shoulders lent him patriarchal dignity.

On our walks we often met him in the neighbourhood of Merchiston Castle. When he came in sight, marching as if

leading his clan into battle, and carrying a tall, silver-mounted stick, his name was whispered back the length of the croc so that no girl should inadvertently be deprived of a sight of the majestic form in progress. There are, I believe, still fervid Scots who raise their hats when passing the Field of Bannock-burn; I am glad to have been fortunate in meeting Theodore Napier, that picturesque anachronism, a man who, loyal adherent of the Royal Stuarts, made annual pilgrimages to Culloden, Fotheringay, and Bannockburn; not long after, he returned to Australia, to his estates in Melbourne, whence he had come on a visit to Edinburgh in 1895, a visit that lasted till 1912.

As we passed Merchiston Castle, girls who had begun the study of logarithms were reminded by the inscription over the gates that they were invented by John Napier of Mer-chiston, that versatile man who also invented a calculating machine, and an early form of tank for land warfare, who improved pumping machinery for coal-pits, and who developed fertilisers for crops. This information was given to me by the late Professor Douglas Young, famous Scots poet and Greek scholar, former Chairman of the Scottish Nationalist Party, and ambassador of the Scottish way of life, who was said to have developed a thirst for knowledge at an early age, and was said to have been found at the age of two, seated in a small chair at the gate of his home in Merchiston, reading aloud from the Book of Job to passers by.

On Sundays we walked to Grange Parish Church in a croc, the Principal and members of the Staff bringing up the rear. The mistresses on weekdays were dressed in the prevailing mode, in shirt-blouses tucked into belted ankle-length skirts. On Sundays we admired their elegant costumes and fashion-able hats. When Chanticler hats were the latest thing due to the influence on British fashion of a current French play, I remember our French mistress appeared in one which was crowned with an arrangement of curved iridescent green tail-feathers.

I never discovered how often the young maids in our school

were allowed off the premises, but we, the pupils, were permitted to spend every third Saturday with friends, on condition that, in a conventional note written in French, we indicated where we would be spending the day and with whom, and provided we were called for and escorted back in the evening. There was an unwritten and unmentioned rule that the escort should not be a young man.

From my first Visiting Saturday I was escorted to the door by the son of the house, a douce young man very correctly dressed, who held a responsible position on the staff of the *Scotsman*. My dor-mates, seeing him from afar, accused me of being 'fast'. I did not understand; I had not before heard the expression. I was to hear it many times in the school-years ahead.

A natural interest in boys could not be prevented, of course, but we were persuaded that it was naughty to indulge in talk about them, and to correspond with them was most improper. Naturally, some girls did, coaxing day-girls to post their letters. Any girl who in this way carried on a correspondence with her best friend's brother, or with her own brother's best friend, was thought to be very fast indeed, though parents were probably aware of the harmless friendship.

After I left school, my sister, still a child at fourteen, was reported to the Principal by a mistress who had seen her walking back to school one Visiting Saturday accompanied by a young man, and she was severely reprimanded. My mother, hearing of this, wrote in righteous indignation to inform the Principal that the young man was a family friend, and that he accompanied my sister with her full approval.

On Visiting Saturdays it was against the rules to enter places of entertainment or to ride on tram-cars, lest we pick up a germ or something equally nasty. It puzzled us why we were considered liable to run this risk only on Visiting days, never on Saturdays when we went to Murrayfield to play a match, riding on the open top of a tram, exposed to wind and weather and not a bit the worse. Long-suffering friends had

not only to devise permitted ways of entertaining us, but to walk with us everywhere, or take a cab.

Cabs *were* permitted; I still get an imaginary whiff of the dusty interiors, the insanitary cushioning of the ancient cabs in which we rode, and which, it was wickedly rumoured, were sometimes used to convey patients to the Fever Hospital. The upholstery in railway-carriages was not much better; we were warned not to rest our heads against it. A multitude of germs must have lurked in these forms of transport.

However, the rule that excluded trams in favour of trains was responsible for memorable Saturdays which my sister and I spent at Gullane among the sand-dunes, at North Berwick, and in Rosslyn Chapel where a hostess with imagination took us to gaze with wonder in our eyes at the beauty of the Prentice Pillar. Legend says it was carved by an apprentice in the absence of his master who, on his return, struck the lad a fatal blow from insane jealousy and was hanged for causing his death.

Below the chapel, overhanging the river, we saw the ruins of Rosslyn Castle with its dungeons and kitchens, and a primitive hoist to the banqueting hall. Our attention was drawn to the gutters which carried hot fat from dripping carcases roasting in the enormous fireplace and was used eventually in their lamps.

It was a long walk to our Mecca, Princes Street, from Marchmont and Morningside where lived our parents' elderly friends whose hospitality we from time to time enjoyed. They were disinclined to walk so far so we were usually sent out by ourselves. Princes Street on Saturday morning was, in the early years of the present century, like Regent Street in London's West End in Victorian times.

It was fashionable to be seen there among the elegantly attired pedestrians; there were no hatless men or frumpish women in that quarter.

Marjory Fleming (Scott's 'Pet Marjory') wrote of it, 'Quean Streat is a very gay streat and so is Princes Streat, for all the lads and lasses, besides bucks and begars parade there.' The

famous street, as I remember it, ran between a long row of very superior shops on one side and beautiful gardens on the other.

There were no multiple shops then, and the goods displayed were of the finest quality. Now, alas! most of the buildings have succumbed to what has been sadly described as the March of the Multiples.

We school-girls found it amusing to watch the regular promenaders who met their friends by arrangement at Maule's Corner, a favourite rendezvous at the West End, and often saw some of the more sophisticated day-girls in their weekend finery mingling with the regulars who strolled along with eyes alert for admiring glances. They stood in groups on the pavement, chatting to chance-met acquaintances, had coffee in Mackie's, strawberry ices in MacVittie's, strolled the entire length of the street, and even found time to glance at the enticing displays in the windows of world-famous establishments not yet designated stores.

The statue of Allan Ramsay gazed down on the ever-changing panorama from his pedestal above the Floral Clock (and its cuckoo) which was new in 1903 and has never ceased to interest and amuse passers-by as it sluggishly and jerkily ticks away the hours.

It was a leisurely promenade of leisurely people in those days, and the parade continued till the one o'clock gun sounded from the Castle, when everybody checked the time on their watches, an automatic gesture that never failed to amuse strangers, and the time-ball on Nelson's Monument on the Calton Hill dropped at the same moment; they then turned homewards or went to lunch in Jenners'.

The gun and the ball worked independently, but were first synchronised in 1861. Sometimes the weather made things difficult; the gunner at times had to set off the gun by hand because frost had jammed the electrical mechanism, and there were days when the time-ball was thrawn and dropped in slow motion.

Those were the days when Edinburgh's shop-windows still

displayed elegant garments called mantles, tea-gowns, and opera-cloaks. The shops were fitted with long counters of polished mahogany behind which stood tiers of mahogany drawers with brass handles.

By the time I left school, however, they were all being modernised, and the overhead railways which carried bills and money from all departments to the unseen cash-office and brought back the change, had been replaced by silent fittings.

I used to haunt the Arcade in Princes Street where, surrounded on three sides of a cul-de-sac of small souvenir shops, was a music-stall. There one could buy sheet-music for tuppence, and hear one's favourite selections played by a lady who sat at a piano hour after hour churning out the requested melodies as effortlessly as a modern record-player. There I purchased copies of operatic gems which I treasure, and blessed the name of Mozart Allen.

Sometimes my sister and I wandered up The Mound to the George IV Bridge and, looking down, saw barefoot children playing peevers on the grimy pavements far below. We occasionally spent a Visiting Saturday with two sisters, one a retired teacher, the other a veritable Martha, careful and troubled about many things, who lived in Bruntsfield and were as silent as their flat.

In one room was an immense draught-screen gaily covered with old-fashioned Christmas cards, picture-scraps of golden-haired maidens soulfully clasping a dove, a kitten, or an arum lily to a rosy cheek, and pictures of Queen Victoria at every phase of her long reign, wearing a crown, the Ribbon of the Garter, and a vast amount of diamonds.

Near it, on a small table, lay an embossed leather photograph album with brass clasps and pages decorated with coloured flowers; a stereoscope with velvet-covered eye-pieces and a pile of picture-cards; and a glass paperweight with a snow-scene inside; when shaken, the snow flew out in a blinding storm against which tiny figures appeared to be battling. It reminded us of the Glen in Winter.

[111]

In an adjoining room stood an upright piano with a fretwork panel backed by folds of amber silk, and ornate candle-sconces. The height of the piano-stool could be adjusted by twirling the plush-covered seat on its spiral column. I never wearied of turning over the pile of music-sheets, always finding something new, for sight-reading was my delight. In this way I learned to play Ivanovich's 'Donauwellen', the waltzes of Strauss, and many classical fragments.

A tiny room off the sitting-room was a feature of Edinburgh flats. Little more than a closet it held only a bed, and was lit and ventilated by a window high on the wall which opened on to the common landing.

My father often occupied such a room when attending the General Assembly, though he occasionally stayed at the St Andrew Hotel, which was full of ministers that week, or at the Cockburn Hotel, which advertised itself as 'combining all the comforts of a well-regulated home at a moderate tariff. NO SPIRITUOUS LIQUORS.'

When friends called on us at school on Visiting Evenings they were shown in to the so-called Small Drawing-Room, really a practice-room, which contained a second-rate piano and a row of bentwood chairs. There were no pictures, no flowers, no fireplace, no curtains. It would have been pleasant to receive our guests in the Large Drawing-Room, furnished as it was with a fine piano, chintzy chairs, pictures, book-shelves laden with well-bound books which only Sixth Form girls might borrow, and a thick carpet. There Miss Robertson received her guests and held her Afternoon At Home Days.

Saturdays In, as opposed to Saturdays Out, were little different from week-days; true, there were no classes, but there was prep. in the morning, and the usual walk in the afternoon, but apart from these commitments we were free to relax in our formrooms and to gather round the piano to strum 'Chopsticks' and that other tune which we picked out with our forefingers for the traditional chant from the back-greens of Edinburgh . . .

O can ye wash a sailor's shirt
O can ye wash it clean?
O can ye wash a sailor's shirt
An' lay it on the green?

Yes, I can wash a sailor's shirt,
I can wash it clean,
I can wash a sailor's shirt
An' lay it on the green.

We could also enjoy the music of 'Peter Pan' and Strauss's 'Waltz Dream', and frequently rent the air with popular choruses such as 'When we are married we'll have sausages for tea', 'By the side of the Zuyder Zee', and 'My lassie from Lanca-sheer'.

We could have a book out of the school library which was a cupboard-like room off the dining-hall, filled with well-stocked shelves and staffed by senior girls. For lack of space it was impracticable to examine the books on the shelves, so we selected them by their authors and titles in a hand-written catalogue.

In this haphazard way I first chose *Alf's Button* by W. A. Darlington, and later discovered the stories of Amy le Feuvre and Louisa M. Alcott, the *What Katy Did* books of Susan Coolidge, progressing by leaps and bounds to Hall Caine, George Meredith, Thomas Hardy and Rider Haggard. Uncritical and indiscriminating, I read with equal enjoyment the works of Thackeray and L. T. Meade, of George Macdonald, a best-selling novelist in his day, and John Strange Winter.

Sweets, normally kept under lock and key, were available on Saturday afternoon, a silent period when, under supervision, we sat with steadily munching jaws reading our library books. When time was up we passed round once more to our immediate neighbours our personal box, then handed it over to be locked away till next day, Sunday, when the same procedure was in force. Those of us who lacked doting aunts to provide us with fancy boxes of chocolate, laid in our own

store of sweets and were gratified to discover jelly cuttings in William Low's grocery store in Newington Road, adjacent to Mitchelhill's Bakery where we sometimes bought an un-sanctioned iced cake. Jelly cuttings could be obtained plain or sugared, and for some unexplained reason, these harmless and inexpensive sweets were subsequently banned.

Slang was frowned upon, but in private we continued to express our ill-temper by being waxy and ratty; exciting or amusing events were still ripping, topping, and killing; to buck up was to make haste, while copy cats, swots and stews, and beastly rotters have long since had their day. We did a lot of bagging . . . bags I this, bags I that, but for the life of me I cannot recall what there was to bag.

We had some odd little customs . . . we said 'Rabbits' three times last thing at night on the last day of each month, and 'Hares' three times before another word was uttered in the morning. It was an incantation to bring good luck for the whole month and was taken seriously. We were quite distressed if we forgot to say it; that put an end to any hope of getting a present during the month, or even to having a wish granted.

If two girls by chance made a simultaneous exclamation they at once, without saying another word, hooked pinkies and remained linked till someone could be signalled to use a chop-ping movement and break the link and the spell. I rather imagine a wish was made during the silence but its substance was never revealed for that would have cancelled its influence.

To enliven winter Saturdays, girls in a Form or Dor would present a play into which all threw themselves with energy and goodwill. It was a combined operation, fun for everybody, especially the performers. Seats were tuppence, threepence if reserved. One penny was charged for a handwritten pro-gramme . . . naturally, they were tuppence coloured. The money went to Foreign Missions. Missionaries home on fur-lough came to tell us of their work in foreign fields. In support of Missions, we, as Junior Fellow-Workers, organised a Sale of Work which was one of the highlights of the Summer Term. Towards this effort my mother always sent an enormous box

of double lilies from the Manse garden. In those days one could depend on receiving a parcel on the day after posting, and every year, as sure as a promise, the lilies arrived, fragrant and fresh, on the morning of the Sale.

Impromptu concerts and variety turns were welcome diversions. I remember a Toy Symphony when the youngest girls performed Schubert's Marche Militaire and a rondo by Mozart, with Ruth at the piano, and I dutifully pinged a triangle in all the right places.

The Cake Walk was a negro dance staged by professionals but considered unsuitable for dancing in private houses or the ballroom; Mattie, however, often amused us by her interpretation of a Cake Walk as she pranced in reverse the length of the schoolroom, leaning back as far as possible without losing her balance, and continuously flapping her hands at chest-level. It was an inept and quite innocent performance.

Dorothy did a Skirt Dance as popularised by Maud Allen in her much-discussed classical style, but, unlike her, she wore a flowing dress of accordion-pleated crêpe-de-chine.

Dramatic poems only come to life when they are spoken, acted, or sung. A burlesque of one was presented one evening when four senior girls gave an impromptu performance of 'Lord Ullin's Daughter'. It was pure farce and none of us, doubled up in our seats, could ever forget the ballad after witnessing that wildly rocking boat (a clothes basket) the boatman rowing madly (with a broomstick) two frantically clinging figures, and Flo, the narrator, rocking the boat with one hand while declaiming from the book in the other, 'One lovely hand was stretched for aid, and one was round her lover'.

Once or twice in a term we had what were termed Musical Evenings. We sat on the carpet in the Large Drawing Room in our party dresses, with needlework in our hands, while a chosen number of our companions performed for the gratification of the Principal, the Staff and ourselves.

Some class-mates I remember were the sisters Gulielma and Christelle; Mary, who in the Third Form closely resembled

Tenniel's Alice; Janey, my lifelong friend, who gave considerable assistance to her father when he compiled an impressive history of the ancient parish of Auchterderran; Amy, my church-going partner and the first coloured girl I ever knew; Flower, who married a prince; and Enid and Eve, whose father and his forebears for generations had filled the double role of Laird of Troquhair and Parish Minister of Balmaclellan. One, George Murray, was in no way disconcerted by the Disruption of the Kirk in 1843, but continued, in his parish in the wilds of Galloway, to enjoy a sporting life and to compose long sets of verses, including a poem about 'The Auld Kirk o' Scotland', the refrain being

> The gude Auld Kirk o' Scotland
> She's nae in ruins yet.

From time to time in our school, parties were arranged to which every one of the organising group contributed and themselves prepared. Liberally, the contents of many cans of fruit were tipped into bedroom basins; Chivers' jellies were dissolved in others with the co-operation of Cook who supplied boiling water with a tolerant eye on the ploy. In the same way, fruit drinks were made in bedroom jugs. Feasting in form-rooms was followed by dancing in the dining-hall, for which programmes had been painted and dangling pencils attached in correct ballroom style. (Little pink programmes with little pink pencils were part of the social scene till the outbreak of the First World War.) Small girls approached with awe the Head Girl and their own idolised mistresses with a shy request for a dance, inscribing their names on programmes and all set to claim their rights at the appropriate time. Party dresses were mainly of white sprigged or dotted muslin, lightly starched, or of jap silk with insertion and flouncing, and we all wore French sandals and cotton gloves.

We waltzed sedately to 'Sobre les Olas' and 'The Chocolate Soldier'; the Barn Dance and the One Step were often repeated during the evening; and we romped through the Lancers to medleys from Gilbert and Sullivan's operas, 'The

Country Girl', and the lesser-known 'Havana'. Among the juniors the figures were apt to become a hopeless muddle, in spite of helpful cries from seniors . . . 'Ladies in the centre', 'Visiting', and 'Corners'; the Grand Chain frequently tied in extricable knots reduced one to helpless laughter or to exasperation according to one's mood. Polkas invariably ended in a gallop to the strains of 'John Peel', a spirited rush from one end of the room to the other. There can never have been any lack of volunteers to play the piano for dancing; we never had a hired band or gramophone records. Fraulein played 'The Blue Danube' at all our parties in a gay, extravagant way, with more verve than I have since heard. She wore on these occasions a black silk dress, trimmed with tiny velvet bows, which displayed her fine shoulders, and rustled like the wind among autumn leaves when she moved. She loved to dance a waltz, too, in bouncing, flamboyant style, holding up her full skirts with one hand. The Monitors' and Sixth Form At Home was one of the Fancy Dress events of the School Year. Once an original pair arrived in the garb of an Organ Grinder and his Monkey, which reminded me of an old print at home, probably a Baxter, 'Italian Boy and Monkey', which I still treasure because it was framed in his youth by my artistic grandfather, and must now be at least 150 years old.

At the end of the School Year we had a Grand Fancy Dress Party in the gym. Costumes were elaborate and beautiful, and the party ended with 'Haymakers' and the singing of 'Auld Lang Syne', when tears were shed by some girls who were leaving school and would next appear as Old Girls in long skirts with their hair 'up'.

On Old Girls' Reunion Day, a Saturday in May, the Old Girls occupied the dining-hall and we school-girls seated on the floor in the gym revelled in a picnic lunch which invariably consisted of a mutton pie, three inches across, still miraculously hot from the bakery, washed down with mugs of fizzy lemonade. There was, we felt, nothing in the wide world so luscious as a tuppenny pie, rich and juicy, with mouth-

watering mutton enclosed in pastry that was thin on top but thick at the sides to contain the gravy. The correct way to eat it, we were told, was to lift it whole and hold it in both hands while eating. The pies used to be made entirely by hand; they were peculiarly Scottish, and traditionally were delivered piping hot and eaten at once.

It was porridge for supper as usual for us girls when the Old Girls had gone . . . monitors ladling it from tureens to waiting queues after the Head Girl had said Grace.

When we were taken to see *Richard I*, staged by a prominent Shakespearean Company, I was deeply impressed by the atmosphere, by the nobility of the actors, and especially by the dedicated realism of Frank Benson who lay for a lengthy period as still as death on Richard's bier. It was remarked afterwards that he wisely did not break the spell by returning to the centre stage to receive an ovation. Spellbound and wordless, I stumbled from the theatre feeling that Richard had truly died that night.

I remember a visit to the Assembly Rooms in George Street, when we heard about Miss Nicky Murray, a lady of quality, something of a snob, and by all accounts a holy terror, who presided over all the fashionable dancing assemblies about the middle of the eighteenth century. She used to sit on a kind of throne at the far end of the great Assembly Room, and kept a stern eye on the deportment of the young ladies and their partners in the minuet and other stately dances. Only one set was permitted to take the floor at a time.

It was decreed at the beginning of the Season that gentlemen drew for partners; the ladies' fans were put in a cocked hat and each man had a lucky (or unlucky) dip. The lady whose fan he drew had to be his partner for the whole season, and no exchanging was allowed even for a single night. There was always the faint hope that, as fans were easily distinguishable from each other, a man might manage to have a quick peep inside the hat and select the fan he knew to belong to his lady. Nicky insisted on early hours and was such a dictator that, in spite of girlish pleas for just one more

mazurka, she would stop the music and end the Ball with one wave of her fan. As we girls set off on our long walk back to school we tried to picture the final scene at the balls of that era, the sedan-chairs and the link boys with flaring torches who escorted the chair-borne ladies to their homes. They had our sympathy, the frustrated ones, as we hummed the Victorian ballad . . .

> After the ball is over, after the break of morn,
> After the dancers leaving, after the stars are gone;
> Many a heart is aching, if you could read them all,
> Many the hopes that have vanished, after the ball.

When King Edward VII died in May 1910 we were taken to the Mercat Cross to hear the Proclamation of King George V, and to the Castle Esplanade on the day of his Coronation in June 1911.

In May every year the General Assembly of the Church of Scotland meets in Edinburgh in democratic fashion, to choose its Moderator, to discuss life and work in the parishes throughout Scotland, to confer on subjects of ecclesiastical interest, and on matters of world importance affecting the spread of Christianity and to decide on ecclesiastical policy.

The Opening Day of the Assembly was, in the old days, a public holiday; the whole city seemed to participate. Shops put on special displays, and restaurants special menus. The streets were lined with thousands of citizens and visitors to watch the colourful procession of open horse-carriages in which rode the Lord High Commissioner, representing the Sovereign, the Purse-Bearer and Aides, the Tabarded Lord Lyon King-of-Arms and his heralds. They drove along Princes Street from Holyrood Palace, since designated Holyroodhouse, up the Mound to St Giles, the High Kirk of Edinburgh, where they attended Divine Service, and then went in procession to the Assembly Hall in the Tolbooth Church.

In those days the police lining the route wore very grand

uniforms for the occasion; constables wore helmets with shining spikes, there were silver helmets for inspectors, and gilded ones for 'supers'.

When the Right Honourable Margaret Herbison was appointed Lord High Commissioner in 1970, the unique occasion was celebrated in verse by Margaret Marshall. . . .

> Peggy's awa' tae Holyrood
> Tae be the Lord High Commissioner,
> Peggy's awa' tae Holyrood
> Tae represent the Queen.
>
> Peggy's up at the Assembly ha'
> Sittin' amang the meenisters,
> Listenin' tae their confabs
> An' speakin' for the Queen.
>
> Peggy's ane o' us yins,
> The weemen folk o' Scotland
> Wha fill the pews o' Scotland's kirk
> An' care for Scotland's weal.
>
> Peggy speaks for us, tae,
> The weemen folk o' Scotland,
> An' a' wha lippen aye tae Christ
> An' canna thole the deil.

The verses were sent to Miss Herbison, who warmly acknowledged them. They also appeared in the pages of *Life and Work*, the magazine of the Church of Scotland.

There was a continuous flow of ministers of all shapes and ages up and down the Mound during Assembly Week. Their wives sat entranced in the gallery during debates, and attended women's meetings, taking copious notes in preparation for making reports on their return home, and wearing their new Princes Street hats, which prompted one warm-hearted policeman, when asked the way to the Usher Hall, to reply, 'Jist you follow the bonnie hats.'

The Right Reverend the Moderator has precedence in

Scotland for a whole year next to the Lord Chancellor of Great Britain, and before the Dukes. In line with tradition, as becomes a democratic Church, he is popularly elected, his nomination being delegated to a committee chosen by the Assembly. Usually a minister is chosen who has served his apprenticeship as the convener of an Assembly committee, distinguished himself in a professor's Chair, or has proved to be an outstanding preacher. He has a strenuous year of office ahead of him. His function is to act as Chairman during the Assembly, and to visit during his term of office a large number of churches at home and overseas, taking them greetings from the Assembly, and encouraging ministers and elders in their work. He also represents the Church of Scotland on national occasions and is always seen in court dress, a custom which dates from the sixteenth century when the Moderator was required to attend the Scottish Court at the Palace of Holyroodhouse (the name is derived from the Holy Rood, the Holy Cross, and should not be pronounced Hollyrood). Tradition has it that the Moderator's dress is a relic of the time when King James I, annoyed at the sombre appearance of the ministers who attended his court, decreed that they should wear proper court dress. The only two people entitled by custom to wear court dress while on duty are the Speaker of the House of Commons and the Moderator of the General Assembly. The lace for the Moderator's dress is made by women in Chingleput, an Indian country town thirty-five miles from Madras, a legacy from the former Church of Scotland Mission which introduced lace-making into the curriculum of a girls' school at the turn of the century. The lace school has come to an end, but women who have already been trained continue to supply lace for the Moderator. He also wears as a symbol of office an amethyst ring inscribed with the Burning Bush emblem of the Church of Scotland. It is handed down from Moderator to Moderator.

In May 1966 the Moderator, Dr Leonard Small, made church history when he paid a friendly informal visit to the Abbott of Nunraw . . . a visit recalled by Margaret Marshall. . . .

He pit on his lace ruffles, he pit on his buckled shoon,
He steekit the gate o' St Cuthbert's Kirk
An' he gaed awa' doon.
He gaed awa' doon tae the Abbey o' Nunraw
Where nane o' his ilk had iver been afore,
He gaed awa' doon tae the Abbey o' Nunraw,
An' he tirled at the pin, an' he chappit at the door.
The Abbott o' Nunraw, a wise man was he,
The Abbott o' Nunraw was blythe him for tae see,
The Abbott o' Nunraw, a guid man was he,
An' bade him come ben, wi' muckle charity.
The twa men o' God, the yin untae the tither,
Did talk, an' better talk, as brither tae brither,
Gin the nations o' the warld wad think on sic a thing,
We needna be that feart for whit the years micht bring.

At one time it was customary for the Moderator to give
lavish breakfasts in one of the fine Edinburgh hotels to which
all the delegates . . . ministers and elders, received an invitation
on one morning or another. Monitors and senior girls from our
school were also invited to one of these famous Breakfasts . . .
it was a novel experience. We, who had already breakfasted
at eight o'clock, walked to Princes Street, thus creating a fresh
appetite, and in a luxury hotel joined older guests, among
whom were many distinguished laymen, in an orderly queue
to be announced individually and received by our host the
Moderator. After enjoying a ten o'clock breakfast on a scale
we had never before seen, we formally took our leave and
walked back to school.

It was an exciting time for girls whose parents were in
town for Assembly Week. Rules were relaxed and outings
were frequent. My father attended every year, whether he was
a delegate or not. Sometimes my mother also came; both
parents took an active interest in our school pursuits and
attended all functions to which parents were invited. My sister
and I were proud to show them round the school, and walked
their patient feet all round Edinburgh. Over the years we

trod with them the Royal Mile, every foot recalling some part of Scots history . . . John Knox's House, Lady Stair's House, and the Palace of Holyroodhouse in which the rooms of Mary and Darnley seemed heavy with secrets and the gloom of Rizzio's murder.

We attended Divine Service at Greyfriars, the ancient kirk hung with replicas of the flags of the Covenanters, and saw the Martyrs Memorial, and the statue to Greyfriars Bobby, that faithful Skye terrier who in 1858 followed the coffin of his master, Auld Jock Gray, to the churchyard, and refused to leave the spot till he died in 1872.

We spent enthralling hours in the Museum in Chambers Street, and when on Sunday the noise of church bells filled the city, we attended Morning Service in the High Kirk of St Giles, where we saw the faded battle honours of famous regiments hanging in the Nave.

It was here in 1638 that Jenny Geddes, a Luckenbooth wifie, shouting 'Ye'll nae say Mass on *my* lug! Deil colie the wame of ye!' hurled her stool at the preacher in protest against the Church of Scotland's adoption of Anglican ceremonies. So well aimed was the stool that the preacher only escaped being hit by joukin', and the stool is preserved in the museum of the Scottish Society of Antiquaries.

We knew that Flora Macdonald had once publicly rebuked some brawlers in the shadow of St Giles, and since childhood we had known about Jeanie Deans, who walked all the way from Edinburgh to London to plead with Queen Caroline for the life of her sister Effie, who had been condemned to death for the alleged murder of her infant child. (Scott immortalised the incident in *The Heart of Midlothian.*)

With our parents we climbed to the Castle and feasted our eyes on the distant Forth, the coast of Fife, and the Lomonds, and in the foreground the long stretch of Princes Street and its gardens. We had to have yet another look at the Honours of Scotland, the Crown and Sceptre, the Sword and Jewels, all closely guarded, dating back to the days when Scotland was a separate kingdom; and St Margaret's Chapel, the oldest place

of worship in Edinburgh. In front of it stands Mons Meg, the colossal cannon made of long iron bars looped together. (For its story see page 161.) Many historical snacks were fed us by my father, who was an excellent courier, wherever we went.

Assembly Week was a stirring period in the life of our school. Traditional Visits from the Moderator and the Lord High Commissioner had a certain formality. The Principal, with every member of the Staff (all wearing new dresses for the occasion . . . last year's dresses then became this year's afternoon wear) received the dignitaries and their retinue on arrival, and ushered them to the dining-hall where we girls in white frocks welcomed them with vocal items and pianoforte solos. Their obvious pleasure made the occasions delightful as well as dignified. We felt relaxed when they crossed the courtyard to watch our Gym Display. The younger members of the entourage invariably showed a keen desire to follow our example when we flew through the air with the greatest of ease on The Giant's Stride and ended the display by coming to rest at their feet.

Fraulein was quietly gratified when I was awarded the Lord High Commissioner's First Prize for Piano-playing and, curtseying, received it from Lord Glenconner's hands, stepping backwards as from the presence of my Sovereign. His daughter, Clare Tennant, a very beautiful girl, was among the members of his suite who that day enjoyed a ride on the Giant's Stride. She married Lionel Tennyson, grandson of the former Poet Laureate, who captained England in 1921 in a Cricket Test Match in place of C. B. Fry who was ill. My gold brooch is of a design exclusive to the school . . . the heart of Queen Mary surmounting the Crown of the Holy Rood. It somewhat resembles the seventeenth-century Luckenbooth brooch, which consists of a heart topped by a crown, and was worn as a talisman to ward off the evil effects of witchcraft, and was often given as a love token. It is a mistake to think that magic and witchery were done away with in the Middle Ages. Witchcraft laws were repealed only in 1951, and there are thousands of believers in witchcraft in Britain today,

practising both black and white magic. It is generally the black sort that hits the headlines, with spine-chilling stories of desecrated graves and lurid rituals at midnight. Witches come from all walks of life, and all covens do not appear shivering on a blasted heath. I myself, driving one fine day in Perthshire with a young grandson in 1973, saw a coven of witches in long white robes and cowled head-dresses suddenly appear from a meadow, cross the road in front of us, and disappear among the trees on the other side.

The name Luckenbooth is said to have come from the lucken booths that formed the jewellers' quarters around the High Kirk of St Giles in the Middle Ages, adjoining the booths of the booksellers, the furriers, and others. One booth, by the way, belonged to George Heriot, crony of Jamie Saxth (King James VI of Scotland) who bequeathed his fortune to found the well-known school for boys. He was Jingling Geordie in Scott's *Fortunes of Nigel*. Another booth, I was pleased to discover, was owned by Peter Williamson of Aboyne, who published the first Edinburgh Directory in 1775, and also established a Penny Post.

In Jane Austen's day, Strawberry Feasts were judged a very genteel diversion for young ladies and remained so in my school-days. We received an annual invitation to such a feast in the garden of Dr Paul, who was Chairman of the Governors. Suitably chaperoned we walked in a croc to his house in Fountainhall Road, to eat our strawberries and cream in the sunny garden, with a clearly-embarrassed young assistant minister detailed to move among us with the silver cream-jug. It was always a beautiful day.

Every term produced its own crop of crazes. There was a time when we all took up Esperanto and Pelmanism; the first, it was anticipated, would become a universal language (over sixty years later, hopes are still high). With friends at home I continued to study it throughout the summer holidays and among us my future brother-in-law was called Edwardo to the end of his life. Pelmanism was a system of memory-training of

which we exam-ridden slaves expected great things. It was advocated by the constant use of little grey books, to develop, one assumed, like Poirot, the 'little grey cells'.

One term we all played diabolo with sticks about seventeen inches long, linked by string, and a sort of bobbin called the cone. The object of the exercise, requiring considerable skill and practice, was to keep the cone rotating on the string, throwing it up and catching it again while it was still spinning. The string, kept slack while the cone was spinning, was quickly made taut to toss the cone aloft. As it came down it was received on the tightened string which was immediately slackened and the cone set a-spinning once more. Diabolo was not a new invention; it had been played in China a hundred years before. When the craze was at its height in 1907, the Spinning Bobbin or Aerial Top, as it was variously called, was described in one advertisement as 'the little sprite of mischief which has made willing slaves of kings and queens, princes and princesses, down the social scale to the child playing in the street.'

Everyone at school had a birthday book; you wrote your name in your best handwriting in your friends' birthday books, and they wrote their name in yours. There was room for several names under each date. We all possessed albums of delicately-tinted pages on which kind-hearted mistresses and friends inscribed a few lines of a favourite poem such as Carlyle's lines

> So here hath been dawning another blue day
> Think, wilt thou let it slip useless away?

or draw a little picture in Chinese ink. In return, we decorated pages of friends' albums with copies of the currently popular Mabel Lucie Attwell children, those endearing fat babies with coy smiles and cute captions; and pen-and-ink sketches of Hilda Cowham's long-legged school-girls, or perhaps Dana Gibson's renowned Gibson Girls, willowy ladies with generous bosoms, narrow waists, and gracefully-curved backs.

The delicate pictures in blue and silver by Jessie M. King

were admired and copied by talented seniors, who were aware that she and her husband, E. A. Taylor, were largely responsible for establishing the colony of artists at Kirkcudbright. The colony that made the town famous is no more. Jessie M. King in her black cloak and buckled shoes was a familiar figure. There have been inevitable changes and the artists are gone.

Towards the end of the Christmas Term, busy little fingers were engaged in making simple gifts. A pen-wiper was then a necessity on every writing-table, and many a father received one contrived from small circles of scarlet flannel, lovingly notched by nail-scissors, and sandwiched between circles of felt. A pad of shaving paper in an embroidered cover so that there was no mistaking its function was another suitable gift for a father; for mothers and aunts hat-pin heads were ornamented with blobs of coloured sealing-wax, and little whitewood boxes were carefully painted. They were sold ready-stamped with a design to be completed by poker-work, painting, or carving. Ribbon Work and Pen Painting were more elaborate crafts practised by senior girls in the seclusion of the Sixth Form Room.

Unlike most schools of that era we were not awarded prizes for our scholastic achievements. Instead of a Speech Day or Prize Giving we had the End Concert to which parents and friends were invited. We marked special occasions by singing the School Hymn,

> Jesus calls us o'er the tumult
> Of our life's wild restless sea,

and the School Song, which was still the Harrow School Song, though some years later one was specially written and composed for the school. 'Forty Years On' was a grand song for singing; with enthusiasm we shouted every one of the double verses, and the fervent, if ambiguous, cry

> Follow Up!
> Till the field ring again and again
> With the tramp of the twenty-two men!

Racing downstairs on Breaking Up Day, we would find Grieve, who lived in the lodge at the front gate, surrounded in the courtyard by a chaotic array of luggage. There were domed trunks covered in shiny black leather; Saratoga trunks, also with curved lids whose contours and shaped battens suggested an upturned boat, and fitted with brass corners and hinges; there were corded tin trunks painted yellow outside and blue inside, and leather portmanteaux of various sizes. In actual fact it was far from chaotic, for Grieve had arranged it for speed in loading, and he, with a long list in his hand, marshalled without error or delay, the steadily moving procession of horse-drawn cabs, informing each driver who circled the yard and drew up at the steps, which railway-station he was bound for. Our names were called, our luggage heaved into place, in we jumped, and off went our cab, making way for the next. A jolt over the ridge that was the bolt-socket of the gate was the thrilling bump that told us we were really on our way, rattling up Kilgraston Road towards 'Cally' or 'Waverley' where before long we found ourselves deposited in the care of good-natured porters who accompanied us to the correct platform, installed us in corner seats, and appeared to be content with a modest tip.

For Ellie and me, the first part of our journey passed quickly but the latter half was slow. There were no expresses on the Great North of Scotland at a time convenient for us. Not long after leaving Aberdeen we made a point of leaning from the window to greet the friendly face of the painted statue of Rob Roy. We supposed him to be a figurehead from a vessel owned by a Peterhead family, one of whose members was connected with the paper-mill at Culter, but some people are now of the opinion that he was originally a wooden figure of a Highlander that in Dicken's day stood outside the door of a reputable tobacconist, similar to the Red Indian of American shops. The dear little chuffing train stopped at every station . . . their names come crowding back, not necessarily in the right order . . . Milltimber, Drum, Park, Banchory, Crathes, Glassel, Torphins, Lumphanan (and that curious cutting at Tillychin,

50 feet deep and a quarter of a mile long, known as Satan's Den), Dess, Aboyne, Dinnet and Cambus o' May . . . we looked out at every one, counting them off. Running through wooded glades, over moor and through farmland, the train puffed fussily across the Muir o' Dinnet along that glorious scenic stretch from Cambus o' May to Ballater. The snell air was like a tonic; we leaned from the window for the last mile, impatient for the first glimpse of the hills of home and the dear folks waiting to greet us. Steam was shut off as we rounded the bend, we began to slow down, and, with a white banner of smoke floating behind, the train came to rest in Ballater Station.

At school we were seldom taken to a concert hall or a theatre, nor did we visit Edinburgh's libraries or museums which are among the best in the world. Its ancient university and medical school confer degrees which are held in high regard the world over, and it was inevitable that, prior to leaving school, we seniors should discuss among ourselves university life to which many girls looked forward. My father hoped that I, too, would consider it, but I had other plans. In those days, at Edinburgh and other universities there were studious men and women who eventually attained high places in many walks of life. There were also the so-called Chronics, men who stayed for years beyond a normal course, not much interested in achieving academic distinction, or even a Pass. Life to them was leisured and free; the university had few rules and no regimentation. One of these young men, the son of the revered minister of St Giles High Kirk, late on summer nights often marched down Kilgraston Road playing his bagpipes all the way from Marchmont Road to Blackford Hill. Hearing him from my little corner bed, I was carried in imagination to the Glen, and the skirl of the pipes echoing among the hills. The end of that era came in August 1914; students, capped and uncapped, foregathered in very different circumstances, many to pass, as Dr George Fischer put it, 'through glory to oblivion' . . .

[129]

> The ne'er-do weel who did not care a jot,
> The Honours Man who always thought he thought,
> Alike from pulpit and from pub have passed,
> And equal daisies mark their funeral spot.

When the time came for me to leave school, I realised that the dividing line between school-girl and adult woman was alarmingly definite and sudden. It marked for me the end of five years of hard work, of happy hours on playing-fields, of fears of failure, thrills of success and hopes for the future. Overnight, as it were, one had to turn a pigtail into a bun (mine was more like a scone) and wear a long skirt. Day-girls, with their mothers' help with sundry hair-pins and combs, had mastered the art of putting up their hair, but I, with other boarders who had floundered through adolescence garbed in unattractive clothes, on the day I left school, pinned up my hair with no style, and placed on my head, very self-consciously, a hat as big as a dustbin lid (cart-wheel was the current description) which I had bought in Princes Street to be in the fashion. Hats were large that year in belated imitation of those in *The Merry Widow*, which resulted in the vogue for Viennese music and 'Lily Elsie hats'. I looked and felt absurd in mine and a few weeks later discarded it. Community life with its rules and regulations and herding together is not the best preparation for communal life. We who had led sequestered lives, who had worked and played and moved with alacrity to the summons of an exacting school-bell, discovered that to emerge as adults was like coming from a nunnery into a strange world. We could parse and analyse, read Molière and Virgil and sing 'Die Lorelei', but we had no experience in thinking for ourselves, no idea of the world outside our narrow limits.

> All that talk of number, tense, and mood,
> Of rhymes and rules
> For gerund and for genitive . . .
> We had done with them for good.

Unsophisticated, gauche, with no clothes sense and no regrets I left school and set myself rather ineptly to the business of

growing up. Malcolm Muggeridge has said that the twin perils of recollecting one's childhood are sentimentality and self-pity. If, in spite of my efforts to be objective, I have failed to avoid these pitfalls, I crave indulgence.

CHAPTER V

A STUDENT
IN DUNFERMLINE

'It is a false supposition that school-days are those of unalloyed carelessness and enjoyment', said an old Scots worthy, deprecating in his pedantic fashion the notion that they are the happiest days of your life, and I, for one, agree with him.

I left school in the very hot summer of 1911, and all my happiest days were yet to come. 1911 was a royal year. The Investiture of the Prince of Wales and the pageantry of the Delhi Durbar followed the Coronation of King George V and Queen Mary in triumphant succession.

That autumn I began my training at Dunfermline College of Hygiene and Physical Training, and the years I spent there were mentally stimulating, physically wearing, and completely happy. I found myself engaged in work which I enjoyed, with companions of my own age with similar tastes and ambitions.

Each new subject was a challenge. Absorbed in the study of Anatomy and Physiology I realised that, had it occurred to me earlier, I might have found great satisfaction as a student of Medicine. A brief history of the College says that

the Carnegie Trustees early turned attention to the subject of child welfare, and one of their first acts was to introduce scientific methods of physical training into

schools. A College of Hygiene was instituted in 1905; the medical inspection of school children was begun a year later, and this led naturally to the establishment of remedial clinics. In 1909 the Scottish Education Department officially recognised the College as a centre for the training of teachers in physical instruction. In 1912 Andrew Carnegie, the town's far-sighted benefactor, laid the foundation stone of new buildings, and in 1921 it became a national institution under the wing of the National Committee for the training of teachers in Scotland.

It was a tradition at College that senior students should give practical help to newcomers, so, on arrival, each junior acquired a 'mother' whose unofficial duty was to guide her in the purchasing of such things as text-books and hockey-boots, directing her to the best shops, and generally assisting her to adjust to College routine. I was grateful to the good-natured Irish extrovert who mothered me for a year and gave me a pattern to follow when I, in turn, had to mother a junior.

The members of the medical and teaching staff were friendly and approachable; it was encouraging to be treated as an intelligent adult. There was freedom, discipline, justice, and a few reasonable rules, mostly self-imposed.

The long hours spent in the gymnasium, in clinics and lecture-rooms, were thoroughly agreeable, as were the years ahead when we eventually graduated to taking classes in schools in the town and surrounding neighbourhood.

There were strikes in 1911 and 1912, but they made little impact on us students, earnestly engaged as we were in daily exercising every muscle strenuously, methodically, and rhythmically, poring over unfamiliar text-books and serenely unaware that the Prime Minister had coined a phrase, 'Wait and see', and that Income Tax had risen to the startling figure of 1s. 3d. in the pound.

With a comfortable bedroom, congenial room-mates, a cold bath every morning and a hot one every night, I was in

clover . . . far behind was the spartan life of boarding-school!

We walked from the Students' Hostel to the College, where all lectures and practical work took place, starting at nine o'clock with an hour in the splendidly-equipped gymnasium. Lectures followed, then back we ambled in twos and threes, to take our places in the dining-room with its ladder-backed, rush-seated chairs, to tuck in with hearty appetite to a vegetarian lunch of nut-cutlets, lentil rissoles, rice patties, or Scotch Woodcock, with fresh fruit and a brown Wedgwood beaker of milk. Our meals were carefully balanced, at a time when a balanced diet was not given much consideration.

Cook, stout, middle-aged and Irish, with hair that Somerset Maugham would have described as 'suspiciously black for her age', could neither read nor write, but she was intelligent, with an excellent memory; when Miss Hay, the housekeeper, gave her verbal instructions regarding quantities and method, she produced extremely palatable meals.

Afternoon activities included games at Venturefair Park where Gregson, our patient coach, took over. He it was who encouraged tenacity in hockey, and coached me so well that at my first International Trial I was among those chosen to represent the Midlands Region under the Scottish Women's Hockey Association. He took pride in our team's successes, kept Press reports of all our matches, and gave us merciless but constructive criticism when play fell below his accepted standard.

At the end of my College career he assured me that I would undoubtedly be selected to play for Scotland in the following season, but, as things turned out, nothing came of it. By that time I had gone into voluntary exile in Perthshire, forgotten, and completely out of touch. I was destined never to wear the colours of the Scottish Thistle, and played no more first class hockey.

At College, lacrosse, which called for speed on the field and a new technique to be mastered in throwing, passing, and catching the ball, was played in spring, and cricket in summer, occasionally against Men's Elevens. Again, my turn of speed

assured me a place in the First Eleven as it had done at school. In some quarters, smiles still accompany any mention of women's cricket, but the College Eleven was considered really good, and the advice quoted in a cricket report of long ago would not come amiss today. 'Learn to defend your wickets, play with a straight bat, be resolute, determined, and practise unceasingly.'

We had the most wonderful freedom in our dress; the minimum of underwear included a cotton garment with built-up shoulders, firmly buttoned down the front with the bone buttons associated with the Liberty bodice of nursery days. By no means so dainty as a brassiere, nor so glamorous as today's bra, it was called a bust-bodice, and though it made no pretence at offering support, it served to conceal the contours of the figure, and that was then all-important.

At lectures we appeared in blouses and pinafore dresses, and on the games field wore brief divided skirts, except when we Midlands representatives played another Region at Murrayfield, or on some other sports ground, with spectators; we then reverted to ankle-length skirts with green braid round the hem. 'Goalies' of that day were known to save many a goal for their side by quick knee-bending, smothering the ball in skirt-folds before it could pass between the posts.

For gym we wore square-necked tunics of fine navy cloth, with box pleats back and front, velvet across the front yoke, and a girdle of broad braid which was tied at the side. The tunic was hand-tailored, as was the rest of our outfit, by Mr McKelvie Robertson in the High Street, who came in person to take our measurements and later attended us for fittings.

The entrance hall of the College buildings was floored with mosaic, and from the lofty ceiling hung baskets of fresh flowers. I seem to remember that there were even flower-baskets overhanging the swimming-pool, known as The Pond, well out of reach of the rings on which we delighted to swing, and then to drop with a splash into the Deep End.

It was not, however, an amusing experience for a doctor's cook who once dropped fully-clothed into the middle of The

Pond. The occasion was a Fancy Dress Ball, organised for charity by the town's leading hostesses, and held in the College by permission of the Trustees. There was dancing in the gym and a number of maids from private houses served supper in the lecture-rooms. Their work finished, they explored the buildings and, discovering The Pond, decided to have some fun swinging on the rings. One, more timid than the rest, unwillingly persuaded to Have a Go, panicked, lost her grip, and fell shrieking into deep water. Her hysterical sobs could be heard echoing round The Pond long after she was rescued, comforted with hot towels, and wrapped in warm blankets.

The swimming-bath was then the best in Scotland, six and a half feet deep at one end, and about three feet deep at the shallow end for children and beginners. It was long enough and broad enough to be appreciated for training practice by promising international swimmers. It was equipped with high diving-boards and spring-boards, and had a supply of metal saucers which were thrown in for divers and underwater swimmers to recover.

We students went to The Pond for lessons from Miss Robertson and Miss Pirrie, muscular ladies who dangled a novice at the end of a pole hooked in a ring on the luckless beginner's back. After swimming-practice, if we emerged with chattering teeth, we soon recovered after a hot shower and a brisk rub-down with a hot towel, which induced a feeling of lightness and well-being. Wet towels and swimming-suits were thrown down a chute to the nether regions where a mysterious mechanism dried everything in no time at all, and returned it clean, warm, and neatly folded ready for use on the following day.

Swim-suits were dowdy one-piece stockinette affairs, reaching to the knee, and buttoning close to the neck. Close-fitting caps of ugly red rubber effectively kept dry our long hair.

My first appearance at The Pond was marred by an experience which did nothing to help me to learn to swim. I was held underwater and half-drowned by the College clown. It took me a month or two to overcome my fear of the water, then I

went ahead with other learners to collect, in due course, certificates for Life-Saving and distance-swimming which were an essential part of the Course. I was lost in admiration of local students who from childhood had been real water babies in that very Pond; they were polished performers and enchanting to watch.

Dunfermline, 'the auld grey toon', sprang up around the abbey founded by Margaret, the wife of King Malcolm III. It is one of the loveliest Scots towns and a pleasant place to live in, with the sea and the hills not far away.

It was because in his childhood he looked longingly at that forbidden Paradise that Andrew Carnegie, when he became a multi-millionaire, bought Pittencrieff Glen and the land around it, and gave it to Dunfermline so that all the towns-folk, and especially their children, could wander freely there at any time that took their fancy and enjoy the delights it had to offer. He, a dedicated golfer, did not linger in Dunfermline to play golf, as he might have done, but after that magnificent gesture, returned to New York, where he built himself a bungalow on the St Andrew Golf Club grounds before his retirement to his Scottish home, Skibo Castle. It was said he always had two caddies . . . one to carry his golf-clubs, the other to give him a helpful push up hills when required.

In Pittencrieff Glen we students in our free time strolled down rustic paths where birds and squirrels would come and feed out of our hands, and over broad lawns where, on occasion, to the accompaniment of strings in 'Greensleeves', we performed in costume Old English processional dances.

Carnegie gave wonderful gifts, including organs and libraries, to the whole of Scotland; on his birthplace he showered gifts, beginning with Pittencrieff, where wolves and bears once had roamed, and the monks from the abbey had dug for coal. To cope with his generosity the Carnegie Trust was formed, and, under it, various educational establishments were set up, including the College.

Still the only one of its kind in Scotland, after many years in the town of its birth, and Second World War years in

Aberdeen, a magnificent new College was built at Cramond, near Edinburgh, and opened by the Queen Mother in 1966; the students, well aware of her favourite pastime, marked the occasion by presenting her with the latest type of salmon-fishing rod; and in 1970, 'the bonny lasses from the Gym College' carried in the medals at the Commonwealth Games in Edinburgh. It was amusing to be reminded on that occasion that when the College was first established, the local children found the idea of a College of Hygiene highly diverting, and made a point of chanting as the students went by,

> High Jean! Low Jean!
> Whaur ye gaun the day, Jean?

In my day we pushed bicycles up the steep New Row. Traffic was mainly horse-drawn . . . vans, milk-floats, vegetable-carts, lorries laden with coal or crates of linen with two powerful Clydesdale horses between the shafts to pull them up the hill to the railway-station; and horse-cabs always on hand for weddings and funerals.

Doctors were beginning to invest in motor-cars, and the Austin Seven was specially recommended for the medical profession. It was odd to see them driving around in the silk hat and morning coat which was then considered the correct dress to wear when carrying that little black bag.

Dr Sturrock could be seen in formal dress, seated behind his chauffeur, his immaculately-gloved hands resting on the professional bag on his knees.

Before long, doctors who drove their own cars realised how unsuitable was the morning-coat and topper outfit and, in country places at least, discarded them for tweeds and an Inverness cape, more appropriate for wear in an open car, completing the costume with a Sherlock Holmes hat with the flaps tied on top. Dr Howie of Strathdon is supposed to have had the first car in Scotland, back in 1895 or 1896. It was certainly the first in the Nor' East.

Dr Crerar of Maryport, whose motor-car, driven by the famous Claud, was one of the first to be seen in the county of

Cumberland (now Cumbria) and Dr Alford Anderson, whose car was the first to appear in Dalbeattie, had twin-cylinder machines that made a noise like a traction-engine when on the highway. Petrol then cost 9d. a gallon.

There was another doctor in Dunfermline who wore a bowler-hat when making his rounds of the wards in the Fever Hospital. As a patient, I recall him wearing a long white coat, unbuttoned and flapping round his heels at every step.

About that time, in a hospital in another region, the matron was found to have moved her bed for convenience; she was sleeping in the same ward as scarlet fever patients, and taking their pulses with the aid of an alarm clock.

I recall that when we patients were recovering from 'scarlet' we were obliged to sit with our feet in buckets of hot water in which a quantity of washing-soda had been dissolved. This was to speed up the process of 'peeling'. Long years after, Molly, one of my fellow-sufferers, reminded me that when our mothers were requested to send old clothes for us to wear in the ward when we were at last allowed out of bed, they responded, individually, in characteristic Scots fashion. Having been informed by the hospital authorities that the clothes would be destroyed in the incinerator, as would all letters and gifts which we had received during our sojourn in hospital, they sent very old clothes indeed. In my parcel was a weird assortment of apparel, including an Inverness cape, while Molly never forgot her dismay at having to appear in a voluminous flannel petticoat with embroidered scallops round the hem.

At College we learned to perform, and in time to teach, graceful dances from Spain and Greece, lively dances from Italy and Japan, artless forms from Sweden and Denmark, the stately pavane, galliard, gavotte, minuet, and mazurka of Old England, Morris Dances collected by Cecil Sharp, Irish Jigs, Scottish Reels, the Sword Dance, and Highland Fling. Relaxing, we revolved slowly in the old-fashioned waltz to the dreamy strains of 'The Merry Widow' waltz by Franz Lehar,

reversing to the melodious strains of 'The Pink Lady', 'Il me disait', Sydney Baynes' 'Destiny', 'The Vision of Salome', Waldteufel's 'Skaters' Waltz', or the rollicking 'Nights of Gladness'. We pranced round the gym in the Edwardian polka, 'the jolliest fun I know', and usually finished with a gay two-step to 'The Policeman's Holiday', with its cheeky whistle and final stamping steps.

I once heard an eminent professor of Child Health expound on the importance of sugar, in some form or other, in the diet of growing children. 'They store it in their livers,' he explained, 'but with their boundless energy the store is quickly depleted, and, Nature seeking to replace the loss, the child turns to the most easily available, if not always the most desirable, namely, sweets.' It all came back to me, the mad rush back to the Hostel from energy-consuming games or dancing, to help ourselves to sugar-cubes which we discovered in a tin on a handy shelf. We helped Nature to replace our loss by crunching them while exchanging uniform for dresses of foulard, velvet or voile, throwing over them our ample gowns of navy serge which were longer and heavier than university gowns; they were cut like pulpit gowns, and were a comfort in cold weather.

Dinner was a substantial meal consumed in leisurely fashion; we afterwards adjourned to the Common Room for coffee and conversation, music, and a look at the newspapers. Entertainment was provided by talented fellow-students. Netta at the piano could turn in a moment from a brilliant execution of a Brahms Rhapsody or a Chopin Polonaise, to a medley of popular tunes, and also acted as accompanist to soloists in their varied repertoires.

Jessie rendered 'The Rosary' which was very popular at the time:

O Memories that bless and burn,
O barren gain and bitter loss!
I kiss each bead and strive at last to learn
To kiss the Cross, Sweet Heart, to kiss the Cross!

Dora carolled 'The Waltz Song' from *Tom Jones*, and a charming Romany ditty,

> Where my caravan has rested
> Flowers I leave you on the grass,
> All the flowers of Love and Memory
> You will find them when you pass.

a reference to the custom of leaving posies on the camp-site where other gipsies will find them.

We had no fault to find with the sentimental songs of the time. We loved Mifanwy in her wood, Melisande who 'leaned down to the water' to look at her mirrored face, and 'Two Eyes of Gray' that used to be so bright. Ballad-writers of that age knew exactly the kind of song that would send singers and their drawing-room audiences into ecstasies of delight.

Amy Woodforde-Finden, an Indian Officer's wife, set the Indian Love Lyrics of Laurence Hope, the wife of another officer, to the most melting melodies, and her 'Pale hands I love beside the Shalimar' and 'Less than the dust' were rendered on every possible occasion, in our Common Room, as elsewhere.

A song that left a lasting impression on me was Trilby's last words, set to a plaintive melody:

> A little work, a little play
> To keep us going . . . and then Good Day!
> A little warmth, a little light
> Of Love's bestowing . . . and then, Good Night!
> A little fun to match the sorrow
> Of each day's growing . . . and so, Good Morrow!
> A little trust that when we die
> We reap our sowing, and so . . . Goodbye!

We sang with equal fervour Cicely Courtnedge's songs from *The Mousme*, which was running at the Shaftesbury Theatre in London; and a South Country song called 'My dear Soul', which began,

Hast thou heard the turtle-dove in the woods at e'en
Singing to his mate of love all his heart may mean?

We all knew the opening line to Tosti's 'Goodbye to Summer',

Falling leaf and fading tree.

We knew that Irving Berlin had scored a great hit with
'Alexander's Ragtime Band', and a new song sung by Mysie,
'Down in the Forest something stirred' was still taken
seriously.

At half-past eight, or thereabouts, softly humming snatches
from 'Maritana' or 'Merrie England', or a few bars of 'Dear
little Jammy Face', we departed for the Studies where we each
had a desk, to settle down to an evening's study, when Silence
was observed as a matter of course.

There we remained till ten o'clock, memorising, revising, or
studying remedial movements for patients in Miss Holmblad's
Clinique, where only feather-light tapôtement was acceptable.

Those were the days when it was definitely unladylike to
smoke. Once or twice, greatly daring, we smoked a cigarette
in our bedrooms, letting the blue wisps drift up the chimney,
feeling very dashing and well on our way to the dogs.

We had not much time for reading; our studies took up all
our time on week-nights, and at the week-end we preferred
to use our free time in bicycling round the countryside, and
taking trips into Edinburgh.

There was in the Hostel for light reading when required, a
collection of modern novels. I felt that I had outgrown the
'great grey-green, greasy Limpopo River' of the *Just So
Stories*, so I took from the shelves Maud Diver's *Captain
Desmond, V.C.*, the novels of Sheila Kaye-Smith, and of
Stephen McKenna, who was understood to be the most
successful Society novelist of his day. I revelled in the works
of Arnold Bennett, in Booth Tarkington's *T. Tembarom*, and
George Birmingham's *Spanish Gold*, and have never forgotten
the enchanting Mary Kate.

I read Hardy's *Tess*, which as late as 1891 had been reviewed

as an immoral book, and H. G. Wells' *Ann Veronica*, which in 1905 had shocked the respectable public. There was as yet no censorship of literature, but a great deal of effort was used to control, by public opinion, the expression of advanced views of sex and free-thinking. I met for the first time Sophistication and Worldliness in the works of Robert Hichens, Gilbert Frankau, and Michael Arlen; we all made a point of reading *The Green Hat* and *The Garden of Allah* but sex was never mentioned in conversation. I discovered the writings of Elizabeth Beauchamp, whose first book, *Elizabeth and her German Garden* gave her the pseudonym which she retained throughout her career. Ethel M. Dell was turning out books in quick succession . . . looking back, my impression is that they invariably contained a horse-whipping. Devoting, as I have done all my life, every available minute to reading, in my old age I have acquired a passion for more and more erudition . . . reading, reading, reading in a frantic race against Time. Somerset Maugham once said that 'to acquire the habit of reading is to construct for yourself a refuge from almost all the miseries of Life' and declared that he would rather read the catalogue of the Army and Navy Stores, or a railway time-table, than nothing. I have been equally desperate. Years ago, arriving late at a Manchester hotel, I found myself, a chronic nocturnal reader, in my bedroom with nothing to read but the Telephone Directory, and with this for bedtime reading I had to be content.

In my College days it would have been more profitable had I given some time to the study of current affairs in the daily newspapers of which we had an ample supply. I was by no means the only indifferent student of events of the day, and on topics suitable for discussion with the Warden, Miss Moseley, we were not as knowledgeable as we might have been. By turns we sat at her table, and she took it for granted that we had made ourselves familiar with at least the headlines in the papers, and, belatedly regretting that we had not done so, we racked our brains for acceptable topics . . . work as a subject at table, being taboo. Possibly we had read that Sir

Edward Elgar had conducted the first performance of his Second Symphony; probably we knew that the King had unveiled a monument to Queen Victoria in front of Buckingham Palace, and that Emmeline Pankhurst was leading the movement for Women's Suffrage, but when, one evening, into a pool of silence Miss Moseley dropped a conversational pebble . . . 'I see they are trying to patch things up in China', not one of us had a clue to follow. From that day, patching things up in China was often mentioned to fill a gap in conversation, but never in Miss Moseley's hearing. When the hum of voices at other tables became overpowering, it was her custom to ping her little bell and admonish us: 'Kindly modulate your voices.' It was pleasant therefore to be able from time to time to enthuse on the enjoyment derived from a concert recently attended in the town.

The Carnegie Trustees were in the comfortable financial position to command performances from world-famous orchestras, and from some of the greatest musical personalities of the day. I shall always remember a joint recital by Eugene Ysaye, the Belgian violinist (for whom his compatriot, César Franck, wrote a sonata as a wedding-present) and Pugno, the gifted French-Italian pianist. I had never before heard a solo violin (as different from crofters' fiddles as chalk from cheese) and it was my good fortune that the first time I heard it, it was played by a great master. It was a small perfect thing, a Brahms valse, tender and warm and it turned my bones to water; I went back to the Hostel walking on air, with a strange tingling in my spine. I felt so happy I could have cried.

In St Margaret's Hall I first heard that appealing song from *The Marriage of Figaro*, 'Voi che sapete' and, in my mind's eye still see the dark-eyed singer whose name I have regrettably forgotten.

There were, too, lively military band concerts in Pittencrieff Glen, and we attended all the local Amateur Operatic Society's productions, *The Dollar Princess*, *The Arcadians*, and *Our Miss Gibbs*. We sat cheerfully and uncritically

[144]

throughout the show, and returned to our quarters humming their tuneful ditties, 'We are the Dollar Princesses', 'Dear little girl with the bit of a brogue', and 'Why must they call me Mary when my name's Miss Gibbs?'

Cecil Sharp, famous for his research into the lore of forgotten ballads and country dances, gave a concert which I remember, with a contralto to sing the songs he had selected, while he gave a commentary at the piano.

Of all the songs that were chosen to illustrate his talk I remember only two . . . the ballad of Lord Randal, with its mournful refrain

> Make my bed soon, for I'm sick to my heart
> And I fain would lie doon.

and a delicate little song which began

> I sowed the seeds of Love
> I sowed them in the Spring,
> I gathered them up in the morning so soon
> When song-birds did sweetly sing.
>
> The gardener standing by
> He bade me take great care,
> For that under the blossom and under the bough
> There are thorns that wound and tear.

On Saturdays we bicycled all round the neighbourhood, often visiting Culross, the little town that was a Royal Burgh as far back as 1588, whose blacksmith at one time had the monopoly in the making of cast-iron girdles for Scots kitchens. 'I'll gar yer lugs dirl like a Cooriss girdle', was a common maternal threat to rebellious laddies.

Its cobbled causeways reminded us that, by ancient tradition, only the leading worthies had the right to 'the croon o' the causie' . . . lesser folk had to be content to tread on a lower level. We inspected the Palace, the Mercat Cross, and the Abbey, and recalled what we had been taught about the

monks of the thirteenth century who developed coal-mines, and extracted salt from the sea. There was a Snuff Cottage somewhere, from which came the saying, 'Wha wad hae thocht it, noses hae bocht it!'

I remember the forestairs on the kirk brae; when houses were small, and streets narrow, it was plain common sense to save interior space by having stairs built outside the main walls leading to an upper floor. A 600-year-old cottage was known as the House with the Evil Eyes. One of its gables, with two small eye-shaped apertures did look uncannily like a human face. The eyes followed the passer-by wherever he went, and legend had it that evil would befall anyone who looked into them. The National Trust and civic diligence have secured the little township's almost complete preservation as it was in the seventeenth century.

Aberdour was another of our favourite haunts. Its castle was once the home of the Regent Morton, who conspired to the murders of Rizzio and Darnley, and is said to have forged the Casket Letters.

With a few friends I was privileged to be invited to inspect a coal-mine on the outskirts of Dunfermline. We descended in a cage and walked for what seemed miles from the coal-face; bent almost double we clambered among pit-props, crawled along a tunnel with a roof apparently four feet high, and there saw men stripped to the waist working on their backs with picks in their hands. We were shown with some natural pride what was then a modern wonder, an automatic coal-cutter at work, and had to raise our voices to be heard above the din. We each handled a pick and chipped a tiny piece of coal to keep as a souvenir, and then from a deep shaft straggled up a long steep slope into the fresh air and sunshine. We were light-hearted, unthinking young girls, but that afternoon's experience made a lasting impression on us, helping us to realise what coal-miners had to endure in order to fill the bunkers of the nation.

Sometimes we went to Edinburgh by train to visit friends, to do a spot of window-shopping, to attend a matinée per-

formance at the King's Theatre, and on one memorable occasion to see the incomparable Pavlova as the Dying Swan.

It was with his play *Bunty pulls the Strings*, with his daughter Winifred as 'Bunty', that Graham Moffat had a great success in London's Haymarket Theatre. In 1912 we students went in a body to see the play in Edinburgh. It was my introduction to a 'seat in the gods'.

Many years later, when I was haranguing some friends on the subject of this play, and picturing the stricken face of the elder of the kirk who could not thole the idea of 'sic an abomination... a wumman at the plate!' they told me that the scene was laid in Baldernock, in Dunbartonshire, which endeared it to me more than ever.

Those were the days when G. H. Elliot, the Chocolate-Coloured Coon, was 'sighing for the silvery moon', and doing his celebrated soft-shoe dance; when Vesta Tilley was acclaimed for her male impersonations and was in great demand as a principal boy in Christmas pantomimes, when the Vernon Castles were the predecessors of Fred Astaire and Ginger Rogers, and in 1911 the illusionist who called himself 'The Great Lafayette' lost his life in a fire at the Empire Theatre, while attempting to rescue his horse.

I believe it was in that same year that the glamorous French comedienne, Gaby Deslys, captivated a European monarch, who loaded her with jewels and nearly lost his crown and throne.

Although Picture Houses had opened in Edinburgh before I left school, I had never seen the interior of one nor glimpsed a screen till my student days when pictures were shown in a dusty little hall in Canmore Street, in Dunfermline. The pictures we saw had the appearance of having been filmed in pouring rain. They nearly all had this curious effect, due perhaps to imperfect celluloid or worn equipment. As well as pictures there were variety turns of a very amateurish nature, presumably introduced to give the operator time to re-wind his inflammable piece of film. I recall a gawky young girl, who

[147]

had probably occupied the pay-box till her turn came to take the stage, in a nasal whine declaimed

> It's not bekass your teeth are pearly,
> It's not bekass your waist is small,
> I love you, little girlie,
> Bekass I love you, that's all!

and a small child stepped forward and announced that her little brother would paint the *Titanic* in the short space of ten minutes, which he did, with coloured crayons, to encouraging applause. One fine June Saturday, staff and students went by train to St Andrews, as guests of Sir John Ross, the elderly Chairman of the Trustees. After a splendid lunch at Rusack's Hotel, we strolled through the streets of the historic town, had a look at the picturesque harbour, and rested where green-and-white breakers washed on yellow sands. Faded snapshots remind me of that brilliant day on the beach overlooking St Andrews Bay, the little rowing-boats we took out, and the bathing. Marian recalled bathing at Aberdeen as a child when the woman in charge of the machines harnessed the horse to your bathing-box and yelled, 'Haud on yersel'!' before leading it down to the water. I recall with dismay how immodest we thought Madge, of generous build and no inhibitions, who, that day at St Andrews, stood imperturbable in her wet swim suit, chattering gaily to the Chairman and all the young doctors while the rest of us, primly draped in towels, hovered on the fringe of the circle.

When I spent a weekend with my friend, Molly, at her home in Dundee, her mother took us to hear the Italian Grand Opera Company from Milan in Gounod's *Faust*, a profound revelation which left me with memories that are still lucid and tender. I can still see the dancing in the market-place, and hear the demoniacal laughter of Mephistopheles. Stout, ageing Marguerite, with her blonde wig and flaxen plaits, trilling the Jewel Song in girlish rapture, did not strike me as incongruous; I was enchanted by her glorious voice as she sat at her

spinning-wheel, and at her window enthralled by Faust's serenade.

Another visit I recollect was to Clydeside with Edith, a school-friend. From the deck of a steamer we watched Lascars unloading tea from the good ship *Pegu*, rhythmically handling the cargo and singing as they worked. We saw great liners go out escorted by fussy little tugs, then, beneath us felt a throb of engines, and with a blast of sirens and a ring of signals we slowly turned into mid-stream and at last were on the move 'doon the watter', with a fresh breeze blowing, seagulls wheeling overhead, and a host of intriguing sights to be seen.

One day we went to Cathkin Braes where Glasgow bairns play in summer; and to Kelvingrove to the Empire Exhibition where I saw the water-chute and scenic railway for the first time (at eighteen!) and can recall the thrill of giddy headlong ascents and rushing descents, Edith and I, like everybody else, screaming with excitement at every swoop and dip. Still at heart the unsophisticated country cousin, a ride on the top of a tram-car was to me of absorbing interest, and it is the recurring memory of milling crowds on narrow pavements, the eternal clanging of bells and shrieking of engine-whistles, combined with the extraordinary variety of sounds that came from the river, that together keep bright my mental picture of Glasgow in the year 1912.

In my second year of training, a young doctor joined the College staff as bacteriologist, lecturer, and Medical Officer in schools. He was not handsome by conventional standards, but he had a broad brow and was deeply tanned. His black hair was thick and his eyes full of laughter. There was a complete-ness about his personality, a sense of purpose and determina-tion that appealed to me, and from his first appearance I paid undue attention to Newsholm on infectious diseases, and liver fluke, tapeworm, and similar oddities had for me a strange fascination. This new doctor, Mark Stewart Fraser, encouraged us in practical work by arranging for us to attend School Clinics to assist him in dressing the cuts, sores, boils, and other

afflictions of the school-children of the day. It was not till my final term that I realised how much it meant to me to be working with him, and how long were the weekends, which he spent at his home in Edinburgh, when no glimpse could be had of his athletic figure striding up Canmore Street with spring in his step.

Hedged around as I was by my natural reserve in his presence, it never occurred to me that he reciprocated my feelings, and when he proposed marriage one afternoon, in a quiet lecture-room where I had retreated for solitary study in preparation for an impending Anatomy exam. there, among the scattered bones, and a skeleton dangling on its stand, I accepted him in a daze of happiness. My friends, when I joined them for tea, seeing me apparently airborne, with eyes like stars, were intrigued, and it was hard to keep our secret, but Mark and I did keep it till the end of term.

In Assembly Week he met my father, and in Princes Street Gardens, amid sunshine and flowers, obtained his formal consent to our engagement. They agreed that our marriage would take place in a year's time. This was to enable me to obtain a Certificate from the Scottish Education Department, to supplement the Diploma of the College which, with the College badge in silver, depicting the industrious spider, would shortly be mine. I still treasure my badge; the College being founded in the Royal Burgh in which Scotland's hero king lies buried, the badge motif was doubtless inspired by the legend of Bruce and the spider. Under it is the College motto of my day, 'Efforts are successes', and the Scottish Lion rampant.

Mark's salary was then £200 a year, but we never doubted we would 'manage'. As a house-surgeon in Paddington Green Children's Hospital he had been paid £1 a week.

Before leaving Dunfermline, I was privileged to visit one of the oldest mills in the linen industry, and to choose much of my household linen straight from the loom. The town was at that time producing two-thirds of the linen woven in Britain. My tablecloths and napkins of the finest damask had exquisite original designs; one bedspread had raised embroidery in an

over-all pattern of thistle sprays. They were treasured and cared for, and lasted a lifetime. Years later I discovered that that same mill supplied King George IV with a seamless shirt which cost him £50, and that King William IV and Queen Victoria had patronised its damask trade by ordering household linen bearing their royal coat-of-arms.

Meantime, I had been invited to tea at the Fraser family home in Edinburgh. No gift from my husband in later years gave me greater pleasure than did the spray of lily-of-the-valley shyly presented to me that day; no ice-cream has ever tasted sweeter than that we shared in a quiet corner of Jenners' tea-room before going to meet his mother. She was at the window watching us walk up the road together. She and her daughters received me very kindly. There was a little schipperke dog, with pricked ears, and bright intelligent eyes, a great family friend, always addressed as Skip. I was admitted to the family circle and invited to spend a holiday at Sandyhills on the Solway, where a house was rented every summer for several months. I was shown the huge hampers and trunks of domed leather which would shortly be packed with bedlinen and towels, table-silver and cutlery, as well as the family's bulky and extensive wardrobe for this annual migration to the seaside, and the collection of homely medical aids which were carried in a Norwegian box, poker-worked in traditional patterns and known as 'Mother's Medicine Chest'. Then followed a long summer holiday together . . . first, in the Glen, where invitations poured in for me to bring my 'intended' to tea. We bicycled for miles visiting friends and favourite beauty spots, then entrained for The Shore, the family name for Sandyhills. It was truly named, for when you had taken a couple of dozen steps from the red-roofed house on the height overlooking the bay, and skipped across the road, there you were . . . on The Shore!

CHAPTER VI

A STRANGER
ON THE SHORE

Grey Galloway of the misty hills and the lonely lochs is a grand
country and some of its loveliest scenery lies along the Solway
coast. The Shore, that is, Sandyhills, near Douglas Hall, is a
stretch of beautiful sand. Our days were filled with golf and
bathing, with flounder-spearing, shrimping, and long walks by
cleughs and cliffs. The sun shone every day; I cannot recollect
a single drop of rain. The Southwick Burn comes down across
the Merse, wide and fast-running, till it is lost in the incoming
tide of the Solway Firth, with the Mersehead and Barnhourie
Sands off-shore. Along the sands which reach as far as Saterness, there are patches of quicksand, shifting and treacherous,
dangerous for walkers. Near the source of the Burn the sands
are apt to feel gluey. Mark told me of an evening when, returning alone in the half-light from duck-shooting, he stumbled on
quicksands and would have lost his life had he not thrown
himself on his back and with the help of his gun levered himself on to firm sand; he never forgot the nausea induced by the
dank odour of the mud.

Mixed bathing was universal by this time but we women in
the house-party were so self-conscious that we wore cloaks till
we arrived at the edge of the water, and left them to wrap

round us as soon as we emerged. My unbecoming two-piece bathing-dress consisted of a tunic high at the neck, and bloomers wide at the knee, with a lot of white braid as trimming.

I was glad to find that I was not expected to grab a leister, to wade waist-deep in the pools left by the outgoing tide, to feel with my toes for dabs and flounders, and having located one, to stab down through the mud to spear it and bring it triumphantly to the surface. That sport was usually left to the men who indulged in it almost daily. There was quite an art in it for the leister was eight or nine feet long, the actual spear being a sort of trident six inches across with barbed points. Mercifully the barbs had worn down with usage and the inevitable striking of submerged rocks in the process of prodding the sand for flounders, on the day that Mark speared his foot and withdrew the spear. The water was intensely cold and he felt no pain at the time. It was only the fact that his foot was bleeding profusely that drew attention to what had happened. Light was made of the incident and the wound healed normally.

Mark told me the historic tale of King James VI who, on his first visit to his Regent's castle on the Solway, called unexpectedly on a family who lived a few miles from Sandy-hills. They were poor but proud; the only fare they could set before their Royal guest was a dish of flounders, but they contrived to serve two courses by presenting first the dark side of the fish, then the white. The King was appreciative of both courses. Smacking his lips, he declared, 'They're baith fine fish, but I think I like the white anes best.'

At Colvend Manse, in their childhood, the Fraser diet had been varied by catching flounders and curing them by the simple method of slitting, salting, and pegging them out on a board which hung outside the kitchen door till they dried in the sun. It was, I imagine, rather salty fare.

I was taken to Saterness (now Southerness) to see Galloway's oldest lighthouse, dating from the 1700s, a stone beacon built to guide ships into Carsethorn and into the tricky Nith estuary

through the shifting channels of the Carse sands and the huge Blackshaw Bank. There it stood, that day in 1913, sombre and stark, in peaceful, unspoiled surroundings; and there it stands today, though Southerness is no longer peaceful or unspoiled.

Three unknown women are believed to have ferried the lovely red sandstone for the building of Sweetheart Abbey from quarries at Caerlaverock across the Nith, and, built into the wall of an old house in New Abbey village, we saw a crudely carved stone which depicts the women in their small rowing-boat. Near the village is a fine plantation of Scots pines which were planted between the years of 1775 and 1780.

We climbed Criffel that day, starting from Loch Kindar, the little private loch where old Dr Fraser and his sons used to fish at the invitation of his friend, R. A. Oswald, the proprietor of the estate. Every year they had one or two days on Kindar, which was a long drive in a four-wheeled dog-cart sitting behind a Galloway cob, from Co'en to New Abbey, some fifteen miles distant. How the lads enjoyed their lunch of cold boiled chicken with lots of bread and butter! Dr Fraser is said to have thrown a beautiful fly. His figure swayed with the movement of the boat, and the cast was a pleasure to watch.

From the top of Criffel (in Kirkcudbrightshire) we looked over the ragged coast of the Solway, Scotland on the near side, England across the pale water, and recalled how important the Solway ports were in days long ago, for legitimate trading, and illegal smuggling, from England into Scotland and the other way round. Kirkcudbrightshire, pronounced Kir-coo-bree-shire, still clings to its old title of The Stewartry, recalling the days when the hereditary Royal Stewarts were the lords.

One day we took the cliff path to Port Ling and Port o' Warren, but had second thoughts about exploring the Piper's Cave, which is very long, very dark, and very dangerous because of a deep well near the entrance.

We all attended Divine Service in the Parish Kirk at Co'en', where the venerable father of the Fraser family had ministered for fifty-eight years; and, as we walked along, many of his

gentle whimsicalities were recalled, such as his liking to prepare
at table with his own hands a salad of lettuce, freshly cut and
shredded by hand, with a dressing of castor-sugar and lemon-
juice between each layer. Even in his young days, when salads
were uncommon, their father had gathered his green things
and himself dressed his salads. They remembered, too, his
preference for crushing fresh strawberries with a silver fork,
then sprinkling them liberally with pepper, and cream from
the brimming glass jug which always stood on the Manse table;
and his habit of shaking a small churn of cream held between
his hands as he paced his study floor while composing an hour-
long sermon. Shaking and sermonising, pacing and turning, by
the time the cream had turned to butter the sermon was not
only prepared but committed to memory, for in those days it
was an affront to the exacting congregation to 'tak' paper
intae the poopit'.

His family has recently been told by a contemporary:

His sermons were no doubt good, incorporating the usual
'Firstly, Secondly, Thirdly, Fourthly, and Finally,
Brethren', but his voice was not strong, nor his delivery
arresting (he was nearly eighty by this time) and with the
lack of air in the church, and the buzz of flies, we
children paid little attention. I waited for him to say 'As
one has beautifully said', and then quote a verse from
Cowper or Newton, and I knew he was approaching the
conclusion of his sermon.

I remember how comfortable we were in church
compared to many; we had a cushion and footstools.
Mother had made the long cushion and covered it with a
length of stair-carpet. We also had a varnished box for
our Bibles, with a little key. No hymns were sung, only
an occasional paraphrase, such as 'O God of Bethel' or
'Behold the amazing gift of Love', but we sang many
psalms.

Regrettably, the little churn was not preserved, nor can the
passing bell be traced, which used to be carried in front of the

funeral procession from the home of the deceased to the kirkyard, being tolled at intervals as the cortège was moving
slowly towards the church.

I heard for the first time how two Aberdeen professors
published a volume of Scottish Sermons propounding a new
theology to which the Rev. James Fraser took exception. He
therefore wrote and published a volume of *Scotch Sermons on
The Old Lines* as an answer to their modern theories. On the
strength of this and other works he was awarded an Honorary
Degree of Divinity, but, to the mystification of colleagues, he
was never elected to the high office of Moderator of the General
Assembly of the Church of Scotland. He must, however, have
been, owing to his age, the Father of the Church for some
years. To the end of his days he would not countenance
instrumental music in his kirk; the praise was led by a precentor whose desk was placed directly under the pulpit, as was
the custom in many Scots kirks, and indeed was continued in
Glenbuchat Kirk on Donside to the end of its usage for public
worship; like David Rorie's 'pawky duke', old Dr Fraser could
not thole the notion of a 'kist o' whustles'. Nine years after his
death a new kirk was built in Co'en', and his widow, with her
family, presented a fine pulpit in his memory, but, she said, she
felt unable to contribute towards the installation of the church-
organ; ever fresh in her memory were her husband's views
on the subject. The new kirk, which accommodates 450
worshippers, was built on a site immediately to the north of
the old one and stands slightly higher. The first sod was cut in
September 1910, and the last service was held in the old kirk in
October. It was a Communion Service at which Sir Mark
Stewart assisted. He had been an elder and had always taken
practical interest in the plans for a new kirk. All the stone
from the old walls were incorporated in the new, and a stone
dated 1771 from the old lintel was built into the boundary wall
at the back. Granite came from the estate of Oswald of
Cavens and red freestone from Locharbriggs Quarries, all local
stone. The chancel has a solid granite interior, and on the
pulpit of red stone, rising three feet high, is carved the text

[156]

from which Dr Fraser preached his last sermon . . . 'Search the Scriptures'.

As an authority on plants and flowers he was known far beyond his parish boundaries. Fellow botanists came from all over Britain to make his acquaintance, to be shown the rare plants of the district and the treasures of his garden, including some which he had brought back from his travels abroad. His name and works are mentioned in most books of his time which bear on the trees and plants of the British Isles, notably in *Famous British Botanists* and *Famous Scottish Gardens*.

He was a most abstemious man, but in his old age favoured a nightcap of toddy, that is, Scotch whisky and hot water, sweetened.

His sons recalled, with affectionate amusement, how in his later years, when he wished to administer a well-deserved slap to the children of his old age, it was his custom to support his right wrist with his left hand, so giving the necessary power to his right arm, at the same time admonishing them in the strongest words of reproach of which he was capable . . . 'You stupid gomeril!'

They also called to mind how as children they, all seven of them, used to crowd round him, on his return from Presbytery Meetings in Dumfries, eagerly enquiring, 'What have you brought us, Father?' To this his invariable reply was 'I've brought myself, is that not enough?' . . . and presently, from his tail-coat pocket he would produce the expected bag of sweets.

At one time, in that part of Galloway, shortbread was used at the Communion Table instead of white bread. Farmers' wives took butter to the Manse some days before the Sacrament, and the minister took it to the baker who used it in the making of the shortbread. Dr Fraser, with his silver hair, conducted the Communion Service on the old lines. Everything was done with dignity and reverence. Afterwards the members of the Kirk Session were entertained to lunch at the Manse. On one occasion, it was remembered, Mr Bentham, one of the elders, remarked appreciatively, 'Good broth, these, Mrs

Fraser! I'll trouble you for a second helping.' Broth, always referred to in the plural, was invariably followed by a gigot of mutton and Manse rhubarb with a milk pudding . . . often it was hominy, with lashings of cream.

In those days tokens were distributed on the Fast Day by elders at the kirk gate to those who intended to be present on the Sunday. Many communicants travelled six or seven miles, as the folk in Glen Gairn did, to be present at the Lord's Table. No hymns were sung, nothing but the grand old metrical version of the Psalms of David, and a few favourite paraphrases.

Country ministers were at that time expected to 'pit up a prayer' for favourable weather to suit the farming community. To pray for rain, or for an end to it, for a drying wind, or for less of it, was a delicate business, requiring shrewd judgment on the part of the minister, who was well aware he could not please everybody.

There was a day when Sandy was overheard grumbling about his new-sown turnips that were badly in need of a shower. Advised a neighbour . . . 'Gin ye speir at the meenister he wad mebbe pit up a prayer', to which Sandy morosely replied, 'It's no verra likely he wad pray for rain for *my* neeps fan his ain hay is no' in yet!'

When my father, as a young man, spent some months in Orkney, he heard of a minister who from the pulpit appealed to the Almighty at the time of approaching hairst . . . 'Lord, send us a guid soughin' wind that will ripen the strae, and winna hairm the heid; but, O Lord, gin ye send us sic a rantin', roarin', reivin' wind as ye sent us *last* time, ye'll play the verra mischief wi' the aits!'

I learned about the making of Dunlop cheese by hand at the neighbouring farms and developed a taste for the creamy white cheese with the thin rind, a distant relation of Cheddar. (At that time it was seldom seen in England as it did not travel well.) I heard how a whole cheese, weighing thirteen pounds and over, imposing in its fitted cover of crochet lace, sat on the Manse sideboard at all times. It was sliced across with a long

thin-bladed knife and the top retained as a lid, till the cheese, a whang of which was eaten with good appetite at most meals, and by the weans at any odd time, had all been consumed. When the cheese was soft a special scoop was used to dig out a portion. I have the ivory-handled steel scoop to this day.

Among the rocks on the Castle Hill of Co'en', near the mouth of the Urr, there is a lone tombstone which marks the grave of a shipwrecked smuggler in 1791. Co'en' in olden times was full of smugglers, the trade being winked at by otherwise high-minded people. Secret cellars existed in all the big houses; under the Manse dining-room one was discovered which could be entered by a trap-door hidden by the carpet.

Heston Island, in the Solway Firth, a wind-swept outpost of Galloway, played an important part in the long history of smuggling that was carried on in the days of Dirk Hatterick and his merry men, as told by S. R. Crockett in *The Raiders*, a yarn of breathless adventure that at one time headed every boy's list of favourite books. Crockett knew every inch of Grey Galloway, every rock path and wild glen. Alford Anderson, who was present at a banquet in Dalbeattie in Crockett's honour in 1906, told me how the author revealed that evening that the Rathan of his tale was not in fact Heston, as everyone had supposed, but was derived from Rathlin, an island off the coast of Antrim, where Robert the Bruce is said to have learned a lesson in patience and perseverance from a spider. There are other places where this legend persists; one, I believe, is in Glen Trool, and another near Kirkpatrick-Fleming.

At the Dalbeattie banquet the regulation repast included turtle soup, turbot, sirloin of beef, chickens and ducks; an unusual event at a September gathering was the 'playing in' of a haggis by a piper in full Highland dress who, at the top table, was offered the customary glass of whisky. This he downed with no heel taps and continued his march round the tables before 'piping out' the haggis. This custom is followed at Burns' Suppers all over the world on 25 January, the date of the poet's

birth. The toasts at Dalbeattie were numerous . . . the King, Queen Alexandra, The Prince and Princess of Wales, other Members of the Royal Family, and the Imperial Forces. Every speaker who proposed or replied to a toast, in a lengthy speech contrived to eulogise Crockett, and to make some reference, directly or indirectly, to his books . . . to 'the land that is fragrant with bog myrtle and peat', to 'Grey Men' or 'Raiders', or to 'deeds of treachery that echo on the moss hags and caves'. The Guest of the Evening made a brief and witty speech, which was followed by more Toasts . . . to Galloway, to Galloway Raiders, and finally to the Chairman. The guests sang 'He's a jolly good fellow' and 'Auld Lang Syne', and the function was over, at what hour is not recorded. In those days, in Scotland, a banquet was a banquet was a banquet.

Many years later, Sam Crosbie, a close friend of the Fraser family, explored every nook and corner of Heston's rock-bound coast in a rowing-boat, and in one small cave found several shelves where smuggled goods had undoubtedly been hidden. A great cave on the south-west side, he felt assured, had been the chief rendezvous of the smugglers. As well as storing their contraband stock in the caves of Heston, these cunning men sometimes sank it in the Solway, leaving floating buoys to mark the spot. The Isle of Man, less than thirty miles distant, was the main starting-point for the smugglers, who operated with fleets of small boats carrying spirits, wine and tea. Landing was well-organised, for pack-horses with panniers to take two casks, were kept waiting at a dozen different points along the shore. On a coast that had so many shifting channels, local knowledge was worth any number of enforcement officers. Local fishermen with their intimate knowledge of the tides often enabled them to avoid capture, so the smugglers prospered, as did the locals, few of whom were opposed to the trade. There were also legitimate trades which are mentioned in a memory aid which was useful for Co'en' weans and others at school:

> Kyle for a man,
> Carrick for a coo,

> Cunningham for butter and cheese,
> An' Gallowa' for 'oo'.

Mark and I spent a sunny afternoon at Castle Douglas, the breezy town that used to be called Carlingwark (only the loch retains the name) where on market days farmers and their wives clip-clopped into town in two-wheeled gigs with brass candle-burning side-lamps, and where once lived a burly blacksmith called Mouncey, who had six equally brawny sons and a noisy wife. In his forge he prepared for King James II a huge cannon to batter the neighbouring castle of Threave, then in the possession of the Douglas family. The cannon was given the name of Mouncey's Meg, an allusion to the roaring habits of the smith's wife, and after figuring in many battles down the centuries, it was brought from the Tower of London in the reign of King George IV and as Mons Meg, that great cannon now sits on the battlements of Edinburgh Castle.

Our favourite walk, however, was up by Fairgirth, where young Aylmer Gray, in Samuel Wilson's ballad (published in Nicholson's *Historical and Traditional Tales of Galloway*) took his hounds to pursue the deer over Barnhourie Lee. In Fairgirth House there was at one time an ancient staircase closed at the foot by a door of solid oak studded with iron nails. It was said that a tenant with a taste for modernisation had the nails removed and covered the old door with wallpaper, a deed, if it were true, akin to near sacrilege in the eyes of lovers of antiquities.

On one of our early walks I was introduced to Belted Galloways, those neat black cattle of an ancient and distinguished polled breed with a pure white band round their middles. (In years to come our children were to refer to them, not as Belties, their local name, but as 'the cows with their Liberty bodices on'.)

A contemporary minister and friend of the family believed with Keats that Co'en' was the scene of *Guy Mannering*, being the only place that satisfied the conditions of the tale; only lack of printed evidence that Scott visited the parish pre-

vented him from proving it. Mark and I often took the road that Keats walked nearly a hundred years before, in July 1818, when he wrote to a friend, 'There was a spot close to the pathway, and there, without a doubt, Meg Merrilees often boiled her kettle. It was among rocks, brambles and broom, with a profusion of honeysuckle, roses, and foxgloves, all in the very fullness of blossom.' There Keats sat down and wrote, 'Old Meg she was a gipsy', and the spot to which he referred was possibly close to the pillar of silurian rock, known as 'Lot's Wife', which rises with dramatic effect from the salt-marshes of Southwick Burn, where gipsies were often seen seated round their camp-fire; or it may have been at the Needle's E'e, a cave-like rock formation forty feet in height, dwarfed by the cliffs which are five times as high. This was also used as an encampment from time to time, and was not far from Southwick Bank where lived Aleck Aitken and his wife, Libby, who before her marriage had been the children's nurse at Colvend Manse for many years. She was a little bird-like woman with a cheep of a voice, and had been the type of faithful servant who became attached to a family early in life and remained in their service for a lifetime. When I first met her she was at the stage when she expected a daily visit, in the holiday season, from one branch of the clan or another. Loud were her lamentations if a day passed without her greeting and offering the warmest of welcomes, along with newly baked scones and honey, to a few small Frasers. I came to know this worthy couple well in their cottage, the middle one of three, with its fuschia hedge, and montbretia, phloxes, and 'red hot pokers' (Kniphofia) in the front garden. Aleck was employed as estate carpenter by Sir Mark McTaggart Stewart of Ardwell and Southwick, whose name was given to Mark at his christening, and also to our younger son. He was the much revered friend of both our families. When my father and mother left Glen Gairn in 1918 to make a new home at Southwick Manse, Southwick was a separate parish; in old Dr Fraser's day Colvend and Southwick was a combined parish as it is at the present day. Our children, therefore, recall

the fact that their grandfathers on both sides of the family ministered in Southwick.

Sir Mark was a Conservative MP in eight parliaments, and fought many a ding-dong battle with the Liberals (there were only two parties in those days) and is well remembered in the Stewartry of Kirkcudbright to this day, particularly for his practical interest in agriculture, his kindness and under-standing as an employer, and as a devout churchman and elder of the kirk. Aleck Aitken was a craftsman of the old regime, giving always his best work, using only the best materials. The articles of furniture which he made to order, in his spare time, in his well-equipped workshop at the head of his backgarden, were constructed of solid oak, finely finished, and well-nigh immovable. He had many of the qualities lauded in 'The Village Blacksmith' . . . each morning saw some work begun, each evening saw its close, and he might have been described in Longfellow's words . . .

> His brow is wet with honest sweat,
> He earns whate'er he can,
> And looks the whole world in the face
> For he owes not any man.

On one occasion, when advanced in years, he trudged to Dal-beattie and back, a total distance of twenty miles, to refund a newsagent who had underchanged him by some trifling sum, his reason for speedy correction of the mistake in the bill was, 'There'll be nae dirty ha'penny come intae this hoose.'

On his daily mile-long walk to Southwick House, with his bag of tools on his back, he passed through Caulkerbush, a clachan which got its name from the Dutch 'busses', smuggling vessels which used to put in there at high tide to have their hulls and keels overhauled and caulkered. The word 'caulker' was still applied to the metal protecting rims on the wooden soles of the clogs in which children clattered happily to school, and which many adults also found a most comfortable and useful type of footwear. The bridge over the Southwick Burn, near Caulkerbush, was the time-honoured place where the

[163]

young men forgathered of an evening to exchange news and views; like the lads in the one-time popular song they were 'Standing on the corner, watching all the girls go by'.

Aleck made coffins for the whole neighbourhood, which Libby lined with white dimity, with a finish of white rick-rack braid. Frugally, she saved the clippings and made from them well-shaped bibs for all the babies of her acquaintance. She also knitted bootees of so excellent a pattern that even the most persevering infant could not succeed in kicking them off.

She had a fund of stories relating to her former charges in the Manse nursery, and used to recall that one of her daily duties was to scour with white sand their wooden pottie.

Until she was old and frail she scrubbed daily the wooden seat of the earth-closet in her cottage garden, which Aleck replenished as regularly with the fresh green bracken which grew thickly on the hillside behind the house. He did the same service for Miss Wilson, who lived alone next door, and had a certain standing in the parish, for her father had been a noted sea-captain who was always spoken of with deep respect.

Libby used the words 'ocht' and 'nocht' for anything and nothing; children were 'weans', and one of her quaint expressions was, in reference to people of small stature, 'They're nobbut the height o' twae scrubbers.'

Aleck at all times ate sparingly, declaring, 'I maunna wrang masel'.' When ready for bed, regardless of visiting neighbours, he would take his lighted caunnel and make a determined move to the foot of the stair, with an imperative, 'Come on, noo, Leezbeth, there'll be nae word o' this i' the morning,' and everybody took the hint.

Libby's thoughts frequently turned to her years of contented service at Colvend Manse, and she liked to remind us that the Minister's Lady had two maids to do the cooking and cleaning, a nursemaid (Libby) to look after the children, and a governess in the schoolroom. None of the children went to the village school; in due course all went to well-established boarding-schools.

The coachman and gardener lived in cottages in the grounds,

and there was an elderly man who helped to harvest the crops on the Manse Glebe, and who appears in contemporary photographs to be wearing one of the minister's old soup-plate hats.

It would not have been considered fitting for the Mistress of the Manse to do more than to instruct her maids, and herself to undertake only light duties in the house; but it *was* thought to be right and proper that she should personally look after her poultry, cure her pig at Michaelmas, stuff her Christmas goose, and make jams and jellies, conserves and preserves, chutneys and liqueurs, which for centuries have ranked as the duties of a lady in her garden and her still room.

On holiday at Sandyhills, where I learned so much about the family, a considerable amount of time in the evenings was spent in planning golf-tournaments on a small scale, which later took place on the small nine-hole golf-course, which the Frasers had planned, designed, and inaugurated some years before, with the blessing of Willie Fernie, a well-known golf professional from Troon who paid them a visit and viewed the plans before the work was carried out. He found it unnecessary to make any alterations, and, by degrees, by draining marshy ground, removing stone walls and gates, and by clearing great clumps of whins and bracken the course took shape. It never aspired to be more than a family holiday course, but over the years it has been improved and extended and has given pleasure to large numbers of golfers. The greens at first were small, but not so small as were those on a neighbouring course where a golfer complained that he could not see one of the greens because a cow was lying on it. While the men folk were discussing handicaps and tournaments we women were often engaged in shelling shrimps in the kitchen, a lengthy job when the catch had been plentiful; but when songs round the piano were the order of the day I was pressed into service to accompany Malcolm who, in his rich baritone, demanded, 'Trumpeter, what are you sounding now?' or implored, 'Speak, SPEAK, *SPEAK* to me, Thora!' while Mark, who had had some lessons from Signor Ricci in Dunfermline, preferred to call on Mary to call the cattle home across the Sands of Dee,

or to sing of the heroic little Midshipmite. Kenneth's favourites were taken from a bound volume of old songs which had been treasured from childhood, and which I now possess. One, a sad little song about a mother's vigil at the grave of her child had a most appealing refrain . . .

> Fair, fair, with golden hair
> (Sang a lone mother while weeping)
> Fair, fair, with golden hair,
> Under the willows she's sleeping.

Another was a cheerful ditty sung by Mr Christy's Minstrels about a cottage on the wild prairie where lived a lovely child known to all as Rosalie, the Prairie Flower.

> Fair as a lily, joyous and free,
> Light of that prairie home was she,
> Everyone who knew her felt the gentle power
> Of Rosalie, the Prairie Flower.

A third was a stirring song dedicated to the Exiles in Europe of the Confederate States of America, which began

The despot's heel is on thy shore, Maryland, my Maryland!
His touch is on thy temple door, Maryland, my Maryland!
Avenge the patriotic gore that flowed the streets of Baltimore,
And be the battle queen of yore, Maryland, my Maryland!

The tune is from a Haydn composition called the 'Emperor' quartet. It would be interesting to know how it came to be used for that song of the Confederate States, and more interesting still, how it came to be adopted for a rallying song for a political party in Britain today.

Round the table at our leisurely meals, there was a constant flow of reminiscences of the old days in Colvend, resurrecting for my benefit anecdotes of local worthies, like the old man at a parish 'spread' (what was vulgarly known as 'a good feed') who was reproached for pouring rich cream over his portion of roast duck and calmly asserted, 'Cream's maist guid for a "thin"!'

They recited a fragment of a modern ballad descriptive of a funeral bean-feast,

> There was ham and lamb,
> Beer by the bucket
> And imported cham.
> And you never saw
> Such a divil of a jam
> When they all sat down.

and recalled, with mischievous glee, the night when an old body fell from her gig on her way home from a party, and was discovered lying beside a burn with water lapping near her mouth, while she in imagination resisting further offers of hospitality muttered, 'No' anither drap, neither het nor cauld!' They told me about their father's friend who went to a Dalbeattie tailor to order a suit of clothes, and asked to see samples of a dambrod pattern. Dambrod is the old Scots word for a draughts-board, so what he was after was large checks. Having been shown all the cloth in the shop, and still demanding a dambrod pattern, the exasperated tailor snapped, 'Man, I can dae nae mair! That's the damdest broadest pattern in the hale o' Dalbeattie!' The granite of Dalbeattie in the Valley of Urr, was once known all over the world, and several hundred men worked in the quarries at Craignair Hill. Alford Anderson, whose wife was a Fraser daughter, had a large and lucrative practice in Dalbeattie. He and one other doctor in the town looked after the health of patients over a wide area, extending roughly between Castle Douglas and New Abbey. He had a one-cylinder Lion-Peugeot of which he was justifiably proud, with the door at the back and tyres without treads of any kind. If the car stuck on a hill, a sprack or bar could be inserted in a wheel which prevented it from running backwards. Seeing him set off with his man, Gourlay, at the wheel, I became familiar with the names of some of his patients, landowners of ancestral estates that tripped off the tongue like an epic poem . . . Chalmers of Kipp, Dudgeon of Cargen, Herries

of Spottes, Maxwell of Munches, Oswald of Cavens, Stewart of Shambellie.

Like most doctors of his day he adapted his fees to suit his patients' means and mode of living, charging anything from half-a-crown to half-a-guinea a visit. Even so, in some households, and not always the humblest, the doctor was the last to be paid, It was not uncommon for a working man to call at the surgery to seek the doctor's services at his wife's approaching confinement, with money in his hand belatedly to pay for attendance at her previous one. This was before the National Insurance Act of 1911, when the worker paid 4d. a week, which was deducted from his wages.

On one occasion the doctor was about to deliver the latest baby of a rather simple soul in her wayside cottage, and enquired, for his records, the name of the father. 'Deed, I cannae tell ye, doctor', replied the simple soul, 'Ye see I hadnae time t'see the name on the cairt.'

In the builders' yard opposite Alford Anderson's surgery were figure-heads which had once adorned the prows of wooden ships which came up Urr to the Port of Dalbeattie. When iron was substituted for wood, figure-heads lost their importance and were consigned to breakers' yards.

The Solway schooners loaded their cargoes of coal and lime at Whitehaven, Workington, and Maryport on the Cumberland coast, and ran up to the creeks on the Scottish side of the Solway Firth, where the cargo was delivered and a return cargo loaded. Guided by the light of Heston Island, the schooners entered the estuary of Urr and, following the channel close to the shore, moored off the village of Kippford, where at one time the Cumming Brothers built sloops of up to 800 tons, as large as any vessel then afloat. Their last ship, launched in 1884, was lost at sea off the coast of Newfoundland. Sam Crosbie once told me that his great-grandfather built one of the thatched cottages which, in the middle of the last century, formed the beginnings of The Scaur, as Kippford was then called on account of its situation on the slope of a

hill. Later it was given the name, Kippford, because a ford across the river was near the estate of Kipp, but old people, like Libby and Aleck, still gave it its old old name, The Scaur. Heavy wooden posts still to be seen sticking out of the mud were put in for mooring the schooners which trafficked up and down the river to Dalbeattie for cargoes of granite from Craignair, and for stone quarried nearby and loaded at the old pier. Sailing up the river from Kippford must have been a ticklish business because of the uncertain channel and no help from the shore; but at Palnackie a team of horses would be waiting to tow the vessel up Urr with the rising tide. Palnackie was then quite an important port, with a dock cut into the river-bank; Dalbeattie could actually be reached on a spring tide though Urr was little more than a ditch at that point. The Solway schooner may be said to have come in with the flood and to have gone out with the ebb; it has long since passed and the only relics of its passing are those posts in the mud at Kippford, which is now the home of the Solway Yacht Club. Races are held frequently in the summer months, and the regatta in August draws hundreds of spectators.

The course which leads out of the estuary into the Solway Firth calls for smart handling, and to see the colourful small craft sailing with the lee gunnels nearly under is a fine sight. In a stiff breeze a wetting is the order of the day.

One fine day in 1913 Mark and I walked to the Mote of Urr, where the Court held its councils and made new laws when Galloway was an independent state. The Mound somewhat resembles Tynwald Hill in the Isle of Man where the ancient Tynwald ceremony, linked with the Norse Kings, takes place every year, and all the laws that have been passed by their Parliament during the previous twelve months are promulgated. At Corra Castle, miles from the Mote of Urr, Mary, Queen of Scots, in her flight from Langside, is supposed to have rested on her way to Dundrennan and England, and the boulder known as the Steedstand is where she reined her horse. Mark and I had tea on more than one occasion at

Edingham and at Corra, prosperous farm-houses beside the ruins of their ancient castles. If the Queen of Scots did in fact rest at Corra, it is likely that she crossed Urr at the very ford from which Kippford takes its name, for it was the best over the whole length of the river and in use centuries before bridges were built.

We were made welcome at the firesides of parishioners who had known the Fraser family when their father was alive . . . the Buchanans, McDiarmids, Boyds, and McLellands, and, of course, the Sinclairs, whose father had been the Manse coachman. There was Janet, who seldom smiled, and John, her brother, always cheerful and uncomplaining though blind . . . obliged to tramp round the countryside selling packets of tea, his sole means of livelihood. No compensation was paid in those days to a stonemason who had lost his sight while splitting stones.

On an afternoon visit to the McDiarmids at Rockcliffe we met a lady who was doing exquisite embroidery, using hair-fine silks to copy on delicate gauze the beauty of butterflies. In some indignation she related how she had given a present of embroidered dinner-mats to a friend, who had actually *used* them at a party, and a drop of gravy spilled on one fragile mat had ruined its beauty for all time.

Mrs Fraser looked back on an incident at the house when old William Sinclair returned from Dalbeattie without the minister. When she emerged from the front door to greet her husband she found William shaking a travelling-rug in a puzzled way and muttering, 'He's no' come't!' Later it transpired that Dr Fraser had gone into a shop and slammed the carriage-door behind him. William, half-asleep on the box after a long wait, imagined that the minister had entered the carriage and drove off, never stopping till he drew up at the Manse door. He was promptly sent back the way he had come, to meet his irate master who had started to walk home. 'He's no' come't' became a family saying in a variety of situations.

Dr Fraser often told his sons how his father, who lived to

[170]

the age of ninety-four, fought at Busaco, then described as 'the bloodiest battle in history', and how his mother, after the Peninsular War, walked barefoot from Grantown-on-Spey to Edinburgh Castle, to buy him out of the army. This remarkable woman had two brothers who were in turn appointed surgeons to King George III. One who served in the Navy, took laudanum as a pain-killer in increasing quantities, and built up such a resistance to the poison that he was able to drink it as other men drank rum.

One evening at Sandyhills the Frasers told me of their father's first visit to Paris when, about to retire for the night, he discovered that his room lacked an essential comfort. He rang for the chambermaid and requested her, in halting French, to bring him a pot de chambre. Puzzled for a moment, at last she comprehended and, saying brightly, 'Ah, oui, M'sieu, une vase de nuit', ran to fetch one.

Their mother also looked back on an evening when as the very new bride of the minister she had gone with him to a very grand dinner-party in their honour at one of the mansions in the parish. It was an era of lavish hospitality and there were many landed proprietors whose houses have long since been converted to hotels. On the occasion which remained forever in her memory she wore her wedding-gown of white satin, and white kid boots over which she had slipped for comfort on the long slow drive, a pair of fur slippers. Midway through dinner she realised she had forgotten to remove the slippers. Resourcefully, she kicked them off leaving them under the table. She was very young, too shy to claim them on departure, and could not now recall how or when they were restored to her.

Still fresh in her memory, however, was an afternoon when she had drawing-room tea with an eccentric titled lady who, with the long sugar-tongs, fished out her gardening gloves from the massive silver teapot where she had absent-mindedly placed them, then placidly continued to pour tea; and she remembered meeting a nervous young assistant-minister who confided that he had been offered very meagre

fare at the breakfast-table of a miserly hostess, and had assured her timidly in answer to her query, 'Oh, yes indeed! Half an egg *is quite* too much for me!'

Many years later, when I myself was a staid married woman, she revived her reminiscences and told me of her personal experience in the days when childbirth took its natural course, and there was no analgesic to relieve a woman in labour. In attendance at the birth of her first child was an untrained local midwife whose unswerving belief was that it would be fatal to allow the young mother to fall asleep after the baby was born; so, prolonged and exhausting though labour had been, she kept watch at her patient's bedside, occasionally giving her a little shake, and anxiously enquiring, 'Ye're no' sleepin' noo?'

Do country folk still go a-slomming in September, I wonder? Searching the hedgerows for sloe or bullaces, as they are sometimes called . . . those hard, blue-black, acrid berries from which, it is hard to believe, under generations of careful cultivation, our finest plums have evolved. Sixty years ago, at Sandyhills, we made sloe-gathering something of an occasion.

Wearing old clothes, strong shoes, and leather gloves, we sallied forth with baskets and thick sticks, choosing a fine day when the sloes were black with a purple sheen on them. Protected as we were against the fearsome prickles, we soon had gathered many pounds and trooped back home for the ceremony of making sloe liqueur, a refinement for connoisseurs, which Mrs Fraser had been in the habit of producing in the back-end of the year in the days when whisky cost 3s. a bottle.

We all sat in a circle round a large stone jar, borrowed from a brewery, each equipped with a silver fork; every single freshly picked sloe was carefully pricked by hand and dropped into the jar. To every 3½ lb. of sloes were added 3 lb. of granulated sugar, and two quart bottles of Scotch whisky. The jar was then corked, sealed, and stored in a cool, dark cupboard, and every day for three months it was thoroughly shaken. When it was uncorked the sloes were shrivelled little

black things, with every drop of natural juice extracted from them, and a beautiful, rose-coloured sirop was strained off into bottles, sealed, labelled, and dated. To drink it at that stage would have been sacrilege. It was kept for at least a year, and the longer it was kept the better it became. I recall some liqueur, ten years old, which in smoothness, flavour, colour, and potency resembled the finest cherry brandy. In Cumberland I later discovered it was the custom to make two or three gallons of sloe gin every back-end, in grey hens, the Cumbrian word for stone jars. This was when the price of gin had not exceeded 2s. 6d. a bottle.

Even today, with gin the price it is, home-made sloe gin is not expensive compared to a fine liqueur. A recipe for a trial sample suggests taking 1 lb. of sloes, 3 oz. of sugar and a pint and a half of gin. Put the pricked sloes in a 2-lb. preserving jar, add the sugar and gin, seal and keep in a cool dark place (but not on stone) shaking occasionally. This is said to be ready to strain and use in three months, so it would be worth trying for Christmas or an Engagement Party. Damson gin can be made in exactly the same way, always bearing in mind that both are all the better for keeping for a year or longer.

Another recipe, guaranteed to be as velvety and potent as any, recommends filling a preserving jar with alternate layers of *unpricked* sloes and brown sugar, adding three or four blanched almonds. The screw-top jar should be kept in a cool place, and topped up with sugar as the top layer dissolves, using about $\frac{3}{4}$ lb. in all. Leave it for three months, then strain off the juice, mix it with an equal quantity of gin, bottle it and leave untouched till next year's sloes are ready for picking. In these days of home wine-making it is worth knowing that sloe wine can be made without spirits by pouring a gallon of boiling water on to a gallon of sloes. Stir twice a day for a week, strain, then add 4 lb. of sugar, and put it all in a large stone jar. When fermentation has ceased, cork loosely for a few days, then cork tightly and seal. Leave it untouched for a year. Strain and use. Sloes make a very good jelly if boiled to a pulp with an equal quantity of apples and strained. Allow

1 lb. of sugar to every pint of juice. Boil for twenty minutes, test, and pot. Sloe cheese, made like lemon cheese, combining the sloes with either carrots or marrow, has a slightly astringent flavour, but in midwinter, when garden fruits are but a memory, it can be useful, and so can sloe and marrow jam made with equal quantities of peeled marrow, sloes, and sugar.

At Sandyhills Mrs Fraser gave me three of her cherished receipts (the old word for recipes) namely, how to make hough soup (pronounced in the Scots way, hoch); how to cure a pig, a lengthy process which she had carried out every year at the Manse, and lastly, how to make sloe liqueur as I have described.

In years to come, when over the Border I had learned to ask the butcher for hoff, I used her receipt on many occasions. It made an acceptable cup of hot soup to offer guests about to face the cold night air. The second, I never had an opportunity to test, but the third, Mark and I tried out within the first month of our married life. We made only a small quantity because whisky had risen in price to the phenomenal figure of 12s. 6d. a bottle! It is pleasant to recall that our one and only attempt at making liqueur was a success, and, sealed for ten years, when sampled it did indeed, in colour and flavour, resemble the finest cherry brandy.

CHAPTER VII

A NOMAD IN PERTHSHIRE

Towards the end of our training course in Dunfermline College we students gave anxious thought to the future and what it might hold for us. Those who were fortunate enough to be offered an appointment before the completion of their training were warmly congratulated (we celebrated the event by a special Post Tea) and enjoyed peace of mind for the remainder of the term.

A clutch of encouraging testimonials gave me the confidence I had hitherto lacked, and sent me home rejoicing; soon after, I was appointed to a travelling post in Perthshire at a salary of £100 per annum, which then was considered a 'good screw'. It certainly seemed a lot of money to me in that Year of Grace, 1913.

My work took me to schools, large and small, over a wide area, extending from Crieff to Aberfoyle and the beautiful Trossachs. One fine day at Kinlochard I drove in a one-horse phaeton round Loch Ard on a narrow road by the loch-side, and had my first sight of shaggy Highland cattle roaming freely on the hills. Laburnum and rhododendrons framed the placid waters of the loch, and beyond I saw the peak of Ben Lomond.

Aberfoyle lies between Loch Ard and the Lake of Menteith, which got its name by mistake. When the district was called the Laigh of Menteith, Southerners, understandably, took this to refer to the loch, and the name stuck. Mary, Queen of Scots, poor mite, was only five years old when, after the Battle of Pinkie, in 1547, she was hustled away for safety to the priory of Inchmahone, an island on the loch. The little garden which she made, known ever since as Queen Mary's Bower, may still be seen.

Now cleared of coarse fish and stocked with rainbow and brown trout, the lake ranks as chief of the new fisheries which increase Scotland's angling potential.

Duchray Water flows from the slopes of Ben Lomond through Aberfoyle to become the River Forth. It was at the bridge over the infant river that a fight took place long ago between the Laird of Duchray's men and those of the Earl of Menteith. The Earl rashly attemped to serve a writ on Duchray and his son, Graham, when he and his followers met them on the road, on their way, as it happened, to have Graham's son christened.

Laying the child on the ground the parties attacked each other with sword and pistol, and when the Earl gave way the christening party picked up the baby and resumed their journey.

In Scott's *Rob Roy* an interesting scene is laid in Aberfoyle when Nicol Jarvie and Osbaldistone arrived seeking shelter at the clachan, and were refused because three 'Highland chentlemen' wanted the place to themselves. The ensuing uproar, when the stout little baillie defended himself with a red-hot plough-coulter which was being used as a poker, is brought to life in the story and the coulter still hangs on a tree opposite the hotel.

The Duke's Road, once owned by the Duke of Montrose, climbs steeply behind the village, and over it I went from time to time to visit a tiny school among the Slate Quarries. From the brow of the road, which links Aberfoyle with the Trossachs, I could see trees fringing the Lake of Menteith, and far-distant

lochs, with Ben Venue and a grand array of other peaks.

I visited frequently the long straggling village of Auchter-arder, which suffered heavily from the intermittent warfare of the mid-eighteenth century, and was burned down in the '15 Jacobite Rising.

I liked the little township of Comrie, which claims the dubious distinction of being Scotland's earthquake centre. Its periodic shocks are slight and I never experienced one.

Every day I set off early from Crieff for some distant destination, returning late in the evening. When adult classes necessitated my staying in some town overnight, kind land-ladies provided me with a hot drink, a feather bed, and a bacon-and-egg breakfast for 2s 6d., my official allowance.

Passing through Buchlyvie and Kippen, I was told the extraordinary tale of the Baron of Buchlyvie, a Buchanan of Kippen, who once styled himself the King of Kippen and did his best to raise the village to the dignity of a kingdom.

From this ambition rose the saying, 'Oot o' Scotland an' intae Kippen', which may now be forgotten, but an old rhyme remains:

> Baron o' Buchlyvie
> May the foul fiend drive ye
> An' a' tae bits rive ye
> For biggin' sic a toon
> Far there's neither horse meat
> Nor man's meat
> Nor a place tae sit doon.

Crieff, once a fashionable spa, was an elegant town with an eighteenth-century air, with Lady Mary's Walk by the banks of Earn, the Mercat Cross, and the stocks beside the Town Hall.

I used to bicycle to Muthil, a village not far away, where nearly all the men-folk were employed on the Drummond Castle estate. The Castle's celebrated Italian gardens were laid out in the time of Charles I. Deep blue violets and white anaphalis have been planted to form a large Cross of St

Andrew and there is a sundial which tells the time in all the great cities of Europe.

The old drove roads from north and south at one time met in Crieff. Drovers and their dogs sent jostling masses of black cattle splashing through the ford near Innerpeffray, and a tryst was held on the slopes of Knock Hill. By the end of the eighteenth century, however, to avoid paying customs in Crieff, drovers took their cattle to Falkirk.

In my modest bed-sitter a large feather-bed occupied much of the space, and into its smothering embrace I sank thankfully at night. There was a table, a chair, a case of stuffed birds, and a sideboard which did duty for a chest of drawers. At a plush-framed mirror painted over with a rustic scene I dressed my hair, peering between the bulrushes.

Bantam cockerels waked me each morning as they hailed the dawn from a garden under my window.

With the cost of my trousseau in mind, I economised on food, buying margarine 'made of choicest nuts and milk', and easily recognisable from butter. It bore no resemblance to present-day products, and cost only 6d. a pound!

From holidays I returned laden with Gairnside fresh eggs, honey, butter, and home-made jam.

My lunches on my wanderings in Perthshire were mainly of the glass-of-milk-and-a-bun variety; occasionally I indulged in a plate of soup for 6d., or a two-course meal for 1s. 6d. in a Trust House.

Travelling across country as I constantly did, I often had to spend tedious hours at small junctions waiting for trains . . . Crieff Junction was one.

When I sat, a solitary passenger, in the dreary waiting-room, reading or sewing to while away the time, I little thought that in a few years that dismal spot would become Gleneagles, a busy station and a world-famous resort, with championship golf-courses and a luxury hotel on the hill. In the Maclaren High School in Callander I had the privilege of planning the basic equipment for the new gymnasium, and of dictating the use of suitable footwear on its all-but-sacred

floor. The School honours the name of Duncan MacLaren, a local lad who not only made good but did good, and was proud to give his support to the founding of the School. A feature of its Sports Day in my time was the Fiery Cross relay race. A cross of two sticks was passed from hand to hand as was done in the distant past when it was a flaming torch of resinous pineroot, a blazing emblem which was carried for miles over moor and mountain to summon the clans in time of emergency. One of the last occasions when this was done was in 1745 when it was carried up the Pass of Leny, and glanced, like lightning up Strathyre', hence the interest it held for MacLaren young students of history. During that long hot summer of 1914 we were happily indifferent to the sensations of the day, the fashions and fads, sumptuous parties in high places on the one hand, and on the other the struggle for Women's Suffrage, with anarchy and spies abroad. We did not realise we were approaching the end of an era, the climax of what came to be known as 'The Age of Edwardian Elegance'; we thought, if we thought at all, that we were living in a safe world.

Golf had long since got into its swing in every part of the country; men played in Norfolk jacket, knickerbockers, and thick stockings, preferably hand-knitted, turned over below the knee with a fancy top. Magazines carried advertisements for Sandow's Strength-Developing Institute, an impressive gymnasium where body-building exercises were carried out, and showed the magnificently muscled Sandow clad in a leopard-skin. Nearly everybody ignored Lord Roberts who was, they complained, forever harping on the growing menace of German militarism, and warning of war on a world-wide scale. They laughed at him for a scaremonger, a quaint little man with an allergy to cats.

Every age has its dance crazes, usually heralded at their first appearance as decadent and sure to deprave the young. The waltz, the polka, those favourites now of 'Old Tyme' dancing, were considered very daring when first introduced in Victorian days, and the dance that hit the country just before the First

[179]

World War was the languorous tango . . . at first declared disreputable, it later became fashionable and respectable. In that quiet town by the River Teith, with Ben Ledi rising in the background, we danced it at MacLaren School parties, a mild Scots version far removed from its lowly negroid origin, but with a faint note of glamour. Some of the school-mistresses appeared in seductive flame-coloured tango gowns, very daring because they revealed the leg to the knee by a slit in the side seam. Ribbon bands were worn low on the forehead, with an aigrette poised in front.

On Saturday night in Crieff, my landlady's daughter and I sometimes had a jaunt to the Pictures which came to town once a week. In a small hall with a crowd of small boys in the front seats, who had probably taken a jam-jar to the grocer and got a penny for it, their price of admission, we sat on hard forms at the back, listening to their yells of pleasurable anticipation.

We waited . . . and waited . . . and waited. The Show which had come some distance from its previous one-night-stand, was invariably late in starting, but at last came the whirr of the projector and things began to move.

If a breakdown occurred in the middle of a picture, as it often did, the youngsters sent up disgusted cries of 'Ah . . . a . . . ah!' and were extremely restless while repairs were being effected.

Meanwhile, the pianist, who never stopped playing through-out the programme, even pounding away with one hand while drinking a cup of tea, strummed a lively selection of tunes to make the waiting tolerable. She had an amazing repertoire of melodies appropriate to every kind of picture shown on the screen, changing smoothly from the Post Horn Galop for galloping horses to romantic waltzes played softly for Love's Young Dream, the fade-out of a tranquil sunset over the sea, or the familiar caption . . . Came the Dawn. . . .

Very popular were slapstick comedies in which custard pies flew through the air to disintegrate messily in the victims' faces. On the screen there was a constant flickering (hence 'the

flicks') and we also suffered from the inevitable woman-in-the-seat-behind who insisted on reading all the captions aloud. Pearl White appeared on the screen in a series called *The Perils of Pauline*, and there was a serial film called *Fantomas*, in which the heroine was periodically left in the grip of a villain in black, with eyes glaring from a Ku-Klux-Klan type of head-dress. After seeing him exert his fiendish power in each spine-chilling episode, we clung to each other as we crept through the darkened streets, thrilled by the fantastic deeds of the ghoulish Fantomas and fearful of unpleasant reminders of knavery in every shadowy corner.

When Mark and I lunched at the Hydro on the day of a cricket match at Crieff's well-known public school, a fashionable crowd of Old Boys and their girl-friends filled the other tables, and I was intrigued to see that one stylish young woman wore on her left ankle a gold watch set in diamonds. One could not avoid noticing it for she found it necessary to extend her ankle at frequent intervals to consult the watch.

Many of my week-ends were spent in Edinburgh and Perth. One day in the Fair City which was once Scotland's capital, Mark and I climbed Kinnoull Hill, a vantage point which gives easily the best view of Perth, and from the top we admired the gracious spread of Strathearn, the Ochils and the Grampians, and the silvery Tay meandering through the Carse of Gowrie, twisting through fields like patchwork pieces sewn together with hedges and drystane dykes till it broadened on the distant shores of Forfar and Fife.

South Gillsland Road, in Edinburgh, was then a cul-de-sac ending in stunted shrubbery. The three-storey houses stood on a slight eminence with colourful displays of rock-plants in their sloping front gardens.

A flight of steps led to the front door. This quiet terrace, facing a wide open space, had no service road at the back, therefore no back entrance. All trade deliveries were made at the front, and the Newhaven fishwife, with her creel supported by a wide strap across her forehead, on her weekly visit came through the front hall to gut her fish at the kitchen sink.

Edinburgh now, as then, is a city of contrasts. It has its graceful Georgian terraces, and the fishwife with her creel still, I believe, goes on her selected rounds.

A pleasant room on the ground floor was used as a study, and gave access by a french window to the long narrow garden which ran up to the wall which enclosed fields, now the grounds of George Watson's College for Boys.

One night, when I was staying there, alarming cries were heard in the night, like those of a woman in great distress. They appeared to come from the fields, and the men of the house, having notified the police, went out to investigate. With a constable carrying an acetylene lamp they searched along the boundary wall but found nothing to account for the noise. The policeman suggested that the eerie cries might have been those of peacocks which roamed the grounds of the Mental Hospital not far away.

The dining-room was on the ground floor across the hall from the kitchen. There were two bedrooms, a bathroom, and the drawing-room on the first floor, and three bedrooms on the top floor.

Bells in all the rooms, connected by wire, rang in the kitchen with resounding clangour. There were wide grates in the living rooms for the coal fires which were lit every day. Coal, delivered and carried through the hall to the back of the kitchen premises, had risen, I was told, from 10s. to 20s. a ton. There were no gas or electric heaters in any of the rooms, no central heating, and, of course, no electric blankets on the beds.

The maids were trim figures in coloured print wrappers in the morning with plain linen caps and aprons. In the afternoon, a black 'stuff' dress with a starched muslin apron and a frilled muslin cap, was correct for the maid who waited at table, and opened the front door with dignity to show callers up to the drawing-room.

One of these callers was Mrs Pagan, who had the gentle charm of an aristocratic Victorian lady. With her silver-grey corkscrew curls framing her face she wore a black poke bonnet

with velvet strings tied under her chin. She must have advised her cousins, two Pagan sisters who lived in Crieff, that I was shortly to become a member of the family, for they formally called on me and left cards. They owned one of the early motor-cars which they entered by a half-door at the back like a wagonette and were driven by a chauffeur round Crieff. They had a pleasant house overlooking the river, and when I had tea there I was impressed by the massive Victorian silver tea-service, and the large pink embroidered tea-cosy which was replaced after use in its muslin bag hung behind a tall folding screen.

The cook at South Gillsland Road helped the housemaid to turn out the rooms, which entailed a tremendous cleaning of brass and copper, and polishing of furniture. The vacuum-cleaner required two people to operate it—one manipulating a sort of bellows in a square upright box, the other steering a nozzle on a long tube.

A whole day was devoted to the cleaning of table-silver, and the candle-snuffers, snuff-boxes, toddy ladles and other antique trifles on the Silver Table, which was a feature of the drawing-rooms of that day, and which, with sundry pieces of lacquer ware and the rosewood solitaire board, complete with striped glass marbles, were family heirlooms.

The cook and the housemaid also did the family wash. Followers were not encouraged; it would have taken more courage than was possessed by the average young man of the times to ring the front-door bell and be admitted as a kitchen-caller.

My future mother-in-law had always been a kindly and capable mistress of a staff. At Colvend Manse country girls stayed for years without thought of change, leaving only, like Libby, to be married. In Edinburgh she had no 'servant trouble' till the outbreak of the First World War, and things, domestically, were never the same again.

The making of munitions and other forms of war work caused an acute shortage of domestic help. Frequent changes in the household were due to the fact that, for a long time,

[183]

mistresses were unable to accept lower standards and poorer material for training.

Mark's unmarried sister was a perfectionist in everything she undertook . . . in chocolate-making, in photography, needlework and cookery she had attended special classes and had attained professional standards, pursuing all these subjects as hobbies. Her interest in a subject was apt to wane once she had mastered the technicalities; she then sought new crafts and new techniques to master. She could not tolerate less than perfection in herself or in others, and waged a losing battle with wartime youthful maids who failed to carry out her precise instructions.

On Sundays we all walked to Morning Service at St Michael's Church . . . I secretly proud to be accompanied by Mark in traditional Sunday garb . . . silk hat, morning-coat and striped trousers, and carrying dove-grey gloves and a silver-mounted walking-stick; his mother in black silk, with a bonnet such as Queen Victoria wore in her latter years, and Annie and I in conventional 'Sunday Best'.

The venerable Dr Wilson, a kindly figure with a long white beard, always read the banns of marriage before announcing the opening hymn, proclaiming that, 'There is a purpose of marriage between . . . bachelor, and . . . spinster, of this parish', following the formal announcement by praying 'May the Lord bestow His blessing upon this union.'

There was a legend that on one occasion, in an absent-minded moment, he prayed, 'And may the Lord have mercy upon them.'

Annie disdained to attend Evening Service in St Michael's, to listen to the outpourings of any young Assistant Minister who would occupy the pulpit at that hour. She invariably attended Evening Service at The Barony, or some other church where, she said, she was sure of hearing a good sermon.

One church where that was guaranteed was Free St George's. Dr Kelman, Dr White, and Dr Black had all been, in their time, powerful preachers in that pulpit, and the famous

[184]

organist for over forty years was Alfred Hollins, first of the prominent blind organists.

I heard him play on numerous occasions. He was a lecturer, a composer, and an Honorary Doctor of Music of Edinburgh University, a remarkable example of the attainment of great proficiency, full of vigour and feeling, in spite of total blindness.

One day Mark took me to climb Arthur's Seat by way of the Royal Mile and the open reaches of what was then the King's Park. We passed by St Margaret's Well and St Anthony's ruined chapel, and began the ascent of the great slumbering lion which seemed to brood over grazing sheep in the Park. At the top Mark told me how he once got up at dawn to attend a Service held there on the 1 May, undertaking the stiff but invigorating climb with a group of student friends who joined the enthusiastic small congregation on the hillside, while the glory of the dawn streaked the Pentlands, tinting the waters of the Forth and piercing the cap of smoke above Auld Reekie. Far away, while they sang their Morning Hymn, Berwick Law could be seen standing sentinel over the North Sea.

Another day Mrs Fraser took me for a drive in an open carriage in the Park which we entered at the Palace of Holyroodhouse and drove round the base of Arthur's Seat and out by Salisbury Crags; and as we bowled quietly along, she spoke of her father, James Pagan, LLD, who occupied the editorial chair of the *Glasgow Herald* from 1856 to 1870. He had joined the *Herald* as a young reporter from the *Dumfries Courier*, and later wrote and published, among other works, a history of Glasgow Cathedral which is still considered one of the best of many such histories. There is in a brochure issued in 1958 by the *Herald* to mark the 175th Anniversary of its first publication, a fine tribute to this remarkable man, in whose years of office the *Herald* grew to the full stature of a daily newspaper, and who was responsible for purchasing the present *Herald* buildings. His younger daughter, Eliza, married James Kennedy, a successful Glasgow businessman, descended from a long line of noted agriculturists. He acquired the

beautiful estate of Doonholm, three miles or so from Ayr, shortly after the death of Baron Blackburn of Killearn, whose home it had been for nearly forty years. The fine stone-built mansion had then required an indoor staff of six maids, a butler, and two footmen; outside were grooms, gardeners, laundrymaids, and a dairymaid. The gardens included a vinery, several hot-houses, and an old walled vegetable garden. James lavished loving care on his three hundred acres, and delighted to extend and improve them. He had an amazing knowledge of woodland and ornamental trees and shrubs, and was proud of the fact that the grounds and terraces grading downwards to the curving and gently mur-muring Doon were, for the most part, laid out by William Burnes, the father of Robert Burns, in 1759 and succeeding years. Doonholm, with its far-famed gardens and its noted herd of pedigree Aberdeen Angus cattle is still the much-loved home of young Kennedys.

Meantime, in Edinburgh, I was learning more and more about the interests, past and present, of the man I was to marry. Until his graduation he had been an enthusiastic Rugger man, and a member of the Mounted Blacks until they were disbanded. While still a student he had spent part of every vacation wandering all over Scotland with a camera, photographing wild birds on their nests, but he no longer had time to pursue this hobby. His intention had been to write a book on birds and to illustrate it with original photographs but the project was never completed; a collection of albums, and lantern-slides galore, representing hours of patient observation from elaborately constructed hides, still testify to the activities of more leisured days. As colour photography was not yet within his grasp, he had coloured some of his slides by hand. Glass lantern-slides in general had to be marked with two white spots. They were shown on a screen by a hand-operated old-fashioned magic lantern. The operator had to work in a darkened room or hall and had to handle each slide twice, once to insert it and again to withdraw it, and the two white spots clearly showed the right way up.

[186]

Mark was also, like his father, a keen botanist and, roaming the Pentlands with a vasculum, had made a collection of prize-winning plants. When he graduated he was appointed in an honorary capacity to assist Mr E. B. Jamieson, Senior Lecturer in Anatomy, by demonstrating to students dissection of various parts of the human body. For this duty he was issued with a black velvet skull cap which out of respect for the dead he was required to wear while dissecting. Students were reminded that the 'cadavers', which lay covered on the tables till the demonstration began, were once human beings and were to be treated with the respect to which a human being is entitled. Mr Jamieson was famous for his marvellous dissections, chiefly on the brain, and for his *Illustrations of Regional Anatomy*, a compact book which became a classic, and was carried in the pocket of many a medical student who referred to it fondly as his Wee Jamie.

As Editor of the Edinburgh University Students' Magazine, and as a Resident in Professor Chiene's Ward in the Royal Infirmary, Mark had, with permission, published in *The Student* the Professor's noteworthy Address to the Faculty, called 'Looking Back', in which he traced the history of the Infirmary from 1860 to 1907. Subsequently it developed into a brochure with illustrations. The Professor was delighted with the production, for the original material was enhanced by photographs painstakingly collected from numerous sources of surgeons of a bygone day and nurses who were untrained but devoted, with inborn skill. The creator of Sherlock Holmes, Sir Arthur Conan Doyle, modelled Holmes on his friend, Dr Joseph Bell of Melville Crescent, Edinburgh. I was acquainted with his nephew, Benjamin Bell, who was a Writer to the *Signet*. Ben's sister, Laura, was a school-friend of Annie Fraser. Together they ran a Girls' Club on the strict lines of the Girls' Friendly Society, but managed and financed by former pupils of the celebrated St Leonard's School in St Andrews, which was founded in 1877.

There never was a lovelier summer than in that year 1914, one to remain long in the memory. From March onwards one

can hardly remember a rainy day; larks were singing in cloudless blue skies in May and June, and it was blazing hot in the early days of July; or so it seems to me, in my own version of 'Looking Back'.

The date of our wedding had been fixed and arrangements went on apace. To be on the safe side of the law regarding residential qualifications we had the banns of marriage proclaimed, not only in our home churches in Edinburgh and Glen Gairn, but in the parish churches in Dunfermline and Crieff where we were at the time temporary residents.

About this time I acquired a copy of *The Woman's Book* which claimed to contain Everything a Woman Ought to Know, a terminological inexactitude, if ever the term was deserved, for nothing, positively nothing, that this woman wanted to know was even mentioned.

From a recent look at the pages of this veritable tome I gather that in 1913, the year of its publication, it was possible to furnish a dining-room for £18, a drawing-room for £22, and a bedroom for £20, which sums covered the cost of essentials in furniture, carpets and curtains.

Advice is given in the book on the wages to pay the butler (£45–£90 per annum), the parlourmaid, the tweeny, and the bell-boy, not forgetting the cook and the housemaid, who were at that time expecting to be paid £22 and £20 a year, respectively. Most of this information I was never required to put to the test, but I made full use of the cookery and household hints in the book throughout my long and happy married life.

Mark at the time of our engagement occasionally smoked a pipe of tobacco, which then cost 5d. an ounce, but, on the whole, he preferred cigarettes, though they had risen in price to 1s. for fifty . . . and hand-made, at that!

Many men were still wearing straw boaters with their striped blazers (shades of *Three Men in a Boat!*) the rest clung to their trilbies, bowlers and flat tweed caps; there was no stigma attached to a cloth cap, and no man went without head-gear of some kind. Most of their suits were dark, worn

with a waistcoat of the same material, and the tailor would, on request, supply two pairs of trousers with the suit.

When Mark first qualified in medicine he had a morning coat tailored for him; it was expected of a doctor in General Practice to be so attired in his consulting-room. All his life he wore it on formal occasions, for the quality was superb, and his measurements never altered, nor was the coat ever out-moded. He wore it on our wedding-day and fifty years later, at the wedding of our eldest grandson, with a starched white shirt (with a highly glazed front), a wing collar, pale grey tie, grey suede gloves, a silk hat, and a walking-stick of polished rosewood.

For formal evening functions men wore full evening dress, described as 'white tie and tails', with a 'stiff shirt', a white waistcoat of pique, and pearl studs, with a white bow-tie (never ready-made) and white kid gloves. Their evening shoes were black patent leather with a flat double bow of petersham silk as decoration.

With a black dinner-jacket (which King Edward VII invented), the appropriate tie was black which had to be tied in a neat narrow bow, a tricky business, but it was not good form to wear a made-up tie.

I bought my trousseau in Edinburgh. In Jenners I chose my lingerie of white cambric threaded with blue ribbon. Coloured stockings were in fashion so I selected several pairs in pale blue. Silk stockings were still a luxury so I invested in three pairs only, crimson, gold, and white for my wedding-day. A German scientist had recently made stockings from nettles, and my nettle-silk stockings in an attractive shade of gold made a talking-point. After war was declared one never saw them advertised again. Experiments were carried out on the production of stockings from odd materials such as the beards of mussels and castor oil beans, but when nylon was invented the hunt was over.

Feather boas were a fashion that was revived from time to time; Queen Alexandra with her swan-like neck wore them with aplomb and made them high fashion in her time. I

possessed a beauty in hackle feathers in marvellous shades of blue that shaded to green.

Annie helped me to choose an opera cloak and two evening-gowns . . . long, filmy, and clinging, which were fated never to be worn owing to the outbreak of war and the curtailment of formal social events, 'for the duration'.

We called at the austere establishment of Miss Gladstone, a Court Dressmaker, whose proud assertion was that no form of artificial sewing-silk was used in her work-rooms . . . all her gowns and mantles were sewn with pure silk. She graciously consented to make my wedding-dress and travelling-costume, and to supervise all fittings in person.

From a book of patterns I chose material for my travel-suit, in saxe-blue, the colour then in vogue, and found in Jenners a charming hat with lots of veiling and ribbon bows, and to complete the outfit, court shoes and white kid gloves which later would be worn when paying afternoon calls and leaving engraved visiting-cards.

All the good-wives in the Glen were invited to tea at the Manse to see my trousseau and wedding-presents, including the silver-mounted tea-tray and biscuit-barrel which were their joint gifts.

The Glen children came to the Manse for weeks beforehand to learn the wedding-hymns.

My wedding was the first to be solemnised in my father's church. In those days country couples in Scotland were married in their own home, in the house of a friend, or in the Manse; this was followed by a feast and a dance in the nearest barn (with music provided by a fiddle or melodeon). There was no honeymoon in those days; dancing was kept up to a late hour, then everybody went to their respective homes.

For some days prior to my wedding it was a case of House Full at the Manse, with every available corner in use as sleeping accommodation. Every cottage and farm-house had previously been visited and a personal invitation extended to every member of each household to a Dance in the School on the Wedding Day.

Tradition decrees that the bride and groom may not sleep under the same roof on their wedding-eve, nor see each other again till they meet in church; after a tiring day at the Manse, devoted by all concerned to dealing with the inevitable last-minute details, the bridegroom was far from pleased to discover that nobody had remembered to order a carriage to take him to Ballater for the night. A five-mile walk at that hour was an exasperating prospect that had to be faced with resignation, if not with equanimity!

So dawned our wedding-day. There was no traditional bridal breakfast-in-bed for me; like my mother and sister I rose early, for there were things to be done . . . hot-water jugs and breakfast trays to carry to guest-rooms, the big dining-table, extended to its full length, to lay with silver and the main items of the wedding-feast, the wedding-cake and champagne to set out in the drawing-room, which was already overcrowded with wedding-presents on view, silver, china, glass, and linen, and pen-painted offerings in the shape of cushions and 'table-centres' from artistically minded friends . . . there were no electrical gadgets, chrome or stainless steel in those days.

My mother had not a minute in which to hover tearfully over me, nor had I time to think romantic thoughts; we were too busy polishing glasses and giving final rubs to this and that.

In a blue overall I was hulling freshly picked strawberries from the Smiddy at Fit o'Gairn when an early guest looked in on his way to the church. My mother, who had organised and planned every detail down to the last silver spoon, was still bustling around when I went upstairs to dress.

The dignified Court Dressmaker had lived up to her reputation . . . my wedding-dress had been made entirely by hand. The inner bodice of kerchief-silk was lightly boned, pin-tucked, and edged with lace. The dress itself was of slipper-satin, and the short train, with a tiny corner turned back with a sprig of orange-blossom was fitting for a little country church where a long train would have been out of place. I had a sprig of

orange-blossom on one shoulder and a coronet of orange-blossom, and with all this I wore satin shoes and elbow-length gloves, and carried a beautiful bouquet which was later sent to Meggie Mitchell who had been bedridden most of her long life.

Carriages arrived punctually and the Manse party set off for church. My father and I were met at the church-door by the Rev. S. J. Ramsay-Sibbald who had known me all my life, and was my father's greatest friend. He waited till my father donned his pulpit gown and St Andrews Bachelor of Divinity hood of violet and white, edged with white fur, then preceded us up the aisle, wearing his vestments as Chaplain to the King, his scarlet hood and cincture and gold-embroidered stole.

The Rev. Archie Thomson, our dear family friend from Corgarff, was late because his mare, Peggy, had cast a shoe, and he had had to lead her for miles across the Glas-choille. Fortunately, he arrived in time to take part in the Service.

My face was veiled throughout the ceremony till, as we turned to move down the aisle as man and wife, my husband raised my veil and kissed me before the whole congregation.

As we drove away from the church I placed on his finger, as he had placed on mine, a gold ring, inscribed like my own, with our initials and the date. He wore it all his life. Again we kissed; it was a renewal of the vows and covenant we had made in church.

Later, I gave him what he had always wanted, a gold sovereign-case to wear on his watch-chain. How could we have foreseen that a month or so later, sovereigns and half-sovereigns would be withdrawn from circulation, and a sovereign-case would thus become obsolete!

We had three Glen pipers who played at the Manse during our wedding reception, James Smith of Recharcharie, and the Coutts boys, John and Joseph, from Morven. Like Robert Buchanan's pipers

> Playing across the heather,
> Backward their ribbons flew,

Blast upon blast they blew,
Each clad in tartan new
Bonnet and blackcock feather.

After the Reception, with the pipers still playing and marching round the house, I ran upstairs to change into my travelling-costume. My bridesmaids and I could hear sounds of great hilarity proceeding from the adjoining room where the bridegroom, the best man and the usher were trying to shed their formal garments and to climb into lounge suits, in a bedroom so small they had barely room to turn round.

When we were ready to leave, the guests in a body accompanied us down the brae and over the footbridge to the Milton where the carriages were waiting. The bridal carriage, which had brought us through the ford on our return from church, distinguished by bows of white satin on the coachman's whip and ear-bows on the horses, was ready to move off. The three pipers were standing by, and as soon as we were seated, at the sudden skirl of the pipes which gave us a truly Highland leave-taking, the horses screamed and reared, but were soon controlled; so, to the strains of 'Hieland Laddie', we drove away to begin a new life, happily unaware that storm-clouds were gathering, and that our trusting belief in a future of unclouded wedded bliss was soon to be shattered by a Declaration of War.

In the stir of wedding preparations I had understood vaguely that someone of importance had been shot . . . an Austrian Archduke in a place called Sarajevo. I did not appreciate the gravity of the situation, and nobody was inclined to enlighten me.

The word War on our wedding-day was never breathed, but that night, in our hotel, we encountered a number of very young Territorial Officers who had been called up because war seemed imminent. They were full of high spirits, excited at the prospect of 'having a whack at the Kaiser'. They spent some hilarious hours in the long corridor outside our bedroom, in a prolonged game of curling, which only came to an end when they ran out of chamber-pots.

In the morning, they told us how eager they were to be in the thick of it; everybody said it would all be over by Christmas, and off they went to teach the Hun a lesson.

Strange scenes, we afterwards read, were taking place all over the country. There was, for example, a great Ball at Arundel Castle, and as the young naval officers who had received their secret call-up, slipped away unobtrusively, there were bound to have been some people 'in the know' who were wretchedly reminded of Waterloo and the Duchess of Richmond's Ball when 'brightly shone the lights on fair women and brave men.'

The German lad, on a walking tour of Scotland, who shared our breakfast-table, gloomily faced the prospect of being immediately recalled to the Fatherland, probably to fight against his friends the Scots who had shown him kindness. We were shortly to find that we had had our white wedding just in time; in the early months of the war it was felt to be unpatriotic to have a full-scale white wedding, but later, when coupons on clothing and other shortages were making themselves felt, it became a matter of pride to have a wedding as near peace-time standards as possible. It was illegal to manufacture confetti, throwing rice was illegal as well as wasteful, and many a couple was pelted with the hoarded small circles of paper from paper-punches in the office. Wedding-gowns were borrowed or hired, wedding-cakes were camouflaged with decorative cardboard covers, no extra coupons were allowed for a trousseau but friends rallied round and every bride somehow contrived to look very smart and very lovely on her wartime wedding-day.

July ended and August Bank Holiday came, and a worried, puzzled crowd gathered in Whitehall; wars in the past had been for professional soldiers, this time, it seemed, we were all to be in it. It was in a severely overcrowded train, after an overshadowed and interrupted honeymoon, that I had my first inkling of what war would mean to the women left behind. The train held hundreds of Reservists, and we shared a compartment with men who shouted and sang, boisterously

concealing their heartache at leaving homes and families in ruthless haste, well-primed with whisky which a crowd of well-wishers had pressed upon them. One man leaned across to tell me earnestly and repeatedly his confident intention, on his return, to pin his medal on 'Wee Georgie's breist'. No one, I believe, had any premonition that Wee Georgie might never see his Dad again, or that the war that was to be over by Christmas would drag on for more than four disastrous years.

CANNY AUL' CUMMERLAN'

It was the Cumberland poet, Jonathan M. Denwood, whose dialect poems are of the homely kind that touch the heart, who declared that 'Canny aul' Cummerlan' caps them a' still'; it was Sir Walter Scott who was married in Carlisle and said, 'The sun shines fair on Carlisle Wa'', and William Wordsworth who made reference to a visit to Merry Carlisle. We were about to investigate the truth of these sayings. Carlisle is an ancient cathedral city with a long and turbulent history; when we passed out of its immense railway-station that autumn in 1914 we discovered it to have many other aspects, and though no longer the scene of battle and Border skirmish it was still a garrison city. Mark had been appointed Assistant Medical Officer of Health at a salary of £225 per annum ('not a bad screw', he said) and was about to join his brother, Kenneth, on the staff of the County Health Department. They had both, on the outbreak of war, volunteered for active service, but it was considered that public health should be safeguarded and so Medical Officers were not then eligible for service in the armed forces. This ruling remained in force till April the following year when volunteers were called up. Meantime they found themselves occupied in the medical examination of

children attending elementary schools in the county. Their journeys were made by train and by bicycle. Their policy was to stay in one place for a period, attending all the schools in that area, bicycling to all within a radius of ten miles or so, and whenever possible it was Mark's custom to search for rare ferns in dykes which bordered the country roads. They had bed and breakfast in hotels, and were given an allowance of 5s. for lunch, and 2d. a mile for cycling. This may have paid for the upkeep of their bicycles (their own property) but was hard-won remuneration, for they carried an immense amount of equipment, including a heavy weighing-machine, a six-foot measuring-rod, and masses of record cards. In those early years of school medical inspection it was far from popular among children, their parents, and teachers. My boyish-looking brother-in-law found in one school that senior girls refused to be examined by 'that boy', and it was not unknown for boys to avoid the ordeal by climbing convenient trees and remaining there, declining to come down till they saw the doctors disappear down the road. Through time, treatment of school-children following medical inspection became a duty by law . . . then followed other special services, dental, ortho-paedic, mental health, and speech therapy, but in 1914 these were things of the distant future.

When the Nursing Association was established in the county in 1897 under the direction of public-spirited women, among whom Lady Mabel Howard was the driving force, only certain areas were covered at first. A Superintendent bicycled all over the county measuring distances by a cyclometer, so marking what she considered would be suitable centres for nurses. Village women were trained and appointed as nurses at a salary which was to be not less than 12s. a week. It was many years before the high standard of the State Registered Nurse qualifications became practicable, but from simple beginnings there emerged a body of devoted women poorly paid and working under difficult conditions who in all weathers attended the sick in their own homes, covering their districts mostly on foot, or on a bicycle. We heard of nurses in the Lake District

who dug their way through snow-drifts to attend urgent cases, and of one nurse who rowed down Ullswater in a storm because the road was blocked with snow.

Mark and I found airy rooms in Victoria Place while we looked round for a home of our own. I have forgotten what rent we paid, but I had £1 per week to do the catering and our landlady did the cooking. One day in the open market I lost my pound note, and grieved for a long time at the sheer folly of literally throwing money away. I was a very inexperienced shopper and had no idea of the quantities required for two people. Packaged cereals were not yet much in evidence, and so accustomed was I to my mother's habit, of necessity, of bulk-buying, that I was apt to buy too much of everything. Although alone for the greater part of each day I was not without friends. Kenneth had lived in Carlisle for some years and I have remembered all my life the kindness shown to me by his friends, the Maxwell girls, Bertha and Vida, who took me on brambling picnics; Eden Richardson with whom I walked in Wreay Woods, Clara Bell who, with Alice Carr, was a friend of Annie Fraser and lived in what was then the only little house overlooking Rickerby Park; Kate Emery and her small yapping dogs, and, of course, the Carr family who had spent many holidays in Colvend. It was the matriarchal Mrs James Carr who took me under her wing and introduced me to the shops she herself patronised. First, at one of the market stalls we bought a basket which she said I would require for carrying small purchases . . . larger orders would be delivered. A small, old-fashioned grocery store, with a huge gold teapot in the window, was kept by two elderly brothers called Baines in one of the lanes off Scotch Street. They wore black frock coats and wing collars in the style of William Ewart Gladstone. They received us with courtly bows and placed chairs for us at the counter. They weighed every-thing, tea, sugar, cereals, etc., and wrapped each item in white paper in the manner of chemists, before ceremonially bowing us out. (Chemists in those days sealed all their little white packages with red sealing-wax.)

Carel Cross has been the centre of the Market Place for as long as records can be traced. There were women sitting on the steps of the Cross that day when Mrs Carr and I went shopping. They were the rudd women, well-known figures who sold pieces of red stone called rudd, which was in general demand for reddening doorsteps. One was known as Snotty-nosed Annie, another Five-fingered Jo, and a third was Ruddy Mary. Business was done round Carel Cross come rain, hail or shine. There were open stalls in the Town Hall square and in the Green Market, and these survived till 1927. Country women brought small stocks of butter, eggs and chickens, set them out on benches and sat near them till all were sold. They also brought posies for sale . . . early snowdrops and primroses, wild daffodils and bluebells, Sweet William, clove-scented stocks, and other old-fashioned flowers from their cottage gardens. The Crescent was still partially residential, but farm-carts stood there on market days laden with potatoes which were sold for 3½d. a stone. The horses were stabled and the carts stood up-ended or with the shafts down, till all loads were sold. Herds of frightened cattle, lowing loudly, were driven down Botchergate, beaten with sticks across their rumps by shouting, perspiring, brutish men known locally as 'bullock wallopers'. They wore official badges issued at the Police Station on West Walls. Newsboys also required a badge, and so did the casual seller of Nicholson & Cartner's coloured picture postcards of prominent parts of the city . . . six cards for 2d.

Jimmy Dyer, fiddler and ballad-singer, accompanied every-where by his collie, Nellie, was a familiar figure in the streets . . . so was Monkey Green with his barrel-organ, but now bereft of his pet monkey, once the delight and the terror of cheeky youngsters. There was Donahue the knife-grinder who pushed his heavy machine through the streets, operating from the kerb-side. There was Lizzie, lame and nearly blind, who sold newspapers, and an eccentric old woman whose name I never heard, who was constantly seen carrying in each hand a heavy open bag which appeared to contain nothing but old

newspapers. She may have been Old Nanny Knockabout of whom I later heard. There was Monday Mary who always had a lidded basket on her arm. It was said that she drew her pension on Monday and used it to quench her thirst, but a more likely explanation of her name is that she was always alert on Monday to pick up bargains left over from Saturday's Market. I heard of other characters, too, in Caldewgate . . . Johnny Hanger Banger, so named because he worked in the smiddy near the old toll-house which I once visited before it was demolished to make room for an inn; the old woman and her blacksmith son had once lived in Colvend. There was also Peggy Sawdust who got her nickname because she collected buckets of sawdust from the sawmill on St Nicholas Bridge to spread on the floors of local pubs at 1d. a time. Outside porters could be seen pushing their barrows through the streets; they met trains and were engaged for the day by commercial travellers to convey their large covered baskets of sample goods from one shop to another. Trams had taken over from the horse-drawn buses for travel in the town, and a few cars had appeared, though horses were still used privately.

The custom of leaving cards was still in fashion, and as a newly-wed I found that many ladies called on me. I studied books on etiquette so that I in return would leave the correct number of cards. It was decreed that when a married woman called or, as in my case, returned a call, she left one of her own cards and two of her husband's cards, that is, one of his was left for the lady of the house; but the lady-caller did not leave one of her own for the master of the house, because ladies do not call on gentlemen . . . gentlemen call on ladies! I was understandably confused when I returned the call of a widow with three unmarried daughters . . . the books gave no guidance, but the kindly lady and I agreed that for me to leave four of my own cards was unnecessary and absurd. One always wore white kid gloves when calling. At first I found it awkward to cope with bountiful wedges of Cumberland plate-cake which was served in all its fruitiness at afternoon tea; I had not been accustomed to dealing with juicy bramble cake

in the drawing-room; pastry in my previous experience had been reserved for meals at the dining-table.

In my wanderings I saw on numerous occasions a statuesque lady who wore a monocle with an air but I never learned her name; there was also a middle-aged couple, the Mounsey-Grants, who intrigued me . . . he in tweeds with the bearing of a country squire, she whimsically attired, with many brilliant scarves floating about her person, and carrying several gay beach bags. They invariably looked as if they were going on a journey, but were in fact making their way to the Crown and Mitre Hotel where they lunched every day.

Inevitably, I became acquainted with a number of the medical men in the neighbourhood . . . Dr 'Basso Profundo' Graham, whose voice enlivened many a social gathering, Dr Aitken, Dr Shepheard-Walwyn, and the surgeon, Cuthbert Balfour Paul, who was Cubbie Paul to Mark and Kenneth when they were boys together in Edinburgh. I was told the probably fictitious story of Dr Lediard who was said to have shouted, 'Go to Hell' from his Lowther Street window when roused from sleep in the middle of the night, and afterwards protested that he had said no such thing . . . what he *had* suggested was that the caller should 'Go to Helm', his colleague who lived in Portland Square.

'Socks for Soldiers' was then the cry—every woman was knitting. I sometimes took my sock to the park and knitted at the base of Queen Victoria's statue; I joined a sewing-party and helped to make pyjamas for the wounded in hospital. I wandered round the city, feeling at times an exciting tug into its past history merely by looking at the street-names, and within the dignified precincts of Tullie House learned something of their story. There was West Walls with its Sally Port, and the Tithe Barn which has stood in its quiet backwater for close on 500 years; Paternoster Row where monks once walked in procession, and St Nicholas where there used to be a hospital for lepers. I learned that as early as the Roman occupation there was a road into the city where Botchergate

now runs, and that the name does not come from Butcher's Gate, as I, in a city of many gates, rashly supposed, but from Botchard, a Flemish nobleman who came to England some time after the Norman Conquest.

When Bonnie Prince Charlie and his kilted army briefly held the city in 1745, it was along Botchergate that the English army advanced to lay siege. There was then, I read, a straw-thatched cottage just outside the city which was blown to pieces by a Scot engaged in firing on the English from the citadel at the English Gate; fortunately for Susanna Pattinson, the widow who owned it, she was away on a visit at the time. I was told that within living memory Carlisle folk on a Saturday night would stroll up and down Botchergate, the rich on one side of the street, the poor on the other. I learned where the Fisher Gate and the Irish Gate once stood, and admired the gate at the Abbey which still stands. Between the streets which bear the name of the East and West Towers on the old City Walls stood the Scotch Gate, on which from time to time was exhibited the head of some marauding Scot.

The Guildhall which was built in 1406 is the oldest civic building in the city. It was an ancient custom that while the Guild Races were on at Kingmoor, the Guild Flags were hung from the windows of the Guild Hall, and the custom is still carried on. The old flags being too fragile to be exposed to the atmosphere, excellent copies are now flown. Once there were eight flags, each representing one of the guilds . . . tanners, smiths, shoemakers, merchants, weavers, tailors, butchers and glovers, each hanging its flag from the window of the room which it occupied in the Guild Hall. Only the shoemaker's guild now carries on the tradition of each year, on Ascension Day, hanging the flag from the shoemakers' room overlooking Fisher Street.

Daniel Defoe wrote a travel book in which he stated, 'The cathedral of Carlisle is very irregular, part of it having undergone the mutilating commands of Oliver Cromwell'. It was General David Leslie who destroyed the nave and robbed it

to strengthen the city walls during the Civil War. Its beauty today, including the famous East Window, shows how magnificently the irregularities noted by Defoe have been overcome. During recent restoration on the south side the masons incorporated two carved heads, in the tradition of bringing into the building something of the outside lives of the craftsmen engaged on it . . . thus, one head is of their foreman master mason . . . the other is of a policeman wearing a helmet and is a tribute to the city policeman, P.C. Russell, who was shot dead while making an arrest.

The Charters of King Henry II and King Henry III granted the right to the citizens of Carlisle to hold a market in return for payment of an annual fee; these charters were lost in a great fire in 1292, but in 1352 King Edward III by Royal Charter confirmed that Carlisle folk had been accustomed to having a market twice a week and a Fair once a year. This was the origin of the famous 'Carel Great Fair' which has been proclaimed every year since then from the Market Cross on the morning of 26 August. Until recently, double tolls on horses, cattle, sheep, and goods sold in the city were authorised to be levied during the period of the Great Fair, and these provided a substantial portion of income to the City Treasury. The Fair was at its peak in the seventeenth century and was one of the largest markets in the North of England at that time. During the Border Wars it served as a meeting-place and a means of communication . . . a man who lived in an outlying village would wait until a party of people making the journey to Carlisle was large enough to shield him from attack from the Moss Troopers. The Fair was a gay and rowdy gathering and a special court was held to deal with offenders. This was the court of Pie Poudre (from the French 'pieds poudres' . . . 'dusty feet') and it remained in existence, though dormant, until all such courts were abolished by the Courts Act of 1971. The Proclamation of the Great Fair continued down the years, of historical interest only. Until its revival in 1975 none of its former pageantry and revelries followed the Proclamation, but that year thousands of citizens

and visitors to the city joined enthusiastically in recreating the atmosphere of bygone days.

During the First World War it was years before it was permissible to cross the drawbridge and enter the Castle. I well remember the first time I saw the pitifully short walk on the battlements where Mary, Queen of Scots, was allowed to pace, and from which it gave her simple pleasure to watch the boys who played football under the Castle walls. Actually her captivity here was not unbearably harsh; she was allowed to ride out each day, splendidly mounted, and to indulge in hunting, hawking, and hare-coursing. There was a gaol in Carlisle when I first knew the city; it was demolished to make way for shops, and prisoners were transferred to Durham. Another prison which was in use was the 'dog-hole' under the Town Hall where petty cases were tried, and the prisoner, who had been kept behind the iron gate at street-level, came up a short stair to appear in a dock in the main hall. This was before the new Police Station and Courts were built. The so-called dog-hole was only an overnight lock-up similar to cells in a police-station, where drunken men were confined, or, as is stated in an ancient order, 'any person who does sett any mastiffe doggs fighting which causeth great disorder in the streets'.

Carel Cross is surmounted by a lion with one paw resting on a representation of the Dormont Book, one of the city's great treasures kept under lock and key in the archives and displayed only to royalty and other important visitors. Fred Webster, the English-born Town Clerk, who affected antipathy to Scots, once told me with a twinkle in his eye that in 1561 a code of bylaws was drawn up and written into the Dormont Book, one of which laid down that no Scot, man or woman, was permitted to walk within the city walls after the ringing of the watch bell. This was rung at dusk, the gates were closed and locked, and the keys kept in the Castle.

From all sides I was soon to be informed that Carlisle is uniquely a city of Family Firms, some still directed by descendants of such sturdy pioneers as Young Laing, a builder,

who came from Scotland and married a Cumbrian wife in the early nineteenth century; Alexander Morton, an enterprising hand-loom weaver from Ayrshire who a century ago founded the firm of Morton's Sundour, described by Jocelyn Morton in his enthralling story of a family (*Three Generations in a Family Textile Firm*, Routledge & Kegan Paul, 1971); the Bucks, whose roots were planted in the early 1600s when Queen Elizabeth I was on the throne; hats made at Carrick's Hattery were worn by many famous people at home and abroad, including the Prince of Wales (later the Duke of Windsor); and Tom Mix, who had one of his enormous cowboy hats specially made for him.

In later years when I was frequently invited to speak on women's work to a variety of audiences it amused me to emphasise at every opportunity that where the men who brought prosperity to Carlisle were concerned the women were undoubtedly behind them. When Jonathan Dodgson Carr first began making biscuits in a small way he almost certainly made the experiment in his wife's kitchen; without a great deal of co-operation and encouragement from her, I declared, how could he have succeeded so well that in the short space of ten years he was appointed Biscuit Maker to the Queen?

It was, I argued, probably because Mrs Thomas Halstead made such delicious boiled sweets stooping over her own hot stove that, in 1859, her husband ventured to found the firm that became internationally known as Teasdale's; and, in 1816, Mrs Charles Thurnam doubtless was actively interested in her husband's project to found their first Library, and the Bookshop that still flourishes under his name. Mrs Hudson Scott's portrait could be seen hanging in the Board Room of the Metal Box Company, so it was evident that she had played an important part in establishing the firm in 1799; and Mrs Joseph Ferguson, nearly 200 years ago, must have shared her husband's anxiety to make a success of his small experimental dyeworks, and his ambition to produce beautiful fabrics.

The great pianist, Adeline de Lara, was born in Carlisle. She played at Marlborough House by Royal Command, and

was presented to the Prince and Princess of Wales, later King Edward VII and Queen Alexandra. In the 1960s she celebrated her eighty-sixth birthday and looked back on a lifetime dedicated to music.

In 1938, with other City Councillors, I accompanied the Mayor to a Service in the little church in Cecil Street which was his normal place of worship. I was amazed and charmed by the exquisite voice of the soloist in the humble choir. Later I learned that Kathleen Ferrier, an unknown singer then living in Silloth, had been engaged to sing on that special occasion. She had recently sung in public for the first time in a Musical Festival in Carlisle, and in years to come became an international and much-loved figure. There have been many women pioneers in social service in the city; Miss Graham and her friend, Harriet Johnson inspired, 100 years ago, the Workshops for the Blind; the forerunner of Maternity and Child Welfare clinics was started by members of the National Council of Women in a little room in Abbey Street and the same band of women founded an Occupation Centre for mentally retarded children out of which grew the modern centre which now cares for some fifty children who are taught by six specialist teachers.

The early interest shown in education by Margaret Sewell and Mary Ellen Creighton is commemorated in the schools that bear their names, though it was Mary Ellen's brother, Bishop Mandell Creighton, whom the City Fathers had in mind when they named the Creighton. Margaret Creighton, no relation but a pioneer in caring for the elderly, had her name given to the first quiet corner dedicated to the housing of elderly citizens.

House-hunting in 1914, Mark and I walked to the pretty villages of Wetheral and Great Corby, and one day had tea at a rustic table under damson trees in an orchard overlooking Eden and the swans. There was then near Burgh-by-Sands, a bridge, the Solway Viaduct, which carried the Solway Junction Railway across the water. It had for years been fighting a losing battle against the fierce tides and the ice

floes which winter storms crashed against it. It was out of use for a long time, too dangerous to cross, and since it was finally demolished there has not been a ferry or a bridge across the Solway.

When Mark had to go to Silloth I went with him, and while he was working in schools I bicycled all round the countryside; in the evenings we enjoyed the wonderful sunsets over the Solway and Criffel and the shore we knew so well. We visited Ewanrigg Hall which was built towards the end of the seventeenth century round the walls of an earlier pele tower. When Charles Dickens and Wilkie Collins were in Cumberland on *The Lazy Tour of Two Apprentices*, so described by Dickens, it was the sight of Ewanrigg Hall that suggested to Collins the opening scenes of his novel, *The Woman in White*.

Back in Carlisle, we formed the habit of going to Her Majesty's Theatre, or to The Palace Theatre, then a Music Hall, once a week. In those halcyon days of live theatre in Carlisle entertainers with great names used to come and delight us by their high standard of performance and by the aura that surrounds such people. They played to packed houses as did Gilbert and Sullivan type of musicals. I have never forgotten, at a later date, Emlyn Williams and Sybil Thorndike in *The Corn is Green*, and Emlyn Williams with Angela Baddeley, in a sad play about an alcoholic actor whose devoted daughter is heartbroken because of his repeated failures on the stage. There was also an unforgettable Pinero play, *His House in Order*, in which a wife suffers much from the unceasing praises heaped on her predecessor to her own detriment.

Variety acts at the Palace were numbered in lights set in a frame at the side of the stage. The turns came on in order of importance, the larger numbers being given to less talented performers till, at the end of the programme, Number I heralded the entrance of the Star of the Evening . . . personalities such as Nelson Keyes, Albert Chevalier, Randolph Sutton, Billy Cotton and his Band, and Margaret Cooper at the piano. Florrie Ford in an elaborate gown, fantastic head-

dress, and carrying a tall, silver-knobbed ebony stick, sang 'O, O Antonio', and 'Has anybody here seen Kelly?' and Bransby Williams, that amazing impressionist, turned his back for a second, and when he faced us again, had assumed another personality. In a lightning performance and a change of hats he enacted a great many immediately recognisable characters.

My last memory of Victoria Place in 1914 is of standing on the front step and watching, with a strange catch in my throat, a company of recruits marching up the street from their assembly point at the Drill Hall to entrain at the Citadel Station for some unknown destination. They were singing 'There's a long long trail a-winding'. That is the picture the song always brings to my mind. The composer's name, I believe, was Elliott; it was his only success.

House-hunting over, we found ourselves in Strand Road, a pleasant corner of the city, with an uninterrupted view across the old race-course known as The Swifts, over the river to the green vista of Stanwix. 'You'll always have this marvellous view', said the house agent. 'There will be no building for the Duke will never sell.' After many years, as it turned out, the Duke (of Devonshire) did sell, and on the parkland where sheep once safely grazed there now stand two large schools which must effectively interfere with the marvellous view.

It was fun to furnish our own home; we bought our blankets from John Wright at Highmore House, which belonged to Charles Highmore when Prince Charles Edward stayed there after the surrender of the city. John Wright's father converted the house into a handsome establishment, retaining its name. Now a multiple store, only a plaque remains to record this tiny piece of history.

Mark's mother, our first house-guest, kindly commended my housekeeping. I proudly produced my mother's crochet and knitted lace which edged my pillow-cases and the top sheet which lay under my Dunfermline linen bedspread. In those

[208]

days the hot pot casserole was brought to the table swathed in a damask napkin, roast pheasant was served with its tail feathers stuck in the usual place, pie-dishes were encircled by a concertina frill of pink paper, and chops had little frilly paper trousers adorning the end of the bone. Salt was bought in huge rough blocks; I shaved it down with a carving-knife and stored it in jars.

Although we lived in Cumberland it was years before I saw the Lake District. We had no car, our friends had no cars; there were a few coach excursions but no buses, and from the train one saw a limited area of the countryside. Once a friend took me in a hired car for my first glimpse of the Lakes, not yet designated Lakeland. We sat on a garden seat facing Ullswater and I have never forgotten the sheer wonder of it.

All too soon, there came the day when we had to close the door of our brand-new home; I went to Edinburgh to have my baby, and Mark went off to Stirling Castle, which like that of Edinburgh crowns the summit of a precipitous rock. Mark's bedroom looked out on a precipice at the foot of which lay the King's Park, where Hugh Gavin, in his youth, was sent to practise when learning to play the bagpipes.

I knitted pure silk khaki ties for Mark on four very fine needles; he wore them throughout his war service. I also knitted, at his request, circular lumbago belts in pure wool to which he clung for many years. Worn over the shirt, they were advertised by Gamages as Active Service Belts, 'Invaluable for keeping the back and stomach warm, and keeping the body clean and free from vermin.' There were also waistcoats for officers in chamois leather for 21s., and the 'Flanders' waistcoat in soft tan leather for 27s. 6d.

Looking very smart in his well-tailored uniform Mark came to see me and our little son, Stewart, in the nursing home. Kenneth, also in uniform, brought me news of the Gretna Railway Disaster. Its prime cause was a flaw in the human element; a signalman, with a north-bound train shunted on to the main up-line, forgot it was there and accepted a south-bound troop train which collided, engine to engine, with the

stationary local. In the ensuing panic the north-bound express was allowed to continue unchecked and ploughed into the wreck. Then the gas used for illumination of trains ignited and in the fire 227 people lost their lives, many of them being members of the 7th Royal Scots, Leith lads bound for Gallipoli. When news of the disaster reached Carlisle, every doctor was notified by telephone, and every single one of them, including the medical staff at the Cumberland Infirmary, proceeded to the scene of the disaster where much valuable and heroic work was done. The result of this exodus of medical personnel was that when ambulances began to arrive at the Infirmary the only medical men there to receive them were Kenneth, all set to report that day to the Royal Army Medical Corps, and Jack Hele, a dental surgeon, who like him, had gone to the Infirmary to see if he could be of help. They did what they could to relieve the suffering of the stretcher-cases who soon filled the wards and corridors and were in great agony. John Thomas has reconstructed 'Britain's Worst Railway Disaster', the memory of which still has the power to shock.

Then came a day when I took my baby the long train journey from Edinburgh to Ballater; Willie Thow met us with his gig and took us up the Glen, and there at the Manse we spent happy and peaceful months till it was thought advisable to take the baby south before winter storms set in. For the next four years he and I travelled the road, stateless persons, staying with friends and relatives in different parts of the country, but always contriving to spend the greater part of the summer in the Glen.

There was still a strong element of abhorrence of all things German, even German dogs and German music. Anything unusual was suspect . . . even golfers waving a club to friends on the Ballater golf-course were rumoured to be spies exchanging signals. I was asked to translate some postcards which I suspect had been taken from German dead and found that the picture on one was a German version of the then popular song, 'When the fields are white with daisies I'll return'.

There was a great demand for sphagnum moss which had

been found to be an excellent absorbent when placed on
wounds. Country folk everywhere gathered it and sent it to
centres for processing. My mother and I gathered great
quantities at the Milton when it was golden green and moist,
spread it on the barn-floor and picked it clean of twigs and
leaves, then packed it in sacks and sent it to Ballater where it
was prepared for dressings in hospitals. When gathering we
used liberal applications of oil of citronella in a vain attempt to
protect our faces, hands and arms from the ferocious midges,
but invariably a plague of the detestable insects drove us
home.

We continued to knit socks for soldiers and to send off
parcels to individual friends in the forces, each of which
contained socks or a balaclava helmet and a tin of sweetened
milky coffee powder, a forerunner, I suppose, of instant coffee.
Our one relaxation was in reading the thrillers of Edgar
Wallace, *The Ringer* and others . . . full-scale novels in yellow
hard-backs which I bought at the Station Bookstall for 3s.
each.

There was a Zeppelin raid on Edinburgh in 1916. Mark and
his brother, Malcolm, were both on leave at the time and
persuaded their mother and sister and the maids to shelter
under the heavy oak dining-table with oval metal dish-covers
on their heads! The men then stood at the front door and
watched the Zeppelin sail overhead and eventually disappear
over Forth where on the beach at Aberdour the entire
population spent the night gazing anxiously across the water.
My school-friend, Lena, and I were staying there at the time
but we and our infants slept dreamlessly through it all.

The cartoonist, Louis Raemaekers, was producing his
arresting pictures daily showing the horrors of war, and
symbolising patriotism. It was reported in the Press that 250
children, aged from six to fourteen, had arrived in Holland
from Lille to be cared for until the end of the war. Friends
wrote to me from Carlisle to describe how in the city and
county they were much occupied with the reception and care
of Belgian refugees. Some Society ladies were thought to be

unpatriotic because they visited German officers who were confined in Donington Hall, and a question was asked in the House as to why these officers were apparently allowed to order their own rations, at a time when the general public was requested to consume as little food as possible. The questioner suggested that pressure be brought to bear on the responsible authority to end the privilege. Another MP wanted to have propaganda to remove local prejudices against certain food. He mentioned that turnip-tops were acceptable as a vegetable in London, but considered rubbish in Edinburgh; swede turnips in Scotland and the north of England were used as a vegetable, but in the south of England as cattle food; eels were loved in London and loathed in Edinburgh; haggis was adored in Scotland and detested in England. There were numerous other ways in which one could prove that tastes differ. The whiting which, for our enjoyment, I used to cook (with its tail curved round into its mouth) was scorned in Edinburgh. 'We only buy it for our cats', I was told.

Standard Bread had been in use in Edinburgh when I was at school but did not seem to last. Now five years later a newspaper article announced that Britain was within measurable distance of adopting by law one kind of bread only, and to meet present requirements it would be sufficient to insist on a 5-lb. loaf of wheaten flour alone, made according to the formula insisted upon by the leading medical authorities in the Standard Bread Campaign.

It was still possible to indulge in modest tea-parties, and in Ballater Mr Ballantyne was a typical gentleman of the day, when elderly gentlemen went calling on Sundays; correctly dressed they went from house to house drinking a cup of tea at each, dispensing and collecting gossip wherever they went. I never heard his Christian name . . . he was just Wee Ballantyne . . . dapper, bright-eyed, with a neat grey beard . . . a favourite at afternoon tea-parties, with his droll, sometimes naughty, stories and slightly malicious wit. Like Charles Murray's Packman, he 'never spoiled a story by considering gin it be true'.

When I see the huge combine-harvesters at work in the cornfields these days in the Glen I think back to the days when a team of women followed the horse-drawn reaping-machine, gathering the sheaves into bands, tying and stooking them. I recall a day at Ardoch when, while gathering, I lost my wedding-ring. In that big field of stubble it could have been trodden into the ground and never seen again. We all spread out and quartered the ground and, to my joy and relief, Mary Ann Hay found it glinting on the surface. That was over fifty years ago and the ring has never since been off my finger. Janet Smith remembers as a child those harvesting days, and Mary Ann's big mare which used to go into the kitchen at Ardoch to get a 'piece' . . . slowly advancing, watching the preparation of the piece, and backing neatly out when she had been supplied. Janet could not have been more impressed had Mary Ann mounted the mare and ridden her upstairs.

Among young girls in Ballater, as elsewhere, the acquisition of silk stockings had become an urgent necessity, worn with care and mended neatly when necessary, unlike munition-workers who, we were told, never mended a stocking but simply threw it away, and bought more.

Penuel, the Village Beauty (her name is said to be of Biblical origin) appreciated the upsurge in wages and gleefully told her neighbours that she no longer bought one blouse but four at a time. Chiffon blouses were advertised by London Fashion Houses as 'Vogue and Value' at 14s. 11d.; in crêpe de chine, with picot-edged frills and jabots they were 'excellent for general use' at 25s. 9d. At Selfridges smart suits were offered for 60s., seal coney coats for £14 14s., and warm winter coats for 50s. There were, in the cities at least, customers for evening frocks. A fashion writer described one of steel grey chiffon edged with skunk, the corsage embroidered in steel and silver beads, and waxed lyrical over the new satin-faced crêpe de chine which made 'the loveliest little evening frocks with a narrow border of fur on the hem and a touch of bright-coloured embroidery on the simple cross-over bodice'. 'We

have gone rather mad on chin-protector collars', continued this writer. 'Every second walking dress is finished in this way; nearly all the high collars are bordered with narrow bands of fur. The correct thing is to have the chin-protector collar that apparently grows on the neck; no fastening, back, front, or side is visible, even on close inspection.'

Fashionable hats were trimmed with miniature laurel wreaths of gold or silvered metal, there were toques of hatter's plush, and three-cornered shapes of black velvet. Russian toques were adorned with motifs or cabochons of platinum embroidery.

The Times reluctantly raised its price from 1d. to 1½d. owing to the rising price of paper and the cost of production, and warned its readers that there would probably be further increases while war lasted. A change in the price of *The Times*, it stated, is something of a national event, but inevitable if the quality is to be maintained.

In 1916 special legislation was passed to enable the State to take over most of the licensed premises in Carlisle. Lloyd George was anxious about the effect that drunkenness was having on the productivity at the important munitions plant at Gretna. The workers, flush with money, poured into Carlisle and became a public menace. There were 4,000 prosecutions a year, and the police had to use wheelbarrows to keep the streets clear. Within a few months most of the licensed premises had been acquired within the city and in the surrounding area; large-scale improvements were under way and the drunkenness rate dropped to the second lowest in the country for a town of its size. Gretna Green was once famous for its smithy where runaway marriages took place, but when King George V and Queen Mary, on a rapid tour of the industrial north, paid Gretna a visit in May 1917, the district for miles around was occupied by an enormous number of war-workers of whom three-quarters were women (called by the Press, if by no one else, munitionettes). They lived in hostels, which accommodated 8,000 girls; there were also

married quarters and bungalows, churches, schools, a hospital, shops and cinemas. All this, quite apart from the vast munition works, took the King and Queen some five hours to see.

In one of the factories the King congratulated a man on his skill with the lathe, and discovered that he was the vicar of a nearby parish who attended to his parochial duties in the early part of the day and turned shells in the afternoon. There were several piquant incidents during the inspection, but what caused the greatest delight to the Royal party was the arrest of a distinguished member of the King's suite by one of the women police. The important personage had become separated from their Majesties in the crowd, and as he was making his way to his place he was seized by the arm by a stalwart lady in blue and forcibly detained. It was only when Queen Mary came to the rescue that he was released from custody, and could tell the story against himself during lunch. Wherever they went the visitors discussed with workers on the spot problems of work and social welfare, and learned a great deal of what was being done by workers at home to help to bring the war to an end. A quick run brought the Royal party to Carlisle . . . King George was the first monarch to honour the city with a visit since King James I of England and VI of Scotland. They were keenly interested in the Gretna Tavern, which was the first of the many State-owned pubs. 'None of that dreadful odour of the pot-house', remarked the King, 'and no sawdust. This is a real club for the working man with food available as well as drink. The two things should be combined as much as possible.'

Every town and village was intent on raising money for the Red Cross. My mother and I, not to be outdone, held a successful garden fête on the Manse lawn to which everybody came; it was the first of many war efforts to be held in the Glen. When Concerts in aid of Limbless Soldiers, Comforts for the Troops, Russian Famine Relief, and other War Charities were the order of the day we held them in the School and each time my mother's piano was taken there on a farm-cart; one

unlucky night we forgot to take candles for the ante-room and the performers in our playlet had to dress in the dark.

At the time of the Russian Revolution in 1917 the Red Cross in Dundee, and probably elsewhere, sold flags to motorists to attach to their cars. They were made of canvas and cost £1, and the money went to help refugees fleeing from Russia. This was the year when Icilma advertised in large lettering The Wet Shampoo for the Busy Worker. 'After a busy day in the office, factory, or in the open air you will welcome a wet shampoo, refreshing, sweetly perfumed . . . wash your hair every two or three weeks in the Icilma way . . . you will be surprised how quickly it dries and how much better it looks!'

In Carlisle a band of voluntary workers who called themselves The Citizens League ran a rest-room and canteen (as they were to do again in the Second World War) and thousands of travelling servicemen were grateful for the facilities provided. When the war was over, with the money they had in hand the League bought, for the benefit of the citizens of Carlisle, the beautiful stretch of Rickerby Park, King Meadow, and Greenay Bank.

One of the economy tips put forward for use in the home was dark aprons for servants, and a vicar's wife wrote from Somerset that she had already started; her two maids were wearing dark overalls in the morning and black aprons in the afternoon. They had given up wearing caps, collars, and print dresses to save soap, starch, soda, labour, and, above all, coal, and the household had given up white tablecloths, all for the duration of the war. ('For the duration' became a kind of slogan, and 'Don't you know there's a war on?' was the inevitable reply to the dissatisfied customer.)

My sister-in-law in Dalbeattie had already discarded all these things, and her maids were now smartly turned out in crimson aprons over their black dresses. Dalbeattie ladies had not yet, however, given up their At Home Days. In the bottom left-hand corner of their calling cards were engraved the words 'At Home, first Tuesdays', or 'fourth Fridays', and on

that day the hostess sat in her drawing-room, at the tea-table resplendent with silver tea-service and her best china, and waited for callers to appear. Wherever one went, one met the same ladies, punctiliously observing their friends' At Home Days, and indulging in a little harmless local gossip over the teacups. I remember a concert in Dalbeattie at which Tot Wilson sang her one patriotic song:

Sandy is handy, very very handy with his gun;
Sandy is handy when there's any fighting to be done,
His love for the Dear Old Country is known to one and all,
And Sandy is handy when he hears the bugle call.

Nobody minded hearing the same patriotic and popular songs repeated on every occasion . . . 'Keep the Home Fires burning', 'Pack up your troubles in your old kit-bag', 'Carry me back to Dear Old Blighty', 'Roses of Picardy', and one about putting the Kybosh on the Kaiser, but Tot's song seemed to be hers alone.

More and more frequently, as the years wore on, I found myself singing

When you come home, dear, when you come home,
No more to leave me, no more to roam.

Roam was perhaps hardly the appropriate word to use in the circumstances. Mark's war service in the Royal Army Medical Corps had begun as Medical Officer to the Argyle and Sutherland Highlanders when he examined all recruits to the Regiment, which figured in every war from the Peninsular Campaign to Korea, and wrote one of the most glorious chapters in Victorian history in the incident of the Thin Red Line at Balaclava.

One day I wheeled our son in his pram up the Castle walk which wound its way up and up, and at the top Mark carried him in to the Officers' Mess where he was admitted as a potential recruit and his health was ceremoniously drunk. (One of the ancient customs of the Argyles is carried out on Hogmanay. A large bowl of Athole Brose is borne by two subalterns and, preceded by a piper and all the officers, is

[217]

carried to the Sergeants' Mess, where a quaich is filled for each officer and sergeant.) Later, Mark was with the Tanks, the Guards Machine Gun Regiment, the Household Cavalry, and the Brigade of Guards, supervising food supplies for thousands of troops, housing, water, sewage disposal, and the control of infectious diseases.

His leaves were golden intermissions that made the desolate stretches apart possible to live through. Many many years later, with our grown-up family, we made a pilgrimage to Stirling, visited his old haunts, saw the room overlooking the precipice which he had occupied, and sat on a still night in the flower-patterned dusk of the Queen Anne Garden, with the massive gatehouse on our right. A lone piper playing in the darkness heightened the atmosphere of expectation; pipes have an ancient language to stir the blood and their music spoke of the long-dead glories and sorrows of Scotland that were about to be recounted. We saw the Palace shine in new beauty as the Castle's long, romantic story was retold with the aid of sound and light . . . an epic tale opening with the Wars of Independence when Scotland was struggling for liberty, ending with King James VI and the brief contact with Prince Charles Edward Stuart. The Palace throbbed with life; it opened its gates to men whose armour clattered in the dusk and whose tread rang on the cobbles, and to merrymakers with rustling silks and dancing feet. We heard Mary, Queen of Scots, singing to while away the hours for Darnley; we heard King James IV enjoying the wit and humour of William Dunbar, his Court poet; and we heard the lament for Flodden. At any moment, we imagined, the doors would fly open and out would tumble a glittering crowd. It was hard to believe that two electronic brains operated the entire performance; this only occurred to us next day . . . at the time we did not give it a thought; it was all so realistic. (But all this was in the distant future.)

On one of Mark's leaves at the Manse he was helping to cut down a tree in the avenue when my father went indoors

suffering from a severe pain which was diagnosed as appendicitis. Four strong men from nearby farms rallied round and carried him on a stretcher down the brae and over the footbridge to the other side of the Gairn where an ambulance was waiting to take him to Aberdeen. Eric Linklater, in his *Fanfare for a Tin Hat,* writes of his years at Aberdeen University when the Professor of Surgery was John Marnoch, so neat and dextrous that his operations were almost bloodless. Professor Marnoch was the surgeon who operated on my father. He was wearing khaki, as was Mark, who had accompanied my father in the ambulance and stayed to assist in the operation at the invitation of the surgeon. While my father was in the nursing-home his colleagues in neighbouring parishes carried out his parochial duties, and afterwards he spent his convalescence with Libby and Aleck Aitken at their cottage at Southwick Bank. He became so well-known in the neighbourhood that some years later he was elected their minister by a fine majority. Sir Mark Stewart was in residence at Southwick House, and his gardener, John Milveen, was a tower of strength when the church was decorated for Easter, Harvest Thanksgiving, and other special occasions. Charlie McKerrow was at Boreland, the Camerons at Shawfoot, the Hallidays at Dunmuck, Maggie and Mary Good lived at Cushat Grove, there were Kerrs at Glensone, Watsons at Roundfell, there were Carsons and McSherrys, Thomsons and Walkers, Dicksons and other long-established families whose names are not forgotten.

Southwick church was an important one from as early as the thirteenth century. King Edward I of England, while hammering the Scots in the year 1300 found time to visit the Shrine of Our Lady of Southwick and give alms. In 1612 David Hope was presented by King James VI to the parish of Suddick and Cow'en (Southwick and Co'en). After some years he moved to Colvend which then became the principal place of worship in the united parish. Services continued to be held at Southwick till about 1745, and the kirkyard is used for burials to this day. The ruins of the mediaeval church lie

in the glen of the Back Burn, and my father conducted many a funeral service in the old kirkyard. Every year he held an open-air service beside the ruins, among those grass-covered graves of worthy folk, who, generation after generation, had lived and worked in that corner of their beloved Gallowa'.

During the nineteenth century there was a demand for recognition of Southwick as an independent parish.

In 1891 [says Walter Duncan] when the fortunes of the British Empire and the Mactaggart Stewarts were at full tide, Sir Mark and his Lady decided to do something beautiful for God. The result, in the words of a former minister of the parish is 'a most worshipful sanctuary, unusual in its beauty and atmosphere of repose'. To the connoisseur it is a gem of Victorian Romanesque; for Southwick folk it is their ain kirk and the bonniest in the countryside.

To conduct baptismal services my father bicycled round the parish carrying the silver christening bowl which had been presented to the church by Miss Stewart, Sir Mark's sister, whose interest in the parish took many practical forms. In country places in Scotland in those days christenings usually took place in the home of the parents; our second son, Mark, was baptised in Southwick church by his grandfather. Libby, carrying the baby wearing the family christening robe, and I, walked from the Manse and found the beadle at the kirk gate anxiously looking out for us. We had misjudged the time and, to prolong the service till our arrival, my father had put up an extra prayer and announced the singing of an extra hymn. At my request, the school-children led the praise very beautifully in the baptismal hymn, 'Father, our children keep, we know not what is coming on the earth'. Later, the baby received from Sir Mark a silver quaich as a christening present.

In the woods around the Manse was a profusion of wild daffodils; these are gradually being diminished as vandals ravish the woods and pick far more than they can carry.

In front of the Manse was the Crow Wood where, night and

morning, crows cawed monotonously from their inaccessible nests, and rose in chattering clouds to fly across the Solway. At times they were seen to be circling at a great height, diving down like bombers, and cawing furiously, a sure sign of rain. At the summit of the Crow Wood was a look-out over the Merse. In the McSherry's Wood there were myriads of bats flitting silently in at the Manse windows, and, literally, hung around till they were chased out.

I think my parents missed the sound of the bees which had hummed in the rafters of their old home. My father's successor in the Glen kept an Italian variety of bees at the Manse. Anna Smith recalls that as a school-girl she met on the Manse Brae the minister who startled her by saying, 'Child, have you seen my Italians?' Quaveringly, she answered, 'No.' Not knowing that he referred to his bees which had swarmed, she visualised swarthy young men with bright head-scarves and gipsy ear-rings, and in fear of meeting them ran all the way home to Balno!

Before the days of organised School Meals many country schools arranged for their scholars to have a bowl of hot soup in winter for a few pence. Southwick School was one of those that supplied the children with barley broth with home-grown vegetables, and whist-drives and other money-raising efforts were held to finance the soup-kitchen.

My parents had one of the early battery radio-sets; my father used to come down from his study to clamp on the ear-phones and listen with rapt attention to the News. My mother listened with great enjoyment to the gramophone records presented by Christopher Stone, the first of the disc jockeys.

At last the war that was to end all wars came to an end; its tragedies, its sad partings and glad reunions were over. We returned to our home in Carlisle, and found our house, as many like us did, in a deplorable state having been let to careless tenants. Our new chintzes and stair-carpet had to be replaced; much French polishing was required to remove spirit-rings from the furniture. Miraculously, my piano had

escaped this indignity. We were constantly discovering fresh evidence of the abuse of our possessions, so much so that when Stewart, aged four and a half, noticed a torn cushion in a friend's house he innocently enquired, 'Have the Roystons been here too?'

None of my old tradesmen remembered me; they looked askance when I asked to be served. Spoiled by years of dealing with munition-workers (not the easiest of customers) shop-keepers' manners had deteriorated. Some were indifferent, others rude. Nobody apparently wanted my custom; it was most disheartening. Even Mark's former tobacconist, to whom he had been a good customer, declined to supply him with cigarettes. In the end we registered with the firms where we had been treated with a measure of civility, but orders were no longer delivered and I loaded the pram with our require-ments.

During the war years the word 'queue' had come into use to denote a file of people waiting in order of arrival for attention and a fair share of some commodity that was scarce; now in common use, it seems we have never lost the habit of queuing.

Mark took up his school medical inspection duties more or less where he had left off, visiting outlying schools on a bicycle with a weighing-machine on the back. Faith in strange old wives' remedies persisted in remote villages. 'I've tried every-thing, doctor, except mouse tea', one mother told him, and went on, 'I couldn't take it myself, so I can't expect her to take it!' Mark hastily prescribed a more palatable cure for her child's complaint.

In Cumberland, in those days, there were always large congregations at funerals and church and chapel thanks-givings, which were followed by a substantial meal of Cumber-land hams and mutton hams, and home-baked delicacies, at which old folk, especially, got together and had a good time. A colleague, a country doctor, told Mark of an elderly patient who was in low spirits and he had advised her to get out among cheerful company. When next he called she informed him,

'I'se dae'n as ye said; I'se been to three funerals an' harvest teas, an' thanksgivin's, an' I'se nae better.'

The Mayor of Carlisle gave a Ball to which we were invited, but lacking a baby-sitter, were unable to attend. Later, the Annual Ball in aid of the Cumberland Infirmary was revived. It had always been an important social occasion for which house-parties were arranged and came from both sides of the Border.

I remember vividly my first Ball. I wore my wedding-dress which Miss Gladstone had cleverly adapted as a ball-gown by removing the train and the sprays of orange-blossom. I wore my wedding slippers, long white kid gloves, and carried a huge ostrich feather fan, then in vogue, made from curled feathers sent by South African friends. Men wore 'white tie and tails', shirts with glossy starched fronts, and white pique waistcoats fastened by a set of removable buttons of onyx or mother-of-pearl. Every man to whom I was introduced invited me to dance . . . that was etiquette. I remember how a member of the professional dance-band stood up at the microphone in the wartime manner, wearing a comic topper, and proceeded to sing a chorus of 'Barney Google'. Cuthbert Balfour-Paul was at once deputed by the chaperones to tell him to desist . . . such vulgarity could not be tolerated . . . it would have lowered the whole tone of the Ball.

There were foxtrots, one-steps, and lancers, but the waltz with its three beats in the bar still dominated the ballroom. Partners invariably enquired, 'Do you reverse?' and as I disliked reversing we waltzed round and round till we were dizzy. On a dais throughout the evening sat the chaperones, Lady Mabel Howard, Lady Featherstonehaugh, and other well-known hostesses and patrons of the Infirmary and supporters of the Linen League. This band of voluntary workers supplied all linen requirements of the Infirmary, including nurses' uniforms, and had a faithful Mending Brigade which met every week and kept the linen in good repair. As a member of the League for many years I collected subscriptions and articles of linen from friends on my list, and

each year our task was to provide a quota of new blankets. The League was disbanded when the Minister of Health, Aneurin Bevan, decreed that voluntary help was no longer necessary. He was wrong, as was soon discovered. There will always be work in hospitals for volunteers, such as today's Leagues of Hospital Friends.

My sister had now completed her training at Dunfermline College and came to work in Carlisle, organising physical education in schools. I recall that she and I, for an exhibition, arranged a gavotte which her pupils danced to the music of 'In the Shadows', and Ena Mitchell, then a very young teacher, sang the words. Years later, Ena became a national figure on the concert platform, with Gerald Moore, her favourite accompanist, at the piano.

My sister and I occasionally went to thés dansants which were fashionable afternoon affairs in the immediate post-war days, sometimes held in private houses where the drawing-room carpet was rolled away from the parquet floor and the hostess wound the gramophone. After a time it did not seem strange to spend an afternoon in dancing. We took lessons in the Charleston which was danced to 'I wonder where my Baby is tonight'.

About that time there was a railway strike and meat and fish became scarce. Our fishmonger could get no supplies except fresh Eden salmon. He had a fair stock of kippered herrings and for a week or longer our main diet consisted of salmon and kippers!

My parents were due to pay us a visit . . . no railway strike could keep them away. They mounted their bicycles and rode all the way to Carlisle, to our great surprise. Later in the week they rode back to Southwick, a total for their cycling trip of approximately 100 miles.

We tried keeping a few hens in the back-garden but that did not work out because when Mary, our domestic help, heard cackling she used to run out and secure the egg for herself, the kitchen door being nearer the hen-house than was the french window leading to the garden! Mary stayed with

us for some years, and accompanied us to Southwick for holidays, where she was immensely popular with the young estate-workers, but when she heard that we were actually going to *live* in the country she promptly gave notice and returned to West Cumberland.

CHAPTER IX

THE COLONY
THAT DISAPPEARED

There came a day when, full of joy at the prospect of participating in a new venture, and also in having a garden for the children's freedom, we left our terrace house to go forward and make a new home in the heart of the country.

Englethwaite Hall was an elegant mansion surrounded by fine chestnut trees, green fields and gardens, and in a quiet corner of the spacious grounds stood Fell Garth, a black and white half-timbered house converted from two cottages, and this was to be our home. The moorland which lay beyond the estate overlooked the wide valley of the River Eden stretching across to the blue and misty fells.

Down a narrow gauge railway line trundled, now and then, a funny little engine pulling trucks of what was known locally as 'alablaster' from the Cocklakes Gypsum Works some distance away.

The nearest village, about a mile distant, was Cotehill, perched on a hill as its name implies, with its church and school, its shop that sold everything, its post-office and pub, and as yet no village hall.

Over 200 years ago, at Wragmire Moss, near Cotehill, a gnarled oak tree fell, not by gale or axe, but from sheer old

age, having weathered the blasts of upwards of 800 stormy winters. It had been used for centuries as a boundary mark, and was an object of significance, being the last relic of the Inglewood Forest, which was ancient before the Conquest, and covered a vast tract of country. It once was full of deer and wild swine, and Edward I used to hunt there with the Lord of the Forest. It had often changed hands, and in times of stress and siege it provided fuel to keep Carlisle's home fires burning. There were, naturally, many thwaites in it. Thwaite is the old Norse word for a clearing, preserved in place-names to this day. Thus I learned that Englethwaite had its origin in a clearing in the Inglewood Forest, and Fell Garth meant the field on the fells. Adam Bell, Clym of the Cleugh, and William of Cloudesley who feature prominently in Border Ballads, were outlaws who lived in Inglewood Forest, that dense wood that extended from Carlisle to Penrith, and which, in after years, was also frequented by Robin Hood and his followers who occasionally came there from Sherwood, in Nottinghamshire. According to certain authorities Adam Bell and his band were contemporaries of the father of Robin Hood.

Mark had long made a special study of tuberculosis, and had been appointed Medical Superintendent of a recently planned Industrial Colony, one of the first to be launched in England, for the care of ex-Servicemen and others who had contracted tuberculosis. Rehabilitation was to be accomplished by the provision of good food, proper rest, and graded exercise in the form of suitable work in the open air.

Mark undertook this responsibility with enthusiasm and vision, determined to make the venture in all its aspects a success, for the benefit of the maximum number of men, to whose welfare he was wholly dedicated.

In the early stages the men occupied wards in the Hall, which became known as the Hospital, but as time passed and numbers increased, they slept in individual chalets in the grounds. Each man was expected to complete at least a twelve

months' course of special care and training, and longer if necessary. The whole basis of his treatment depended on graded exercise if he was to be fit to compete again in the labour market. After an initial period of two months, as he became able for a reasonable amount of light work, he was encouraged to consider what occupation he wished to follow, bearing in mind possible openings for that particular occupation in his own home town or district. Mark impressed on each man the importance of carrying out the simple regulations at the Colony, for in this way they would not only help themselves but by establishing a live Colony would benefit those who came after them . . . benefits which could not be gained in a Colony in which the spirit of co-operation was lacking and whose rules were constantly being infringed.

It was his policy to come down very hard on any man who infringed his rules against smoking, drinking, and spitting. He continually emphasised to the authorities who were backing the project, and arranging that the colonists and their families were financially cared for during the breadwinner's period of training, that when a man had reached a certain stage, there was nothing so harmful, mentally and physically, as to allow him to think that he was no longer capable of any work; and he affirmed that most people would be agreeably surprised to learn how much work such a man could do to his advantage, given good food and healthy surroundings.

Every colonist was under constant medical observation, and the work he was given to do and his hours of work were carefully supervised. As time passed, it was most rewarding to all concerned to find that men who, prior to admission, had been languishing in idleness, were sufficiently improved in health to resume work in the open labour market, and to carry on satisfactorily.

Colonists had to be in their wards and chalets by 9.30 and at 10 o'clock precisely Mark went his nightly rounds of the chalets, wearing, as he always did around the estate, his old whipcord riding-breeches which had been part of his Army uniform; and his Army greatcoat, his 'British Warm', which

he found a comfort in all weathers. He carried a heavy wooden lantern fitted with a powerful light and an electric battery which Arthur re-charged when necessary.

Besides basic instructions in market gardening and poultry-keeping, men who were ambitious to acquire in due course something in the nature of a small-holding, were given a general idea of elementary carpentry, and this department, which started in a very small way, gradually developed into an industry.

Albert, himself a colonist and a master craftsman, was in charge. A large wooden hut was set up in Big Field, near the Poultry Farm, and there this gentle, silent, middle-aged man worked contentedly, and was happy to train other colonists in joinery. From doing household repairs in the Hospital, and undertaking orders for chicken-coops and wheelbarrows, implement handles and rustic work for small gardens, they embarked on the construction of chalets and poultry-houses, and constructed a large barn for the College of Agriculture and Forestry near Penrith. They also made a workshop for the cloggers, and an office-hut for the Medical Superintendent and his clerk, who was a colonist. It was always difficult for this industry to show a profit, as all the work had to be done by hand. To be self-supporting it would have had to be on a large scale and equipped with up-to-date, labour-saving machinery, and this was out of the question. The country was in the middle of a financial crisis, and economies had to be enforced. Hand-made articles were, of course, more substantial, but competition against machine-made goods turned out on a mass-production scale was formidable; such articles could be bought more cheaply and, for a time at least, served the same purpose.

There was, in those days, a demand for clogs in West Cumberland. Adults in a variety of occupations wore them, and it was customary for children in many villages to wear them to school, for they kept their feet warm and dry. Shoes were for Sundays and for rare party occasions.

Clog-making became an industry at Englethwaite, and in

fine weather the cloggers sat on the steps of their well-equipped hut and worked in the open-air. Clog-making, unlike joinery, can be learned in a comparatively short time, and when the cloggers later undertook shoe repairs, it was felt that any man who acquired a working knowledge of clog-making and repairing, and shoe-repairing, ought to be able to make a living when he returned to his own home district.

After some years, owing to changing social conditions, the demand for clogs practically ceased, but the contracts for boot and shoe repairs kept the cloggers busy, and this work always paid its way.

The three-fold object of establishing industries was to teach the colonists an open-air occupation by which they might support themselves after their stay at Englethwaite; to make the industries pay, so that their surplus proceeds could be used to lighten the cost of the project, and through time to enlarge them so that they might permanently support a number of suitable colonists, and form the nucleus of a Village Settlement. At the outset, the Ministry of Health had been approached for approval of a scheme for developing the Colony into such a Settlement, where married colonists could have their wives and children living with them. Regrettably, a prolonged period of financial stringency intervened, and the scheme never materialised. On two occasions it was proposed to extend the number of beds; again such plans were deferred. Mark deplored these decisions, for he felt positive that if even one of these schemes were allowed to develop the Colony would grow and flourish and become a notable institution of its kind.

He was a keen amateur poultryman and never wearied of showing visitors round the Colony, drawing their attention to the pens of stately Light Sussex and Rhode Island Reds, and the Khaki Campbell and Indian Runner Ducks which needed no duckpond and were amusing to watch, always ending the tour by bringing them to Fell Garth for coffee and a snack of two poached eggs on toast before their departure.

Jock, the jovial, hefty Scot, who was in charge of the seven-acre poultry farm, was well aware of his importance in having to employ a large number of colonists on the farm, for the work was very suitable for men who could only do light work. He was glad to show them how to rear poultry on up-to-date scientific lines. He took great pride in his pens of agile Anconas, White Wyandottes and Leghorns, his day-old chicks, his methods of trap-nesting pullets, and his accurate records of all birds, subsequently retaining only those with a high-laying record and disposing of poor layers.

Our children had bantams in a pen in the garden, and were forbidden to encroach on Colony ground. They had ample space in which to romp, and when friends came to spend a Saturday afternoon in the garden they played cricket on the broad lawn, and indulged in massive hunts and hides in the grottos and secret places in the shrubberies. The Head Gardener was Arthur, lean, wiry, conscientious, with sound, old-fashioned ideas on what constituted good service. His main task was to train colonists in market gardening; this he did so thoroughly that it was noticeable that men trained under him did better for themselves regarding health and self-employment on leaving than those who had been engaged in any of the other occupations. His trainees also spent pleasant hours working on the herbaceous borders and flower-beds which were always gay and sweet-scented. There were beds of wallflowers, primulas, pentstemons, and salvias, and the greenhouses were full of cyclamen, begonias, gloxinias, and other colourful house-plants. Arthur also instructed the men in the growing of tomatoes and cucumbers, in the use of cold frames, and the grading of monster marrows. Under our drawing-room windows Mark's favourite night-scented stock filled the darkening hours with fragrance. Bordering a path was a fine display of the golden flowers of St John's Wort, which used to be called St Columba's Flower, because the saint is said to have worn it under his homespun robe in memory of John the Baptist. When my friends came out from Carlisle for an hour or two, trains permitting, Arthur always

contrived to present them with an enormous bunch of flowers from the well-filled borders, or some of his finest roses. He was a Dorset man who had come north as butler to Mr Maude, a former owner of Englethwaite Hall. From time to time he would recall his buttling days, when he was required to serve delectable home-grown white currants and green figs for dessert, and purple grapes from the vinery, to all of which, in his spare time, he still gave tender care, reserving them for appreciative palates. When Mr Maude returned to his native south country, Arthur, with a new master, remained at Englethwaite in his cottage adjoining Fell Garth, with his soft-spoken, Dorset-born wife and their four sturdy children. She was a notable cook and housewife, who found our northern winds sweeping off the fells somewhat boisterous, and enjoyed what she called 'a nice drop o' sunshine' to remind her of a gentler climate.

They owned a beautiful Old English sheep-dog, named Tess in honour of Thomas Hardy, an amiable well-bred playmate for all the children, like Nana in *Peter Pan*.

When Mark bought an English springer spaniel called Belle, and she had her first litter, Tess adopted the pups and made a point of helping their mother to look after them. It was a charming sight to see Tess and Belle with the puppies and a tumbling heap of little boys of assorted sizes falling about among them on the lawn. We continued to breed spaniels, and our children became so accustomed to having puppies on the premises, all registered at the Kennel Club with impressive pedigrees, that when they were given an out-size toy dog by their 'Aunt Jess' Fletcher, they immediately 'registered' it as 'Eden Brows of Englethwaite' and gave it the pet name of Browser.

In our first year at Englethwaite we had no car, and were largely cut off from our town friends. There were no rural buses in those days, and though we were only a few minutes' walk from a small railway-station express trains thundered through at frequent intervals but few trains stopped. The last

stopping train left Carlisle at 7 o'clock and if we wished to go to a concert or play we had to stay overnight.

Mark retained his active interest in church affairs, and when he attended Kirk Session meetings in Carlisle he was obliged to walk home from Wetheral, a village some five miles distant, where a late train did stop, a tedious walk in darkness on a lonely road. Our boys travelled to their Prep. School by an early morning train, returning conveniently at 4 o'clock. On Saturdays I took the children to Carlisle for their music-lessons and dancing-class, and we lunched in town, a small treat intended to compensate in some measure for their having to sacrifice their one 'free' day.

Our Sunday afternoon walk as a family took us up on the moors, where we were enchanted by the wild life, identifying the calls of the birds, and wondering at the stark beauty of the great stretch of the valley and the distant fells. Unconsciously, we must have felt, like Keats,

'Tis very sweet to look into the fair and open face of
    heaven,
To breathe a prayer full in the smile of the blue
    firmament.

On fine days in November we often found ourselves crunching through forests of tangled bracken. Mark showed the children how inside each stem is a tiny copy of an oak-tree. Choosing a stem that was brittle and uncrushed, where the gold colour of the dry stem blended into the brown of the root, he made a cut with his sharp pen-knife, being careful not to damage the stem. The cut had to be clean, leaving a perfect cross-section, and there, framed by the outer shell of the stem, was discovered the representation of an oak-tree, as shown on page 234. To finish the demonstration, Mark showed us all the seal on his watch-chain, which had belonged to his father and consisted of the identical impression of the oak tree.

Long conversations with the loquacious and weather-wise station-master, Mr Armes, had taught us to observe the helm bar which lay at certain times along the fells like a dark bank

of cloud. The Helm Wind, which we fortunately never experienced, was a bitter north-easterly destructive wind, spoken
of with bated breath in the valley, and dreaded, for when it
swept down on the Pennines it sometimes went on for days.

On our walks we passed by the eerily-named Black Moss
Pool, and the tree-fringed tarns which had their origin in old
quarry holes.

In spite of generous off-duty hours, domestic help was hard
to keep, for town-bred girls could not tolerate for long the
isolation from their friends, from shops, and from the Pictures,
nor were they allowed to fraternise with the cheery young
colonists who passed by, within shouting distance, whistling

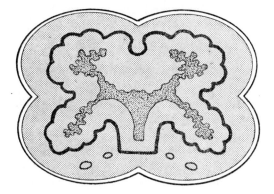

at their work, and that was the last straw. Every few months,
it seemed, I trod a familiar path to Miss Downey's Registry
Office in Carlisle, which had been started in the latter half of
last century by two sisters, Miss Fanny and Miss Lily Downey
and their mother. In its last years it was in the sole charge of
Miss Robertson who retired after fifty years in the business,
and could recall its heyday when, on market days and at the
'term', there were long queues of clients stretching from the
Lowther Arcade out into the street, when in the office they
often worked until 11 o'clock at night, placing cooks, house-
maids, butlers and coachmen in suitable situations. I did not

pursue the policy of a friend who instructed her maids always to refer to The Master (and presumably to The Mistress) but I have not forgotten Lavinia who came to us from Tyneside and stayed with us for many years. She left to care for an invalid mother and called me Madam to the end of her life.

The electric plant at Englethwaite was operated by the versatile Arthur, who was a qualified electrician. It supplied light to all the buildings in the grounds and power to the laundry in Little Field, but there was insufficient power to allow the use of domestic appliances such as radiators.

I had an electric iron, however, a tremendous boon and it was my daily practice to switch on when I heard the engine humming, to tackle the family ironing. There were no drip-dry or crease-resistant fabrics then; our four children wore cottons and linens and all had to be pressed. I seemed to be forever dashing away with the smoothing iron.

Our household linen, fortunately, went to the laundry, down in Little Field, by courtesy of Bessie and her assistant laundry-maid, who constantly assured us that, in contrast to the vast amount of hospital requirements which kept them busy for the rest of the week, ours was hardly worth mentioning.

One year we had what amounted to a plague of starlings. Thousands of them among the laurels and rhododendrons kept up an incessant chatter, dying after a time to a steady murmur like running water. At dusk when they returned with a whirring of wings from their daytime wanderings, they liked to gather at certain points and argue, making an incredible din. The shrubs where they rested were white with their droppings, and after rain the sickly odour was most offensive. At last Mark was driven to fetch his gun and fire a couple of shots into the air, creating pandemonium among the starlings. Alarmed and bewildered they took refuge among the tall trees; twittering, they returned to their perches for a conference, then, in a dense cloud and a deafening cacophony of screeching, they rose and descended on distant stubble fields. They never returned; so ended their five months' stay among us.

At the neighbouring farm of Knott Hill lived Percy Bishop who supplied our little community with milk, delivering it in person with cheerful morning face.

At Christmas a large jug of cream was sent over to Fell Garth by Mrs Bishop, a handsome intelligent woman, who seldom went visiting but was content to practise the house-wifely arts, like Rob Allan's Bonny Bell, 'a tenty dame that spun her oo' an' said her prayers an' bade at hame'. From her I learned the history of many traditional Cumberland dishes, and the method of preparing them, such as Herb Pudding, a delicacy made from a varied bouquet of wild spring greens, the chief ingredients being the tops of young nettles, dandelion leaves, sour docks, tansy, a few blades of chives and Eastermen Giants. She explained how the greens must be sorted, washed and chopped, boiled in a muslin bag till tender. Cooked barley was added, a beaten egg, butter and seasoning. The mixture was put in a small basin to shape it, then it was turned out and served with roast veal on Easter Sunday.

I had never heard of Paece or Pace Eggs till Mrs Bishop showed me how elaborately dyed and decorated they could be. As a child, my sister and I had Easter Eggs hard-boiled and dyed with onion skins or some harmless vegetable dye; we rolled them down a grassy slope till they cracked, then sat down and ate them. But in Cumberland, I discovered, children were given, by friends and neighbours, beautifully decorated eggs, a colourful collection which was displayed in a glass dish till the following year. Pace, of course, means Paschal, and eggs are believed to be the symbol of the Resurrection . . . the Promise of Life to come.

From time to time I saw Mrs Bishop engaged in the preparation of Cumberland hams and mutton hams; she made rum butter for christenings, and nickies, which were plate-cakes (covered tarts) made with a thick layer of currants, the edge of the cake being left plain, with only a nicked top made by light cuts across the pastry.

She told me where I could buy Cumberland's own particular sausage, sold by the yard, and we took such a liking to it we

generally bought a foot or two each time we were in the vicinity of Bothel. Tatie Pot was another of her specialities, containing rounds of black pudding as well as the usual ingredients of spare rib or neck of Herdwick mutton.

Percy Bishop's father was a venerable old man possessed of great dignity. He had a long white beard, wore a John Bull hat, and was a most interesting conversationalist. He was, he told me proudly, one of the Twelve Men of Wreay, a neigh-bouring village, and from him I learned their story. At 6 o'clock on Candlemas Day, 2 February, every year I believe there still meet in the inn on the village green, according to custom since the year 1684, the Twelve Men of Wreay. The founders of this venerable body of responsible local men formed all those centuries ago the Village Parliament, an early form of Parish Council. The Twelve Men acted as guardians of the poor, and continued to be trustees of some educational endowments, with the right to distribute certain charities. It was considered a great honour to be elected to the Twelve and, once appointed, a man held office for life. (The business to be transacted at their annual meeting is now largely a formality, mainly the ratifying of action taken by the Vicar, their ex-officio Chairman.) Afterwards, said Mr Bishop, the Twelve Men shared a simple meal of bread and cheese, bannocks and butter, and ale; they then filled long churchwarden pipes, and spent the rest of the evening reviving ancient song and story, each of the Twelve being expected to contribute to the entertainment.

It was from Mr Bishop that I learned of other old Cumber-land rites and customs, such as telling the bees when their master or mistress died, and placing mourning symbols on the hives. In West Cumberland, at that time, it was still common to find, when visiting a house where there had been a death, that not only were the blinds drawn but all mirrors and pictures were covered up, and a saucer or pewter plate con-taining salt had been placed on the chest of the corpse. The covering of the mirrors was done so that, should the spirit of the departed try to get back home, he would not recognise

his house, nor recognise himself in a mirror, and so would go back to the place whence he came and rest in peace. The saucer of salt was placed over his heart because it was supposed that salt absorbed all evil and so would take away his sins.

Again with the idea that salt absorbed anything harmful, it was usual when going to see a new baby for the first time to take as a gift a small box containing a packet of salt, a silver coin, and an egg, suggesting a sincere wish for health, wealth and long life.

Englethwaite was, on the whole, a happy little community, each colonist looking forward to his next short leave with his family at home, and to spending the 'wage' he had received to encourage him in his work. Austin, in charge of the horses, was a cheery soul, always singing, as the carts rumbled along the back roads conveying varied loads from one part of the estate to another, he could be heard warbling his version of

> I'm forever blowing bubbles, pretty bubbles in the air,
> They fly so high, never reach the sky,
> Then, like my dreams, they fade and die.

One day, when he and a fellow-colonist were engaged in filling hessian sacks with potatoes, he was seen to hold a holey sack up to the light, then cast it aside, muttering with dry humour, 'That'uns got a touch o' T.B.'

Another man was called Tich by his fellows. There was 'on the halls' about that time a comic figure wearing outsize boots who was billed as Little Tich on account of his small stature. The name, to describe a small man, slipped into common use.

The Hall, now the Hospital, at one time figured in educational circles as Miss Nairn's Select Establishment for the Education of Young Ladies, and the building in the grounds that had been their gymnasium was now converted into a recreation room for the colonists, whose Sports Committee organised whist drives, billiards tournaments, and various competitions with prizes provided by well-disposed business

firms. The men occasionally devised amateur entertainments in which they showed considerable originality and ingenuity. I recall a Black and White Minstrel Show with Mr Interlocutor, quick-fire cross-talk and all. When Peter enquired, 'Mr Bones, what is an average?' the answer came back pat, 'Ah tink it's suthin' in de chicken-house, 'cause Doctor him allus tellin' how many eggs a hen lays on an average.' I remember Frank wearing khaki and Mark's military cap with a white bandage round it to denote the rank of a Staff Officer of the First World War; strutting to and fro on the stage with a swagger stick under his arm, he declaimed in the manner of a haughty young lieutenant, verse after verse, of the advantages of being 'on the Staff', including the pretty typists in the War Office, bragging that 'the nicest of them all will put the sugah in my tea! I'm on the Staff! I'm on the Staff!' Mark and I arranged monthly concerts throughout the winter, when parties of talented Carlisle musicians gladly gave their services. These concerts were open to the public and the hall was invariably packed to the door with an appreciative audience, for village life was then uneventful, and Englethwaite concerts ranked as social occasions. Jess Fletcher and I started women's meetings in a small way in the village school, which in years to come grew into a flourishing Women's Institute. One of the first demonstrations was on the making of felt slippers, which was repeated at Englethwaite for the benefit of the colonists. One of our younger members used to amuse us regularly with a somewhat raucous rendering of her one topical song, 'All the girls are busy knitting jumpers'.

Scottish Country Dancing, unlike folk-dancing of many other countries, was always intended for laird and crofter alike. It holds a real spirit of friendliness and, like true Highland hospitality, welcomes all who wish to take part. Dances like 'The Dashing White Sergeant', and Circassian Circle, and the Waltz Country Dance cannot be equalled as an ideal means of meeting old friends and new as one progresses round the room. Scots everywhere remember that we owe the revival of our traditional dances to Miss Jean Milligan and Mrs Stewart of

Fasnacloich, co-founders of what is now the Royal Scottish Dance Society.

One summer all the younger women came to Fell Garth to take part in Scottish Country Dancing, which was undergoing a revival in Glasgow and Edinburgh in an endeavour to make Scotland a dancing nation once more. That summer at Fell Garth we had great fun at the rehearsals of the Eightsome Reel which we had ambitiously decided to enter representing Scotland in a Festival of International Dancing to be held in the grounds of Greystoke Castle.

Every evening they assiduously practised the intricacies of the reel, under the open drawing-room window from which floated the strains of old Highland melodies expertly played by our own Smithy on my piano. Every girl mastered an individual reel-step for her solo performance in the ring, and on the day of the Festival they were foot-perfect. I was proud of my team as they marched on to the field in their feathered bonnets and buckled shoon, their tartan sashes, borrowed kilts, and home-made sporrans, for which I had sacrificed a bearskin rug! They looked so striking in that pastoral setting, and danced so beautifully, that the judge awarded them top marks, then reluctantly withdrew a mark because it was pointed out that the repetitive dance had over-run, by half a minute, its allotted time; but the Cotehill Sixteensome, complete with banner, was unofficially voted the sensation of that scene of pageantry beneath the stately castle walls.

When we bought our first car, a snub-nosed Morris Cowley of a somewhat bilious shade of green, we were at last able to attend church in Carlisle, to visit friends, to join theatre parties, and go to an occasional Ball, returning in the early hours of the morning to a chilly house. I find it amusing to look back on those dancing days when I wore flesh-tinted silk-stockings and cami-knickers with a very short lavender georgette dance-frock with a petalled hemline. I remember, too, a favourite blue summer frock which was patterned all over with Mah Jongg figures in white, a reminder that the game of Mah Jongg was then all the rage. How youthful I felt

with my hair shingled in the latest fashion! Before permanent waving was invented, feminine hair in Carlisle was marcel-waved by Monsieur Le Gall, the only ladies' hairdresser in the city . . . very autocratic, very French, who styled our hair in ridges with hot tongs. These were heated over a gas flame, and when Elise Le Gall did the waving she used to swing the tongs rapidly in the air to cool them before use.

We danced the Charleston that year, and sang 'If you were the only girl in the world'. We heard something of the Bright Young Things and of flamboyant young males who had broken out into flannel Oxford Bags, flapping and voluminous, measuring twenty-five inches round the ankles.

Mark, who as a young man had once owned a temperamental Swift, drove the Morris in the slow, careful manner whice had been proper in those earlier days, and remained an excessively staid driver all his life. Cars had wide running-boards that went out when stream-lining was invented; there were times when forgetfully we left a camera or a brief-case on the running-board, and it was still there when we arrived at our destination.

A neighbouring vicar had also acquired a car, but he never master-minded the technicalities of motoring. He seldom took his car on the road without encountering trouble, and drove in constant fear of meeting another vehicle. He gave due warning of his approach by frequent pressing of the rubber bulb of his motor-horn (as his wife complained, 'He goes horning all the time!') and was liable to run backward on a hill, and to entangle with a holly-bush as he manoeuvred in at his own vicarage gate.

Eleanor Elder, a relative of the Frasers, both she and Mark being of Pagan stock, with her husband, Hugh Mackay, the well-known singer of Gaelic songs, toured the provinces with the Arts League of Service, taking culture to the masses. Jack Lowson, who acted under the name of Hubert Leslie, and his sister, Agnes, toured with them. We saw their performance at Her Majesty's Theatre in Carlisle, in the drama, *Campbell of Kilmohr*; Sara Allgood, an honoured guest, sang, 'I know where

I'm goin' '; Susan Richards acted the lively ballad, 'Soldier, soldier, will you marry me?', and Hermione Baddeley, a tiny figure in a short wispy cobweb of a dress, danced like an autumn leaf in the wind to Hugh's unaccompanied singing of 'Dance to your shadow'. Hugh specialised in the singing of Hebridean songs (he was 'Hebs' to his fellow-actors on that account) and Port a Beul.

Ballads brought to life by Eleanor and the other members of the team were 'The Bonnie Mill Dams o' Binnorie', and 'The Keeper' with its gay refrain, 'Hey down Ho down, derry derry down, among the leaves so green, o!' I recall the pathos of Charles Murray's 'The Whistle', and Sea Shanties which were a special feature of Arts League programmes. John Masefield's short story 'The Western Islands' was suggested for their consideration by the venerated Pagan aunts in Edinburgh but we in Carlisle never saw it performed.

The Theatre eventually closed; John Laurie and Leslie Phillips were the last established actors I saw play there, when Leslie borrowed a large Gladstone bag that had belonged to Mark's father for his part in *Charley's Aunt*.

There was a large meeting of the Carlisle Medical Society one summer which Mark and I attended. First, the members paid a visit to the Dispensary in Chapel Street (Carlisle's oldest charity) which was founded in 1789 by a local medical man, Dr John Heysham. To commemorate the centenary of his death a tablet was unveiled by his descendant, Mary Sybil Mounsey-Heysham. Then we went on to Lanercost to honour the memory of Dr Addison. The Addison Ward in Guy's Hospital is named after the great eighteenth-century physician who for thirty-seven years was an unselfish and tireless worker in that famous London hospital. We visited Lanercost Priory where he lies near a yew tree in the churchyard not far from Gilsland and the Roman Wall. The only spa that was ever developed in Cumberland was Gilsland, which was a well-known watering-place in the last century, being visited by many famous people, including, of course, Sir Walter Scott. It

was there that he first met Charlotte Carpenter, and at the Popping Stone popped the question. Later, they were married at Carlisle, in St Mary's Parish Church, then the Nave of the Cathedral. We all went across the valley to Naworth, one of the strongholds on the Border, and were received by the slim and elegant Countess of Carlisle, who later became the wife of Walter Monckton.

Meantime, cars were parked in the surrounding Great Park where cattle were grazing, and we emerged from the Castle to find cows munching and tearing to ragged fragments the hood of our Morris Cowley car. It was made of a kind of heavy waterproof material on a folding frame, which could be raised or lowered by hand, preferably by two people, one on either side of the car. The hood was up at the time, with its plastic side windows slotted into position. A theory was voiced that the hood in its manufacture was partially stuffed with straw to prevent wear and tear to some extent, and the cows were seeking the straw which lay between the layers of the fabric.

As time went on, the number of Cumberland men available for admission to Englethwaite inevitably decreased; a large number had received their full period of special care and training, others were unfit for Colony regimen. Mark was eager that other Authorities should be invited to send men for treatment to the Colony, which was the only one of its kind in the North. He was positive that they would gladly accept the available beds, and the cost of maintenance would be shared by them instead of falling entirely on Cumberland and the Ministry. His pleadings were all in vain. It was conceded that much valuable work had been done among some 200 colonists, but it was uneconomical to carry on. The decision was that as soon as the men in residence had all received a satisfactory period of treatment and were fit to go home, the Colony should close. So colonists and staff, like old soldiers, gradually faded away. The wastage was heart-breaking; fertile fields lay fallow, cultivated gardens became overgrown; the Hospital and Fell Garth stood empty and bare, the grounds desolate and, in an

appallingly short time, the busy bustling colony had disappeared. Mark's last word on the subject was to hope against
hope that, as the country's financial position improved, Village
Settlements would be established in many districts throughout the kingdom.

He still had much work to do; the universal fight against
tuberculosis continued with unabated zeal. The conquest of
the scourge is a fascinating success story. Even before the
Second World War it was being overcome by improved
methods of diagnosis, better general living conditions, and the
widespread use of special clinics. Then came the dramatic
impact of new drugs; combined with antibiotics, chemicals
were discovered which sought out and killed the germs, and
a continual fight went on to eradicate infection by immunising
children. It was Mark's life's work and he lived to see the day
when he was happy to say that the disease was now comparatively rare; but he maintained to the end that there were
dangers of becoming complaisant about it . . . it remained a
world health problem, and both the public and the medical
profession must remain alert.

CHAPTER X

BE JUST AND FEAR NOT

'Be just and fear not; let all the ends thou aim'st at be thy country's, thy God's and truth's.' (motto under Carlisle's City Arms)   William Shakespeare

. . . And so we came to live in Harraby, the Hairibee of the Border Ballads, which was a hamlet with only forty-six inhabitants when the last great oak in the Inglewood Forest was laid low. Travelling along the busy London Road it is hard to picture the village as a quiet country spot disturbed only from time to time by Scots raiders, or, later, by the rabble pouring forth from Carlisle to witness the execution of some reiver on sinister Gallows Hill, or, later still, by the excitement and bustle at the toll-bar gate as the stage-coaches passed through on their way to and from Carlisle. Harraby owes its origin to the powerful Engayne family who, after the Norman Conquest of the area, became Barons of Burgh. One of them had a farm beside the old Roman road and called it Heinrichby, Henry's farm, which became Henreby, and then Harraby, and 'With its corn-mill and all liberties belonging to it', was given to the Prior of Carlisle by Henry's son, Radulph, before his death in 1159. That makes Harraby over 800 years old.

Botchardus, the Flemish nobleman who helped to build

Carlisle Castle in the days of William Rufus, and whose name survives in Botchergate, also gave his name to the neighbouring village of Botcherby.

Across the Petteril was Upperby, another village that still retained its rural atmosphere. When we first knew it, electricity had not yet arrived; housewives coped with black-leaded grates, oil-lamps, and wash-tubs with poss-sticks. Lady Gillford, who was an aunt of Sir Alec Douglas-Home, lived at Petteril Bank and took a lively interest in village life and in the provision of a village hall. These were our neighbours, encountered while we enjoyed settling down in our new home. Hill Crest, a wide house with a verandah and strong pillars supporting a balcony, had been built on the site of an old farm-house, leaving untouched the gable, a steep little staircase and two rooms, one above the other, with uneven floors and cast-iron fireplaces. The date 1712 is still seen over the back-door. We drove into a large yard where horses had been exercised and mounting-blocks were still in place. We entered by a side-door into a tiled hall with a wide staircase and high stained glass windows on one side, and on the other an archway leading to the hall and wide, glazed front door.

When our family saw their new home for the first time they were entranced; they ran through the house, up one staircase and down the other, using the brass knockers on every door, ringing electric bells in every room, and they soon discovered that the double doors on dining- and drawing-rooms could be folded back and with the square hall make one large room which would be wonderful for parties. There was a small window of stained glass in the study . . . the office of the former owner, outside which his men had lined up to collect their pay; our children thought it made an ideal ticket-office for their imaginary train-services. They revelled in the garden and ran wild on the lawn; they lit phantom bonfires, chose places for the swing and the sand-pit, and took turns in pushing the revolving summer-house round and round . . . a ploy that never palled.

I saw myself as the chatelaine of a stately home in miniature,

stepping out on to the balcony to gaze dreamily over the lawn which stretched to the bottom of the garden. I loved the lilac, and the flowering shrubs . . . the buddleia, rhododendrons, Japanese honeysuckle, and the large white globular flowers of the guelder rose, or snowball tree, that hung in profusion near the ancient pear trees that stood guard over the wild garden and its bluebells . . . all that was left of the old farmhouse orchard.

Mark, a born gardener, believed that from the stress and strain of modern living the peace and quiet of a garden have an inexpressible restorative effect on the spirit. He threw himself with enthusiasm into elaborate plans for improving the garden. He built a rockery that ran the length of the lawn and planted a fine array of unusual rock plants; he had the lawn relaid with fine Solway turf, and set up trellises and archways and smothered them with Dorothy Perkins and her kind. He closed the long flight of steps at the bottom of the garden, considering it too precipitous for the children and made a new entrance near the house with graded steps leading to the front door, and when he had stocked the kitchen garden and planted fruit trees he built a greenhouse and spent hours pottering among his seedlings and cinerarias, gloxinias, primulas, and cyclamen. He loved to plant under the windows stocks and tobacco plants that send forth their scent at night, and would often call me to lean out and inhale the fragrance on the night air.

The flagging in front of our home is now of Lazenby Stone, a quartzite sandstone from Lazenby Fell, which, incidentally, was used for the steps at the main entrance to Liverpool's Anglican Cathedral. It replaced the oval setts which, in close formation, formed the pathway; we used them to make a little wall for rock-plants. Outside our bedroom window grew a cherry-tree that every spring was 'apparelled like a bride' in an enchanting mass of white blossom; then a gale tore branches from it and as by that time it was gnarled and old it had to be cut down, and was replaced by a rustic bird-table on which the antics of the numerous song-birds give endless pleasure.

We are amused when we consider that the bath in our bathroom may date back to 1880; I saw a picture of it, described as 'canopied splendour with intricate showers and jets', and went to the Science Museum in South Kensington where it was supposed to be on view. Unfortunately, owing to some unforeseen delay, the Exhibition was not yet open. However, I read elsewhere that in pre-First World War days the kind of bath that was being fitted in houses such as ours was in every respect descriptive of our bath-tub which must now rank as a museum piece. Constructed of porcelain with a tall curved screen at one end, very cosy and draught-excluding, it is raised off the floor on four claw feet. Taps are attached to one side of the screen which is fitted with a shower and sprays, and involves so much labour in cleaning under and over, inside and out, that I would gladly exchange it any day for a modern labour-saving tub, but for the outcries of grandchildren and great-grandchildren to whom its gadgets give unending delight. Stand in the shelter of the screen . . . one turn of the tap releases a hundred tiny sprays of hot water, another turn, and the sprays are deliciously cold pin-pricks, yet another turn brings down a shower of hot or cold water. It is supremely old-fashioned, but the water *is* heated by electricity, the sole concession to progress!

What pleasure we had from our first gramophone in its rosewood case! It had a picture inside the lid of a small white terrier listening to His Master's Voice on the old horn-type of gramophone. There was a handle for winding the motor and a neat clip in which the handle lay when not in use. There was a tiny box of needles for it was advisable to change the needle from time to time, and a fan-shaped brush attached to the arm swept the records as they spun. An old silk handkerchief was kept for polishing the double-sided records which included Beatrice Harrison playing her 'cello to encourage nightingales to sing in the Surrey woods; Ernest Lough, the Boy Chorister, soaring 'on the wings of a dove'; 'The Whistler and his dog', 'In a Monastery Garden', 'In a Persian Market', and several of Gilbert and Sullivan's complete operas.

Our three little girls did the Palais Glide to 'Horsie, keep your tail up', and danced round the nursery table, to 'All the King's Horses' and 'When the Guards are on Parade', and the hilarious 'Village Concert' was a real family favourite.

Mark enjoyed shooting and fishing. From his schooldays in Glasgow, as a sergeant in the Cadet Corps, he had been a crack shot and had a gold medal to prove it; and he wore in his hat the pintail feathers of a snipe which he had shot as a youth. He and his brother, Kenneth, were partners in a syndicate renting rough shoots, and on Saturdays in the season tramped for hours over fields on a Longtown farm, and in the woods at Heads Nook after game with gratifying bags.

They fished at night, wading waist deep in the Esk, bringing home fine baskets of sea-trout.

For many years, on fine Sundays after church we took our family to the Bass Lake, better known as Bassenthwaite, and had a picnic on the shore. Usually Mark fished from a boat. In June there was a striking array of foxgloves on the wooded fells on the far side . . . hillsides as purple as the Glen hills would be with heather in autumn. A Sunday walk we loved was a path through Wetheral woods, along the wooded banks of the Eden, till we came to St Constantine's Cell high above the river, which at one time could only be reached by boat and ladders.

I remember the General Strike which started at midnight on 3 May 1926. For nine days the country was paralysed. Troops protected food lorries, volunteers drove trains and trams. Private cars fetched the mail from Manchester to Carlisle. Mark accompanied Vincent Waddell in his car which, unlike some, escaped damage by strikers.

In 1928 I was thirty-six and for the first time had a parliamentary vote. That was the year of the first Carlisle Historical Pageant. As a family we took part in the episode depicting a Fair and a Runaway Marriage. Mark, as a gamekeeper, carried his gun and game-bag, and at his heels had Belle, our English springer spaniel who passed unperturbed through vast crowds

on the Pageant field; Stewart, accompanying him, carried over his shoulder the old Colvend flail. Elspeth rode daily on the coach from Gretna Green; round the Village Pump I had a crowd of little boys in Kate Greenaway costume carrying earthenware pitchers; among them, Mark Junior, who pulled his small Greenaway sister, Sheila, in a little Greenaway cart, and Jean, at seven months the youngest performer, was carried on the scene every day throughout the week and suffered no ill effects.

My friend, Hannah Stewart, for many years displayed wild flowers in their season in Tullie House Museum for the benefit of children and older nature-lovers. She arranged them freshly picked and clearly labelled, in little glass jars so that we knew what to look for on our country walks.

Cumberland women were noted for their home-made wines long before wine-making became a cult. Hannah was one who made beautiful wines from flowers, fruits and roots without elaborate equipment, and gave me many of her recipes. She made potato, beetroot, and rhubarb wines, wine from burnet buds which she gathered in the meadows, and from the dock-like leaves of the burdock. She made a sparkling apple drink and marigold champagne, and her elderberry wine was made from a family recipe dated 1773.

John Buchan was in fine form when he addressed a large gathering in the Crown and Mitre Ballroom. He finished by telling a story which he appropriately attributed to a Borderer . . . this man arrived at the Golden Gates and demanded right of entry from a dubious St Peter, who went to enquire if he should be admitted. When St Peter returned, the Borderer had disappeared . . . so had the Golden Gates! When John's sister, Anna, came from Peebles to speak to our Literary Society she had some intriguing stories to tell us of J. M. Barrie's life and character, and afterwards told me her golden rules for the woman speaker, ending with 'Put your final notes on four post-cards (paper rustles) for nothing depresses an audience more than seeing a speaker rise with what looks like the script of *Gone with the Wind* in her hand!'

Nervousness makes one liable to effect a spoonerism, like a friend of mine who began by saying that she was 'grately deepful'. That was spontaneous... Beatrice Lillie's spoonerism at the telephone was, on the other hand, I imagine, cleverly contrived . . . 'This is Lady Speak peeling'.

Carlisle's first cinema was housed in a small Public Hall which had once been a Roman Catholic Chapel and gave its name to Chapel Street. The hall was adjacent to the Church of Scotland, then known as the Scotch National Church. There came a day when Mark had difficulty in persuading his fellow-elders to agree to the cinema owners erecting a platform next to the church's gable wall to house their projector for showing the new animated films. The nearness of the picture-house to the church offended their sense of fitness.

There were other cinemas through time; the Lonsdale was the most luxurious. Its Opening Night was celebrated like a West End First Night with an invited audience in evening dress in stalls and dress circle, and the Mayor wearing his chain of office. Small rockeries bordered either side of the stage with little fountains playing among the flowers. The mighty organ rose impressively from under the stage with the organist playing as it rose. Robinson Cleaver was the first resident organist, succeeded by Joseph Seal; both became well known in later life.

Major-General Sir Edward Spears was a cavalryman of the Old School; born in Paris he spoke French like a native. He was Member of Parliament for Carlisle for fifteen years, Mark and I saw a good deal of him and his wife, Mary Borden, the authoress. In the crucial early summer of 1940 he was Churchill's personal representative to the French Premier, and when the French Army capitulated he helped General de Gaulle to escape to London by stretching out his hand as the plane was about to take off, pulling him aboard to the complete surprise and consternation of all who were standing near.

There was a time when Hugh Lonsdale, the Yellow Earl, great-uncle of the present earl, delighted in having an army of

horses and ponies at Lowther Castle. They were his pride and joy. He, who entertained King and Kaiser and a multitude of other guests, would have been honoured to welcome Prince Philip who helped to put back the clock by taking part in Horse Driving Trials, thus reviving a tradition which is so much a part of Lowther history. The Trials took place in the magnificent rolling parkland which the fifth earl had such a large share in shaping. This event carried me back, nostalgically, to an immense garden party which Lord and Lady Lonsdale gave at Lowther in 1935, as a farewell to their friends in Cumberland before they left it for ever, and went south to live. It must have grieved them to leave the Castle with its associations, and the gardens on which they had lavished so much love and enthusiasm. A natural terrace with a superb view ran high above the River Lowther, which they had developed into a long avenue of trees and ornamental shrubs. This, with about a hundred acres of gardens, kept fifty gardeners busy, each with a boy to do odd jobs and run errands for him. On the day of the garden party we moved in a long procession up the flight of steps leading from the Great Park to the stately terrace in front of the Castle, long and wide with ramparts and two watch-towers. We did not enter the famous reception room . . . sixty feet long with a central tower ninety feet high; nor had we time to do more than glance at the stained-glass window which was a gift to the Yellow Earl from the Kaiser in recognition of lavish hospitality, but we passed by the grand staircase, with its many statues, to a door leading to the gardens. There stood our hostess and host . . . she fragile and elegant, he stout, jovial, and ruddy, wearing a panama hat and a comfortable old coat, in sharp contrast to his usual spruce appearance in public when he was never seen without a gardenia and a large cigar.

Two miles of clipped yews were a feature of the gardens which Lord Lonsdale had created in the image of those at Versailles. We saw where the old watering-place for cattle, known as Jacob Croft's Pond, had been converted into an ornamental lake, and where thousands of annuals were bedded

out every year to form a blaze of colour which radiated out from a central hub like the spokes of a great floral wheel. A rock-garden, with lily-ponds, had been created for the Alpine plants and dwarf trees which Lady Lonsdale collected on her travels; this was her special province. In another corner every conceivable sweet-scented flower was concentrated, and, hidden away, we came upon a Japanese garden with masses of water-lilies and irises set among tiny islands. Along hidden paths there were life-size bronze birds, Japanese stone shrines, and scarlet lacquer bridges over water. The Earl, it was whispered, was not content to leave anything untouched for long, and it had been known for him suddenly to order the uprooting of 25,000 rose trees, and to have 25,000 new ones planted in their place.

On the lawns at the back of the Castle a huge marquee had been erected, probably with a parquet floor like that erected in Carlton House Terrace at the time of the Lonsdale Golden Wedding, and probably, as on that occasion, decked with the Earl's racing colours, but of these details I have no recollection; all our attention was focused on the fascinating gardens with their surprises at every turn of the winding paths . . . a last look at the lily ponds and the bridges, then out into the vast park again. Much of the Castle has been dismantled, but the façade has been spared and from any distant angle appears intact on the skyline.

Mark and I were invited to another garden party, this time at the Palace of Holyroodhouse as guests of the Duke and Duchess of Kent. It was a beautiful day and, as usual, the spectacle of thousands of people going to a garden party at Holyrood attracted many other thousands. The green slope above St Anthony's Well was almost as colourful as any corner of the Palace gardens. Mark, like most of the men among the guests, wore morning dress complete with silk hat and pale grey gloves; I had a new hat and long dress for the occasion. Most of the other women guests wore traditional garden party frocks, long, flowery, frilly and flouncy, and we felt somewhat

overdressed when the strains of the National Anthem indicated the appearance of the Duke, as Lord High Commissioner, and he and Princess Marina came out. She was wearing a very simple, very short dress, without decoration or trimming, with a little jacket to match, in that shade of bluey-green which was soon to be universally known as Marina green. As at all Holyrood garden parties, large tubs of thistles much higher than a man had been placed outside the Palace. Large marquees had been erected in the grounds to which we were glad to repair when rain started to fall, but it was not heavy enough to mar a Royal occasion. When the Queen is in residence at the Palace she is attended by the Royal Company of Archers, her Scottish Bodyguard of Scots gentlemen drawn from all over the country but centred in Edinburgh. The High Constables are Edinburgh's leading citizens and claim that they are the oldest police force in the world. Wearing plumed hats and carrying batons, their duties are to keep law and order within the precincts of the Palace on *all* official occasions, but the Archers only appear when the Queen is there in person. Their uniform is green with a black Kilmarnock bonnet and eagles' feathers, and they carry bows. Each man has three arrows stuck in his belt.

In Edinburgh we saw *The Co-Optimists* with Phyllis Monkman, Davy Burnaby, and Stanley Holloway, but I remember more clearly the earlier *Follies* with Pelissier and Fay Compton. In one of them the popular chorus was

> Does the spearmint lose its flavour
> On the bedpost overnight?
> When you get up in the morning
> Is it much too hard to bite?

and in the other it was

> How does a guinea-pig show he's pleased
> When he hasn't got a tail to wag?
> All other animals you will find
> Have got a little tail stuck on behind.
> If you'd only put a tail on a guinea-pig

And finish off a decent job
Then the price of a guinea-pig would go right up
From a guinea up to thirty bob!

Between the wars hundreds of unemployed men tramped the
length and breadth of the land from the Clyde shipyards
seeking work where they hoped they might find it. A large
number passed through Carlisle, and it became known among
the fraternity that the doctor in Harraby lent a sympathetic
ear to a man's troubles. His well-known basic kindness was
proved time and again; he was always willing to listen to the
stories of old soldiers. He could see no fellow-traveller in
distress or pass by on the other side. He earnestly endea-
voured, also, to play his part in the work of the Church, and
served for many years as an elder. On one occasion he addressed the General Assembly in Edinburgh, urging the
provision of motor-cars for ministers in scattered country
parishes to enable them to attend to their parochial duties
over a wide area. The practical work of the Salvation Army
always appealed to him, and the local Band played at Hill
Crest at his invitation on Christmas Eve for many years.

Our friend, the Rev. Mr Watt of Langholm, visited the Holy
Land every summer, years before it became invaded by
tourist traffic. When he preached in Carlisle we noticed that
he carried his pulpit gown in a black sateen drawstring bag,
as ministers long ago used to do. There is in the Folk Museum
at Ceres, in Fife, a carpet bag which long ago was used for this
purpose.

An elderly minister stayed with us when doing duty for our
own minister who was on holiday. He came from a remote
parish in Argyll, and was of the utmost piety. He solemnly
said Grace before having afternoon tea in the drawing-room
and was puzzled by the sight of a chocolate biscuit, the first
he had seen. Mark showed him how to switch on the electric
light by pressing a bulb on a long cord hanging at his bedside,
and noted that he wore a flannel nightshirt and nightcap.
Being taken to church by motor-car was a novelty to him,

though he admitted to owning a motor-bicycle. When asked if he took his housekeeper to church in the side-car he was shocked and replied in a reproving tone, 'Indeed, no! My housekeeper is a respectable woman!' This was in the year 1930, or thereabouts! We concealed the Sunday papers under a travelling-rug on the way home from church, lest a glimpse of them grieve him for our lack of grace and respect for Sabbath Observance.

Lady Londonderry was a great political hostess, and Londonderry House in London was the centre of the political world. In 1935 she was appointed President of the Personal Service League. She invited Lady Mabel Howard to be President of the Cumberland Branch, and she, in turn, asked me to assist her. Lady Mabel was the Irish-born daughter of one of the Earls of Antrim. She married Henry Howard of Greystoke Castle, and over the years of her long life became a true Cumbrian, absorbed in her work as a County Councillor, as an active worker for Women's Institutes and for the League of Nations, and a clever exponent of the Cumberland dialect in local ballads and folk lore. In her young days she had been an ardent rider to hounds and had suffered many severe injuries which had not impaired her courage. She took to motoring late in life and drove herself hundreds of miles, in what she always called her motor, in the course of her public work. The Personal Service League, which from the outset she supported with enthusiasm and activity, was an emergency organisation founded with the main object of alleviating distress by the distribution of footwear and clothing through existing social services to those who were in the depths of misery through unemployment. There were thousands who longed to work, whose talents and skills were wasting in idleness which they hated, and this included the vast mining community of West Cumberland, one of the most deeply distressed areas in the country. Our main depot was in Carlisle, and sub-depots were opened in every town and village in the distressed area. Funds were raised for the purchase of

materials, working parties were set up to make garments and for years contributed splendid support. Gifts of money ensured that no man lost his chance of a job for want of a pair of boots or a suit to enable him to go to work decently clad. Lady Mabel made numerous appeals on behalf of the League; once I deputised for her at a large gathering in Caxton Hall, in London, with Mrs Sydney Marsham in the Chair. I sat beside Florence Horsburgh, then Member of Parliament for Dundee, not yet Dame Florence or Minister for Education, each of us urging the audience for practical help for the relief of the unemployed. As a result of that meeting came renewed help in the way of bales of clothing, blankets and mattresses from anonymous friends in Devon and other non-distressed areas. For ten years the League functioned in Cumberland between the wars. Every day volunteers received, sorted, packed, and dispatched gifts by the truck-load to West Cumberland where willing helpers distributed the clothing and bedding to needy families who were all well known to them. The work was strenuous and compassionate. Harsh critics condemned us for 'handing out old clothes'. In actual fact, much of the clothing was new, and all was in good condition and of such excellent quality that no man, woman, or child felt unwilling to accept it. Our work was never recognised by other bodies set up for mitigating distress . . . to the end they insisted on thinking of it as a distribution of 'old clothes' in the most disparaging sense, instead of being activated by a desire to give practical help where no other help existed. The work of the Personal Service League in West Cumberland receives no mention in official records; voluntary workers do not look for thanks . . . the appreciation of those who received warm clothing, blankets, and boots when these were desperately needed made it all worth while.

Mark was actively interested in the welfare of the unemployed, not only in the county but in the city, helping to promote schemes like the provision of allotments, tools, and seed potatoes. He took a ready interest in the club for the wives of unemployed men with which I was associated. Wool

and materials were purchased to enable them to knit and sew for their families; there were talks and demonstrations in cookery, concerts and plays in which all joined, and every meeting ended with tea and buns. The allotments scheme went on for seven years. In that time a large number of men had made good use of their plots, their families had benefited and it seemed likely that many would continue to take an interest in growing flowers and vegetables to the end of their days.

During the Second World War Mark was fully occupied with Civil Defence matters, training teams of ambulance men all over the county, giving First Aid lectures to citizens in every walk of life (as were a great many of his colleagues) especially in Maryport where he was later Medical Officer of Health. He took part in Gardeners' Brains Trusts and Campaigns where the slogans were Dig for Victory, Grow more Food, Gardens versus U-Boats and similar appeals. As increasing demands for national service were made on the menfolk, special emphasis, as desired by the Ministry of Agriculture, was laid on the part women could play towards making their homes self-supporting in vegetables. 'You can dig just as effectively as men', said a woman speaker from the Ministry, 'and you will find that your bad backs and weak ankles will go.'

Previous to all this we had billeted evacuees from Tyneside; expectant mothers received special care in hastily equipped country houses, there were mothers with young children and a crowd of sad-faced unaccompanied children.

Hill Crest was full of London families who had come north to avoid the blitz . . . four or five women amicably sharing one kitchen, and one night we had our own bomb story. I heard the low-flying aircraft pass over the house and ran out on to the lawn. Something fell which I took to be the wing of a plane from the swishing sound it made, but it turned out to be a stick of unexploded bombs which fell at intervals on allotments over the way. Houses were evacuated, occupants given temporary shelter till morning, when the bomb disposal squad found the bombs and declared them harmless.

Memories of some things in those war years are now blurred, others remain vivid. On the wireless we had Sandy Macpherson at the organ, Tommy Handley and his ITMA team (the name arose from his catch-phrase referring to Hitler 'It's that man again!') and Vera Lynn, the Forces' Sweetheart; pocket magazines were on the bookstalls; Mark had difficulty in obtaining his favourite hand-made Gold Flake cigarettes in their familiar yellow tin box. Men spent fine evenings digging in their allotments, or kept vigil at their nearest ARP post.

I started work on Carlisle City Council which I was to continue for thirteen years. During that period I pleaded for Family Planning, women police, playgrounds for children on housing estates, closed streets for playtime hours in built-up areas, improvement in the social services and many other matters. Demanding as it was of time, effort, and research, work as a City Councillor gave me a great deal of satisfaction as well as frustration. My great friend on the Council was Maud Scott-Nicholson, who found relaxation in her experimental garden, and who in wartime planted carrots and beetroot in her herbaceous borders, rejoicing in their rich foliage. She was a pioneer in flower arrangement long before it became a cult, and followed in the footsteps of Gertrude Jekyll in having all blue, and all silvery-grey, borders.

In those days, when there was an election, either for a parliamentary candidate or for a seat on the City Council, the school-children had a whole day's holiday because many schools were in use that day as polling-stations. They haunted these places and as cars brought voters to the poll they brought their offensive weapons into play. These were newspaper balls as large as footballs on lengths of string, and with these they battered cars on wheels and bodywork. Large crowds used to gather at night outside the *Cumberland News* office where the results of the ballot were shown on a wide screen. Supporters also assembled at each polling-station to hear individual results announced, to cheer or deride the winner, and listen to brief speeches from winner and loser alike.

Another break in the school term occurred when an official

holiday was granted to enable older children to go out to work on farms at potato-picking time.

Since my early married life I have valued my membership of the National Council of Women, and have been privileged to work alongside many outstanding figures in the movement, including Mary Ellen Creighton, an early campaigner for women police; Lady Ruth Balfour, who completed her medical studies in Edinburgh and worked in the Royal Free Hospital in London; Mrs Wakefield, who with her doctor husband did pioneer work with the legendary Wilfred Grenfell of Labrador; and Ishbel, Marchioness of Aberdeen and Temair, an international figure who came from her home in Tarland to speak to our members and instead addressed a mass meeting of citizens in the County Hall. Afterwards, eager to be on her way to join her husband who that day was addressing the House of Lords, her departure was something of a Royal progress. She was met at the station entrance by the station-master in full regalia, and a number of his staff who in procession escorted her to her carriage, with me trotting meekly behind. All she required from me was an evening paper so that she might read an account of her husband's speech to the Lords. 'We Twa', as they were known in the North, all their lives showed deep personal preoccupation with social welfare. The story of the work they did together in different parts of the Empire makes enthralling reading. Their Deeside home was the centre of abounding hospitality as my parents well knew. Incidentally, Lady Aberdeen founded the Women's National Health Association with its crusades against infantile mortality. One of its exhibitions so impressed me as a school-girl in Edinburgh that it awakened what was to prove life-long zeal in the fight against dirt and disease. One of my National Council memories is of a day when I was suddenly called upon to offer up a prayer of thanksgiving for the fact that the Prime Minister had that day returned from Munich after a supposedly satisfactory talk with Hitler. Neville Chamberlain waved his bit of paper in

triumph as he stepped from the plane, and we all thought for a brief period that it was Peace in Our Time.

After a National Council of Women Luncheon in the House of Commons we were in time to hear the usher call, 'Make way for Mr Speaker!' and with the crowd in the Central Hall at Westminster stood still, ceasing our chatter, showing proper deference. The brief procession hurried by; two attendants, the Serjeant-at-Arms carrying the great silver-gilt mace, Mr Speaker in his long wig and black gown. Cabinet Ministers bowed as he went by . . . the only indispensable member of the House of Commons had passed on his way.

I was proud to call that remarkable woman, Dame Caroline Haslett, my friend . . . she whose name will forever be associated with the founding of the Electrical Association for Women, now over fifty years old, with branches all over the country. Caroline as a young woman started work in the London Office of the Cochran Boiler Company, and was so strikingly successful that the directors decided that she should go to their works in Annan for practical training in the intricacies of boiler-making. She hoped to become a fully qualified engineer, which seemed to her the most useful career imaginable. Her knowledge and skill rapidly developed, and she was very proud of the first blueprint that appeared over her initials. She could have made her mark at Cochran's where she had been accepted on terms of complete equality . . . the one thing that mattered was to get the job done. She carved for herself a niche in the masculine world of engineering but never lost her femininity. An opportunity arose for making the path easier for other women when she was appointed the first secretary of the Women's Engineering Society, one of its aims being to promote the study and practice of engineering among women. Over the years she persuaded universities and engineering institutes to open their doors to women, and was called upon to speak at the first World Power Conference held in London, because, it was stated, the existence of women in the engineering world was still very novel. She realised that the widest scope for women at that time lay in electrical

[261]

engineering, and held that education on simple constructive lines was necessary if the untechnical woman in her home was to realise to the fullest extent the value of electrical development for domestic purposes . . . it was out of such thinking that the Electrical Association for Women was born. Although she remained closely associated with the Women's Engineering Society, Caroline's future lay more and more in the world of electricity, and she devoted the rest of her life to the development of the Electrical Association and the freedom of women from household drudgery. She visited us in Carlisle several times. At one meeting the hall was packed to the door; chairs were borrowed from every available source within carrying distance. Panting women, each carrying a chair, sometimes two, bustled to and fro in Fisher Street . . . many women had to stand. Afterwards, Sarah Perkins, Kitty Hunter, and I took Caroline for a stroll round the Castle Walls, a walk she much enjoyed and often recalled in later life. The Caroline Haslett Memorial Trust continues to provide educational opportunities, such as university scholarships and bursaries of various kinds, for a number of young women every year. For the Electrical Association I did an immense amount of travelling all over the country, addressing meetings as far apart as Dundee and Bristol, from the Kingdom of Fife to the Five Towns. It was a rewarding aspect of public life and I met a large number of interesting people.

I met Lord Woolton when he was Minister of Food and was said to have encouraged us all to eat a casserole of all-sorts which came to be known as Woolton Pie. I met Lord and Lady Citrine at a conference. She had been a singer in her heyday and he liked nothing better than for her to be invited to sing on every possible occasion.

I remember occasions when delegates were invited to Lord Mayoral Receptions in the Mansion House, Goldsmiths' Hall, and the Guildhall, and a happy occasion when Edinburgh's Lord Provost with Baillies and Town Councillors in their scarlet robes received us in the historic Assembly Rooms, and the Castle was flood-lit in our honour.

I was in London during the last phase of the War, when Oddenino's were still serving pallid dried egg scrambled for breakfast, when the Royal Court Hotel had its blasted windows covered with brown paper, and at Berners Hotel I was reminded of my father's clerical tailors, Vanheems and Wheeler, whose premises were near by. In my ignorance of black-out hazards I walked the length of Wardour Street to post a letter in Charing Cross Road, and only knew later what possible risks I had run.

In my solitary wanderings round London, eager to see as many places of interest as possible, I inevitably found myself at Buckingham Palace and was reminded of the little Cumberland lad who with others was taken on a visit to London by David Hutchinson. In front of the Palace he demanded 'Whae lives theer?' and when told it was the Queen's home he turned his gaze on the Queen Victoria Memorial and asked, 'And is that wheer she does her weshin'?'

I saw Hatchard's bookshop in Piccadilly and every year visited the Summer Exhibition of the Royal Academy at Burlington House, followed by tea in the elegant precincts of Fortnum and Mason. I called at Brown's Hotel out of curiosity but ostensibly to visit Lady Gillford of Harraby who at one time lived there with her daughter, Theodosia Meade; and visited the Tea Centre which, from the time of its opening in 1946 was recognised as a most successful adaptation of modern exhibition technique to a subject with a long commercial and artistic history . . . I went to Threadneedle Street and the Stock Exchange . . . and sat within the portals of the Bank of England to absorb its atmosphere under the benevolent eye of its top-hatted commissionaire. I had many walks on the Embankment and once found myself in a dark, dank alleyway flanked by high black walls, and a flight of worn steps that led down to the mournful lapping of the river at my feet.

A few months after I saw the Book of Kells which was on loan from Dublin, I was shown it in greater detail by John Hurst in its home-setting of Trinity College. I spent hours in the National Gallery, the Victoria and Albert Museum, the

Wallace Collection, and the Geffrye Museum, and attended Services in Westminster Abbey, St Paul's Cathedral, and St Martin-in-the-Fields. I often got on a bus chosen at random and once found myself in Southwark. When I once boarded a bus at the terminus, unsure of my destination, I said to the conductress, 'I should like to go to Piccadilly, please,' and she replied cordially, 'And so you shall, dear, so you shall!'

I saw *The Mousetrap* soon after it was first staged, with Richard Attenborough in the surprise role, and also saw *Kismet*, a spectacular musical with words borrowed from Omar Khayham and music by Borodin; I even went to the Windmill, the theatre that for years boasted 'We never closed'.

Lunching alone at The Cheshire Cheese I suddenly realised that I was a lone female in an exclusively male preserve.

At Billingsgate I was too late to see the market or to hear any language, but at the Smithfield Show at Earl's Court, after admiring hundreds of beautifully groomed animals, I joined the crowd round the auctioneer's rostrum and gazed in wonderment at the great beasts that came through a door on his right hand. I saw a man take a pocket-comb to give a last-minute touch to his prize bull's forelock before it ambled in, all twenty hundredweight of it, and hides were being given a final polish as a matter of course. Up on the rostrum beside the auctioneer sat his clerk, his head bent over his figures, and his pen moving like a shuttle over the pages of his notebook. I marvelled how he kept pace with the staccato phrases of the auctioneer, who spoke in a bewildering onrush of words and prices, his eyes alert for a gesture here, a nod there; at the right moment bang went his hammer and there was a brief lull till the next fine animal was led in.

I strolled through Soho which, in a sense, provided this country with its first international supermarket, the Soho Bazaar, which operated in the streets until well into the nineteenth century. Goods from all over the world were on sale, and shoppers were entertained by minstrels and clowns while they went from stall to stall. The Bazaar collapsed when merchants moved from pavement stalls to shops, and gipsies

packed up and took to roaming the countryside. On a number of occasions I enjoyed the hospitality of Norman and Dora Pett in their charming home in the heart of the Sussex woods. Dora's plain gold anklet emphasised the slenderness of her pretty legs which had figured daily in the *Mirror* during the war years, when the exploits of 'Jane' were the delight of servicemen and others. Her skirts in Pett's famous cartoons were daily left in a precarious state but never suffered complete disaster.

With the Petts I visited places which I probably would never have entered alone. We lunched at Prunier's, danced at Murray's, laughed together at the Crazy Gang and Frances Day at the Victoria Palace . . . we dined at Quaglino's and reclined on the plush benches of the Café Royal where I sat entranced, recalling H. M. Bateman's cartoons which I had loved for close on twenty years, 'The Guardsman who dropped it', the affronted horse who was offered a carrot while on duty at Horseguards' Parade, and 'The Girl who asked for a glass of milk at the Café Royal'.

I am glad that in Festival of Britain Year (1951) I attended the Chelsea Arts Ball which originated in students dancing in the streets fifty years before, and became one of the highlights of the London social calendar, when thousands of costumed revellers flocked to the Royal Albert Hall to see a sprightly ending to a memorable year. Those who connected the Albert Hall with concerts only, as I did, and knew its reputation for dignity and size, hardly recognised it that night for at the Arts Ball the Hall acquired an Arabian Nights atmosphere, rich in colour, gaiety, and good fellowship. Traditionally, these artists' revels ushered in the New Year with tableaux, preceded by a kilted pipe band, the singing of Auld Lang Syne and the release of a brilliant cascade of coloured balloons. Leading up to all that there was dancing to the music of top-ranking bands, and visits to jolly parties in private boxes. One could join the ceaseless parade in the grand tier and loggias, or take time off from parading and dancing to sit in box or gallery and follow the ebb and flow of colour below. One could sup magnificently

in the gallery, in the Prince Albert Suite, or in one's own box with waiters in attendance. Every year the Ball had a special theme which was depicted on the vast backcloth designed by a famous artist, in a recurring theme of music, and in the towering edifice which occupied the centre of the Hall.

About 6,000 people attended, producing an unrivalled display of fantastic and futurist costumes. Fancy dress was compulsory, and stewards were empowered to enforce this ruling, but for men Venetian cloaks and masks could be hired on arrival and only spurs were barred.

In what might be called the Year of King Farouk, I noticed that an amazing number of men 'got by' wearing a red fez and dark glasses with ordinary evening dress. Not all the decorative girls were artists' models, nor all the bearded men artists; under the green and gold uniform of an Austrian Hussar I knew there beat the heart of an Income Tax Inspector, a modest assistant from Derry and Toms was dressed as a Quaker, I myself was a Spanish lady, and there were many elderly couples circling sedately among the high-spirited youngsters who swarmed over the floor to greet the New Year with joyful noise. Students of Art Schools in and around London spent weeks building elaborate tableaux which paraded round the Hall at midnight, followed at intervals by grotesque Mardi Gras figures. The structures were afterwards pulled to pieces by students of rival schools, the fragments were removed, and dancing continued till 5 o'clock. Thousands of people, who did not want to go to the Ball but wanted to see the beautiful spectacle, used to queue for the Spectators' Gallery and sit there all night, fascinated by the changing kaleidoscope seen far below through a shimmering haze of flood-lighting.

In their private boxes I met Joan Collins and Maxwell Reed, Arthur Askey, A. R. Thomson, the Royal Academician and portrait-painter. (His home is very much the castle of this distinguished painter. He has a real aversion to working anywhere but at home. His studio is a lovely long room in Chelsea and his hobby is sailing his twelve-foot boat in Chichester

harbour.) T. C. H. Jacobs, author of crime and mystery stories, was a kinsman of W. W. Jacobs, whose tales of sea-salts my father used to enjoy. I met a man whose wife was assistant to an illusionist and was regularly sawn in half! I also met George de Piro, the Maltese artist, dressed as a Chinese gentleman, who took snuff with the air of a Regency Buck, and, in his eighties still rose early to get the morning light for his paintings of religious subjects. The Arts Ball is no more, but one who in her fifties attended it five times, will never forget the excitement, the warmth, and the colour.

With Brian Reece I met Eddie Byrne and Alfred Marks. I used to visit Brian and Iris Reece at their delightful Richmond home, where their three children loved to walk in the Park and made friends with war-scarred veterans they met there. Brian died young, fighting with great courage a losing battle against a grievous illness. His early death was a tragedy and a great loss to the theatre.

Gwenda Hurst and I attended a meeting of the Victoria League in the Mansion House and were presented to Princess Alice, Countess of Athlone, who congratulated us on the formation of a Branch in Carlisle; next year, I went with Joyce Woodbridge, and was again presented, and the Princess, with her Royal memory, asked us how the new Branch was progressing. She was wearing what the Chairman laughingly called her wedding-cake hat . . . round and white and deep, its trimming like crisp sugar-icing. With the League I visited Windsor Castle on its cliff rising abruptly from the River Thames. We saw St George's Chapel, the Albert Memorial Chapel, and the State Apartments, as well as the Governor's study with its archway hung with a heavy Persian curtain, and other rooms which are never seen by the public, ending with tea in an attractive small Grace and Favour house at the gates.

I treasure the silver quaich which was presented to me as a souvenir of long years of voluntary service to the city. The coat-of-arms and motto 'Be Just and Fear Not' are engraved on it. When a quaich was on sale at Christie's not long ago

nobody present knew how to pronounce it. Its name is adapted from the Gaelic 'cuach' meaning a cup, and its shape, a shallow bowl with two lugs by which it was raised to the mouth, resembles the English porringer. Though originally a drinking-vessel it was sometimes used in small kirks to receive the offertory, and was employed on occasion as a Communion Cup, or as a baptismal bowl. It was made in a variety of materials . . . brass, horn, pewter, and wood, the latter finished with bands like a coggie; but for Scots aristocrats of the seventeenth and eighteenth centuries the quaich was usually of silver bound with silver hoops. The quaich is often mentioned in literature and history. In *Marmion* the quaich was deep, the liquor strong; Smollett, in *Humphrey Clinker*, wrote that spirits were drunk out of a silver quaff; Mrs Thomas Carlyle, in 1849, spoke of buying two beautiful little quaigs, and Queen Victoria had a silver quaich from which Prince Charles Edward Stuart had drunk.

CHAPTER XI

IT'S THE JOB
THAT COUNTS

The Women's Royal Voluntary Service is a service of the Crown. Her Majesty the Queen honoured it in 1966 with the addition of 'Royal' to its original title, and since then all its schemes are heralded by the insignia of intertwined initials WRVS surmounted by a crown. Back in 1938 when it became apparent that there was going to be a war in the foreseeable future, the then Home Secretary, Sir Samuel Hoare, invited the Dowager Lady Reading, widow of the first Lord Reading, to do something about co-ordinating women's voluntary work in case of national emergency, so when WVS came into being it did so at the express wish of the Government. Splendid organisations already existed . . . all kinds . . . the general covering of all sorts of work was technically there, but additional drive was needed to make women realise that immediate training and practical undertaking of specific tasks was required. Women responded to that drive and came forward in large numbers, and, thanks to the wonderful co-operation of all organisations, work of varying kinds of national importance was undertaken and carried through. Before long the WVS became a service of over a million ordinary women, doing everyday jobs on a national scale,

known far and wide as being able and available to be what they cheerfully called 'The hand-maidens of the Local Authority', doing the work that was nearest, though it was mighty dull at whiles, especially in the early days.

There were always plenty of lame dogs to be helped over stiles. Carlisle, though an important railway and industrial centre, miraculously saw little of enemy attack. It is still an important railway centre but very little remains to show that the Citadel Station was at one time in the unique position of being the junction of seven different railway companies.

This chapter tells of no heroic deeds, contains no special evidence of courage, but is indeed as was said of WVS work in general, 'a proud expression of individual duty knowingly accepted'. The women who made it a reality were housewives who contributed their spare time, their ability, and their knowledge to the service of the community, in the hope that their work would establish something of value to the citizens of the future. After the inaugural meeting in December 1938, months were spent in enrolling women as members, in training in First Aid, Home Nursing, Fire Fighting, Anti-gas Precautions, Ambulance Driving, and so on. When war was declared in September 1939, opportunities for service began to emerge, and we became conscious of a sense of privilege in belonging to an organisation which offered openings to serve our country in homely ways. One of our first tasks was to assemble gas-masks and show adults and children how to adjust and wear them in the emergency that was dreaded but mercifully never arrived. We received with tea and buns and sympathy the first evacuees from Tyneside, pregnant women, mothers with very young children, and children alone, and helped to billet them, many of them in our own homes. We realised that the best contribution that housewives could make towards the war effort was to carry on with home life, to keep a decent home for our own families, and help to build a comfortable and happy home life for the strangers who had so suddenly and from so disastrous a cause, arrived in our midst.

We opened a club for bored evacuee mothers, nursed their babies, and played with their toddlers, and waved goodbye to them when four months later they drifted back to their familiar home surroundings. At a later date we did much the same for soldiers' wives who, with their families, had been brought home from India, and were accommodated in a camp previously occupied by German prisoners-of-war. We soothed and cossetted, advised and helped, listened and argued with the disconsolate and the discontented, and told ourselves that it was the job that counted . . . nothing else mattered . . . not the person or the method, and the greatest disservice a woman could do, at the time, was to consider herself useless.

Our uniform was designed by Digby Morton and at first was familiarly known as Spinach and Beet because the colour scheme was based on green and wine. Wearing of uniform was not obligatory but it had to be earned and we paid for it out of our own pockets. It started modestly with a tweed suit and overcoat, and a plain felt hat, and soon that hat underwent many changes.

It was Winston Churchill who, watching the first WVS parade, remarked somewhat disparagingly to Lady Reading, 'But they're all wearing their hats at different angles' and she swiftly replied, 'I like them like that . . . they are individuals, not to be regimented'. Berets were introduced for Civil Defence, and slacks for salvage and other rough jobs, long before trousers became accepted wear for women. The basic uniform has changed a score of times, each time to become more in line with current fashion, and the unpromising felt hat of early days is long forgotten.

In Carlisle our war did not call for spectacular qualities of daring; it called for calmness, endurance, a capacity not to let anything get us down; for a sense of proportion and a spark of vision that could look forward with hope to a world that would one day be at peace again. For years we manned an all-night service at the railway station to help distracted mothers with terror-stricken families who had fled from blitzed

[271]

areas and were often stranded for hours on their way to take refuge with relatives. We provided hot sweet tea and looked after the children.

One night we bathed eight babies in cloakroom basins. They had spent several nights in underground shelters and were the better for a thorough wash and fresh clothing, poor mites! We shall never forget the stacks of sandwiches which we made with tinned salmon . . . the best quality, which later became a luxury!

Members also helped in rest-rooms where travelling service-men could have meals and a bed for the night. Service women on the move were often given hospitality in WVS homes. Rest Centre teams turned out in full strength when train-loads of mothers and small children arrived at short notice, their destination officially arranged. Soon they were making the weary travellers welcome; borrowed clothes baskets made cots for tiny babies; bleak church-halls became homely places with rows of feeding bottles at the ready, screens were erected for privacy by the simple method of hanging sheets on clothes-lines, and other lines were pegged out with baby garments.

We had to be ready at all times to serve the people who were suffering through the war. We tried to be compassionate and understanding with the wives who arrived from bombed towns with their children, without money, spare clothing or nappies for the baby. All they knew was that their husbands were stationed somewhere in the Carlisle area and at all costs they must be near them. They sat in rows in the WVS Office and waited for someone to find them lodgings, rations, relief . . . immediately.

There was the woman who fled in her pinafore, coatless, carrying her baby, without hand-luggage, not even the baby's feeding-bottle.

Too distraught to move with care, another wife stumbled and broke her leg while descending from a bus at the gate of Hadrian's Camp, and created a problem of temporary accommodation in that all-male establishment.

We discovered that the many tasks we undertook in feeding, driving, or contriving, opened a vision to us of the wider scope of national responsibility and, therefore, the part others were looking to us to play. There was the soldier who had gone absent without leave, and when he did return to camp brought his baby with him, believing that his Welfare Officer would sort out his domestic problems . . . which he did, with a little motherly help from WVS!

There was the girl who had followed her soldier-lover to Carlisle, and who was seen off by a WVS member, with the moral support of a padre, on a midnight train to London to rejoin her husband.

We shall always remember an occasion when we received an urgent message to prepare coffee and sandwiches for 750 people who would be passing through Carlisle that night . . . destination unknown. It was all very hush-hush. A band of volunteers set to work. They worked all afternoon and all evening . . . sandwiches for 750 take some time to prepare! At 9 o'clock the whole thing was cancelled, and canteens thankfully absorbed the sandwiches. Months later we heard that the expected party had been very important refugees who had, at the eleventh hour, been directed north by a different route, but we never heard how they fared for coffee and sandwiches.

The first big exercise in which we were involved, the first of many such practices, was supposed to be the Invasion of Carlisle. Military and Civil Defence Authorities of adjoining counties took part in Combined Operations, and the 'Enemy' was a detachment of soldiers from across the Border. A WVS member is still teased by her family when it is recalled that at dawn when she, her husband, and daughter were setting out to report for duty at their posts before zero hour, she found her house and garden surrounded by the Enemy. To the young soldier sent to capture them she merely retorted 'Nonsense! The battle is not due to begin till 6 o'clock!' and drove on. Subsequently, she and a fellow-officer drove unmolested through the streets wearing gas masks in a supposedly gas-

affected area, being uncertain when it would be 'safe' to remove them. (Incidentally, the Enemy robbed the garden of every apple off the trees!)

At a later stage we were making a great effort to improve our Street Coverage (house-wives in their homes co-operating with wardens) and we held an exercise on a large scale, the first of its kind in the region. Exercise Housewives, better remembered by us as the Rock Carling Experiment, being devised by Sir Ernest Rock Carling, was designed to discover how the Housewives Service, with active members in every street in the city, would respond to an Emergency Call Out. It covered an extensive part of the city where the incident was supposed to have taken place and was attended by high-ranking representatives of Civil Defence from Regional Head-quarters and Officers of the Local Authority.

Judges from other areas observed and made helpful and constructive notes on the quality of services rendered by housewives, rest centre staffs, ambulance teams, wardens, and others who became involved in the exercise.

The demand for books increased during the war years. The blackout resulted in long evenings for some people with little to do; newsprint was in short supply, newspapers and maga-zines were smaller and soon read. Troops stationed in remote areas, and on active service overseas clamoured for something to read. Prisoners of war, fire-watchers, and other Civil Defence organisations needed reading matter. We in the WVS collected books and periodicals from every possible source, but could not cope with the demand. Paper rationing con-tinued long after peace was declared; books continued to be printed in small print and on paper of poor quality.

Workers in our camouflage factory spent hours weaving scrim in official designs on to strong net, working in two shifts, morning and afternoon, five days a week, until the need for the service no longer existed. In three years they garnished just under 3,000 large nets for camouflaging army vehicles, and were proud of the fact that the standard of their work was so consistently high that the Ministry of Supply ceased to

examine their nets, which went straight into action without inspection.

Food rationing was at its most severe in the middle of 1941. An adult was allowed for a week 4 oz. bacon, 6 oz. fat, 2 oz. butter, 8 oz. sugar, 2 oz. tea, 2 oz. jam, an egg if available, 1 oz. cheese and 1s. worth of meat. Apart from bread and vegetables everything was scarce, and we became accustomed in our home-kitchens to devising family meals based on spam, snoek and rabbits. We made carrot tarts and dried egg concoctions. Margarine for sandwiches was made to go further by melting it and beating in some mashed potato. Tips on how to avoid waste and how to stretch the rations were eagerly exchanged, and all the talk among housewives was of the provision of balanced meals.

The war brought welfare foods for expectant mothers and for children, the provision of school meals, and the establishment of works canteens, and housewives learned the value of milk and green vegetables.

From time to time we in the WVS were called upon to weigh, parcel, and distribute to needy persons large consignments of rolled oats, chocolate, milk powder, dried fruit and other scarce commodities which were shipped by Friends of Britain.

Once, at a time when sweets were rationed, we had the joy of taking toffee to every school-child in the city. Lady Reading never failed to express our deep feeling of gratitude to Britain's Friends in the Dominions, in the USA, and other places overseas.

It would be idle [she once wrote] for me to try to tell you how much we value the wonderful things you send us for distribution . . . warm woollies, mobile canteens, delivery vans, food parcels, all of which we have been proud to accept and put to the best possible use. Again and again, when there has been an urgent need for something, you have heard us before we have spoken and come to our aid.

There came a time when no further consignments of gifts could be sent because of the need to save shipping space.

Knitters at home continued to produce large quantities of balaclava helmets, mufflers and mittens, jungle jerseys and sea-boot stockings, and when there was a desperate need for hundreds of pairs of socks for British soldiers in Korea, 'Knit, Knit, Knit!' urged Lady Reading, 'knit in your baths if need be' and we knitted . . . and knitted . . . and knitted! All over the country the click of needles accompanied our every activity, wool winding itself even into our dreams. One earnest knitter brought us what she believed to be a string vest of which she had read; she had knitted it entirely of string . . . it was like a suit of chain mail . . . in fact, with a coat of aluminium paint it eventually served as just that, in a schoolboy's pageant.

Older knitters kept up the flow of squares which others sewed together to make blankets for the aged and infirm at home, and for refugees everywhere. School-children gave us lovely blankets, all their own work. Once, when a consignment of squares from a class of eight-year-olds had been acknowledged, there came a hasty letter from Barbara with a belated offering. 'Dear Madam,' it ran, 'when we left the parcl of squars I had not quite finished mine. Now I am sending it. I hope it will be of some use to the *refuges*.'

WVSs everywhere were official menders and sock-darners to the Army. Members brought their shopping-bags to our Centre, filled them with some of the week's quota of socks, vests, and Long Johns, took them home and in a few days brought them back neatly repaired. Thousands of shoulder-flashes were sewn on to uniform. When we received a frantic appeal to come to the aid of fifty RAF cadets who had passed out, there was no panic. We knew what was wanted . . . not First Aid, merely a band of needlewomen to sew on brand new flashes!

Then came years of austerity when big economy drives were inaugurated. Paper, string, and handy containers were hoarded like jewels, and an executive type was known to

become surly if somebody mislaid his elastic band. Thrift became not so much a virtue as a necessity. Conservation of raw materials was vital, so our energies were directed to salvage, national savings, and making do.

'Hast thou ne'er a brass thimble clinking in thy pocket?' asked William Congreve a long time ago. All through the years we continued to mend and sew, making baby vests from the tails of fine dress shirts, and cutting up the starched fronts for labels for the Clothing Store. We made really attractive garments for children from the most unpromising material. Our needlewomen were invited to send in for competition samples of the clothing they were making for children and silver thimbles were offered to the winners of the most attractive and wearable entries. Charming dresses and trouser suits made from outmoded but not outworn adult discarded wear, went from Carlisle WVS, and to our delight won three thimbles.

In a pile of paper salvage I gleefully discovered an old copy of a well-known magazine for girls published ninety years before. The editor of that day would have beamed benevolently on our seamstresses for he amazingly anticipated the result they were trying to achieve. 'In view of the prevailing distress amongst children, especially for clothes', he decided to institute a competition so that his readers, while showing improvement in their needlework, might also benefit the poor. The work, after being judged would be carefully distributed through children's hospitals and Board Schools in the poorer quarters of London. The garments required included boys' unbleached calico shirts, girls' unbleached calico chemises and drawers, and wincey and flannel petticoats. The cost of material must not exceed 18d. a garment. A competitor had to send with each entry a note from a clergyman or teacher certifying that in the execution of the work, which included buttonholes and gathers as well as the cutting out, she had received no help at all.

Conditions in competitions are much the same today, except that we long ago gave up using unbleached calico for garments to be worn next to a child's tender skin.

The WVS had a great responsibility in holding large stocks of valuable clothing. Every care was taken of it, and its distribution was controlled so that it was put to the best possible use. It was hard and unspectacular work but it meant that all over the country we were in a position to bring warmth and comfort to people who were suffering from the effects of total war. Extra volunteers had to come forward to assist our already large rota of workers in the Clothing Store, when emergencies arose, such as helping victims of the Salford and East Coast Floods. Packing clothing for Hungarian refugees was another busy time, and a few years later came World Refugee Year when Clothing Teams baled over 12,000 garments, mostly for Beirut, and hundreds of layettes were assembled for Arab babies. Many touching incidents occurred during these periods. We remember the old lady who brought us the warm jumper she had just finished knitting for herself; the man who took his only overcoat off his back and thrust it into our hands, saying he could get another, and the girl who brought us her best coat before she had completed the payments on it! Among the needy at home, we have not forgotten the two little motherless boys who sat wide-eyed on a sofa in their fellside home while the district nurse produced, from the parcel of clothing we had sent them, jerseys and shorts, warm vests and underpants . . . and belts. 'Belts!' they breathed, as if in a dream, 'We *prayed* for belts!'

Perhaps our biggest single effort was made when Carlisle 'adopted' Croydon in the nation-wide Re-Homing Scheme. The citizens gave generous sums of money which the City Treasurer received and acknowledged, and large quantities of household goods to help towards refurnishing homes in the much-bombed London borough. The WVS undertook the task of collecting, packing, and dispatching the goods . . . four and a half tons of carpets, linen, cutlery, crockery and cooking utensils. Enthusiastic packers fell upon everything on which they could lay hands . . . even the office teapot disappeared . . . with tea-leaves still in it. Years later, our Croydon fellow-workers who had the job of unpacking, remembered that

teapot and their mild surprise that the kind donor had neglected to empty it first. Before the war ended I went by invitation to Croydon to see what good use had been made of the
loads of china and kitchen ware which Carlisle folk had sent
in an effort to replenish even a fraction of the lost possessions.
I trod acres of desolation overgrown with rosebay willow herb
and buddleia, and picked up a battered kettle from a heap of
rubble, which I took back and placed in my office window.

One of the incidents that will remain forever in my memory
took place one sunny August afternoon in 1945. Jewish
children from concentration camps and the streets and towns
in Czechoslovakia, Hungary and Germany were brought over
to temporary homes in the Lake District. They had experienced indescribable horrors; one, a boy of fifteen, had actually
fought in several battles and been awarded a medal. The
children were flown direct from the continent to Carlisle
Aerodrome in ten RAF Stirlings. There were close on 400 of
them, one a stowaway, and as they stepped off the planes
clutching small bundles, they smiled weakly at our compassionate faces. We had lumps in our throats as we looked at
the wan big-eyed little ones, and heard how they had been
separated from their parents, some of whom had been mur-
dered in concentration camps; the children had swarmed the
streets, homeless and hungry. We arranged them in rows on
the grass and fed them with buns and fruit, milk and orange
juice, paying special attention to the stowaway, who had to be
isolated till seen by a doctor.

Then came trains full of half-starved Dutch children brought
over to recuperate in this country; much later large numbers
of Hungarians arrived, to be comforted, found jobs and
lodgings, and fitted out with suitable clothing. Escorts were
provided for refugees of many nationalities, sad-faced women
who could not speak a word of English but embraced their
kindly escorts with tears of joy. Among the legion I recall a
little old Latvian woman who travelled across Europe from
a Displaced Persons' Camp to come to live with relatives in
Carlisle, an Austrian mother with her baby who came to join

her husband who had found work in Cumberland, and a band of German girls who arrived to work in hospitals and on farms in the county and spoke some English which they had learned in post-war Germany while working with British families. All were met and welcomed and escorted to their new homes. The end of the journey and the handing over of their charges never meant 'incident closed' to the members of escort teams. All were vitally interested in the future welfare of their travelling companions. One was 'our English godmother' to foreign girls working in Carlisle; another said, 'All the refugees I escorted knew I was a friend to whom they could turn if ever they needed help or advice.'

Do they still serve Sauce Eglantine at Balmoral, I wonder? Queen Victoria, who gave it that name, liked to eat it with milk pudding; you and I would call it Rose Hip Syrup, made from the hips of the Sweet Briar Rose boiled in a little water, rubbed through a sieve, with sugar and lemon added. Hips from garden roses and wild roses are rich in Vitamin C and there was a time when vitamin-wise mothers made sure that none of these were wasted. During the Second World War school-children and any adults who could spare the time were urged to go out into the hedges and gather rose-hips which were at their best from late September to the middle of October. They were considered particularly good in the North, because it is a strange fact that the colder the climate the richer the vitamin content. We in the WVS handled literally tons which were dispatched to manufacturers to be made into a rich syrup, a valuable addition to normal diet, and used in school-meals kitchens and hospitals. We advised mothers to give it by the teaspoonful to young children, to give it to the older ones on their ice-cream and breakfast cereals, and to make a party jelly by using half a cupful of the syrup to a tablespoonful of powdered gelatine dissolved in a little hot water.

After prolonged investigation we got our Meals on Wheels Scheme under way in 1948, the meals cooked by our own members and delivered by private car. One driver who upset

a large dish of sago pudding over the leatherwork of the back seat of her car, and had to clear up the gooey mess, has never since cared much for sago pudding.

Over the long years the scheme has grown and flourished, and now functions five days a week, with several vans, a rota of helpers, and food supplied by the School Meals Service. It is not only the fact that a hot meal is brought, ready to eat, to their door, or bedside, that is of benefit to the infirm and sick. Often they are lonely and neglected people who have few visitors; the visit of the Meals Lady, her cheerful smile and word of greeting make more difference than is realised.

Lady Reading, in one of her many amusing stories against herself, used to relate how on one occasion she took a meal to a crabbed old man in a top-storey flat in a tenement in Camden Town. 'You're late!' he greeted her, 'and you're the wrong one, anyway!' This she told to stress the importance of being punctual and dependable. Lonely people look forward to seeing their regular visitor, whether she comes to bring a meal, to do a bit of shopping, to collect a pension, to change a library book, to write a letter, or to do any other little thing that wants doing, such as shifting a wardrobe, hanging a picture or catching an escaped budgie. In the beginning we saw some pathetic cases . . . there was the old couple whose doctor had recommended us to call, who were about to sit down to their midday meal, which that day consisted of a very small meat-pie, intended for one person but divided between them.

On more than one occasion we reported an escape of gas which the old people had not noticed, and once we found a feeble-minded old lady crouching so near the fire that the blankets in which she had wrapped her feet were smouldering. Swift action was taken and she was moved to a place of safety.

When we inaugurated Darby and Joan Clubs we also started a Luncheon Club to which some fifty mobile pensioners came regularly. Speaking of cooking and feeding reminds me of the days when we had Food Leaders and earnestly studied the most practical ways of using rationed foods. Lilian Dowell, my lifelong friend, was our Chief Food Leader and was in the

habit of inviting her neighbours who from time to time were inconvenienced by cuts in gas and electricity, to come to her house and cook their meat-ration on her solid-fuel cooker. One evening when she was out a complete stranger rang the bell, thrust a packet of steak at her husband who opened the door, and said abruptly, 'Cook this, and I'll call back for it when I come home from the Pictures.' To make his meaning clear he added, 'Give it to the WVS woman . . . she does things like that, you know' and, as an afterthought, enquired anxiously 'Will there be chips with it?'

Nobody worked harder than Lady Reading who travelled thousands of miles, visiting WVS Centres, sharing every activity, cheering us on, stiffening our resolution, restoring flagging spirits, continually stressing that 'it's the job that counts'. People looked to the WVS for help, not only in emergencies but also in the day-to-day problems of life. Our advice was sought by a lady on behalf of her friend and faithful companion who was approaching pensionable age. Orphaned at the age of five, she possessed no birth certificate or Family Bible to establish her age which she believed to be nearing sixty. Enquiries were set afoot in Edinburgh, her birthplace, and it was found that she was, in fact, sixty-one, so she received her pension sooner than she expected.

An anxious London mother begged us to contact a runaway couple at Gretna Green and beseech the girl to return home. We found that money was running short and it was not hard to persuade the young man to return to his job and earn some more. The girl, meantime, looked after by WVS friends, was eventually put on the night coach to London and, the parents having relented, a happy wedding took place soon after with parents and relatives present . . . the picture that WVS had steadily painted. A grateful letter and a piece of wedding-cake were received from the bride's mother. We gladly responded to every worthy appeal, and shopped for birthday gifts and flowers which we delivered to wives, mothers, and sweethearts on behalf of their men who were still far away. Unusual requests for information included how to send a food parcel to

China, clothing to Budapest, a transistor radio to Pakistan, and how to get a twenty-first birthday cake baked in Hong Kong. All were safely accomplished.

The history of our work in hospitals dates back to the early years when our assistance was first sought in helping to get ready the first Military Hospital in the city. Over the years we operated Trolley Shops, acted as Play Ladies in Children's Wards, drove cars in the Hospital Car Service, and arranged outings for patients in Geriatric Wards. One such outing was affectionately remembered as The Day we went to see The Queen, when patients from three hospitals were taken by Mary Birkett to see Her Majesty pass along the road to Appleby. The coaches were parked at the entrance to Lowther Castle. The Queen, having been told in advance of the expedition, had promised to pass slowly, and when she saw the coaches her car slowed to a crawl. It was a wonderful moment!

We were instrumental in obtaining a push-chair for a three-year-old boy who had been in plaster from birth, and was beginning to sit up for a short time. Billy, with his nurses, made a royal procession round the hospital block; he and another little boy were so tiny that both could sit comfortably in the push-chair; they were taken on a tour of the wards and had a great reception wherever they went.

Feeding helpless patients, tidying lockers, carrying trays ... any little job that would relieve the hard-pressed nursing staff was gladly undertaken. One member went to a hospital three times daily for eleven weeks to feed an old lady who refused to take food from uniformed nurses. This member and her sister at the same time cared for the husband and sister of the difficult patient, feeding, dressing, and putting them to bed ... truly an outstanding example of good neighbourliness.

The mobile telephones which we presented to the hospitals proved a tremendous boon, appreciated by staff and patients. A doctor brought in with injuries received in a road accident was thankful to be able to speak to his wife in Glasgow and to assure her that he would soon be all right; another victim of

an accident owned a chain of garages and spent his first evening in the ward telephoning instructions to all his managers. An old country woman, rushed to hospital for emergency treatment, was fretting about affairs at home. When the telephone trolley was being wheeled past her bed she asked 'What's that?', then 'Could I speak to John?' Presently the connection was made and she who had never before used a telephone, conducted a lengthy and highly audible conversation with her son. When she had instructed him where to find her pension book, the rent book, and her teeth, she lay back on her pillows with a contented smile, saying, 'I'se be aw reet noo!' and from that day never looked back. Occasionally, a patient was inclined to monopolise the telephone, forgetting that others were waiting to use it, like the teenage lad with a host of girl-friends whose calls had to be rationed to three a night. As well as amusing incidents the WVS staff often experienced heartache from cases such as that of the bank manager, the last of whose nightly calls to his wife was 'just to say I love you' . . . next day he died. A lady who had suffered a long and painful illness had never had the strength to make telephone calls, but, the day before she died, said she would like to speak to her family who lived at some distance. She was propped up in a comfortable position and left alone to make her call, the telephone lady returning in time to hear her say, 'Good night, my darlings, it has been lovely to hear your voices.' In such circumstances, the real worth of the service was demonstrated.

A shopping service which is still greatly appreciated has been functioning since 1956 in a small hospital where all the patients are sadly handicapped. It is a trolley shop with a difference, for the goods for sale are not sweets or biscuits, but nightdresses and bed-jackets, cardigans and stockings, soap and talcum powder. Fully ten or fifteen minutes are spent with each patient so that she can make a slow and careful choice, and if a shawl is not the right colour, or soap the right scent, an order is taken and delivered next day. It gives these devoted friends such pleasure to see the contentment it brings

to the handicapped to be able to do their own shopping and choose their own things; they also read to patients, write letters for them, and read the clues in crossword puzzles to a blind lady who is a wizard at solving them.

Ashridge Park, where WVS Courses were sometimes held, was an immense castellated Gothic mansion built for the Duke of Bridgewater as the Bonar Law College, an institution dedicated to the study of Conservative principles. When it was a Centre hired to educational bodies for short courses, Clough Williams-Ellis did the conversion. At conferences one met eminent personages with important messages to give and words of encouragement to speak. Eleanor Roosevelt was a very great woman, most eloquent when speaking on the Bill for Human Rights. Her wonderful smile lit up her countenance like sunshine.

Whatever our day-to-day activities, we never forgot that Civil Defence was our primary concern and in realistic tourneys practised every phase of the Care of the Homeless under emergency conditions, which training has since proved of immense value in various civil disasters.

In 1945 the war in Europe was officially ended . . . later the war in Japan was concluded. Throughout the country these events were celebrated in memorable fashion. In the midst of our jubilation we were urged to bear in mind that for our Forces in the Far East war was still a reality. Many WVS members had been working overseas in Leave Clubs and Rest Camps being responsible for the welfare of men and women of the Forces. At one period eight Carlisle WVS members served overseas at the same time in different Clubs; Mary Taylor, the last to come home, had served at the Hook of Holland for eleven years. At home, too, WVS managed the social side of NAAFI clubs as well as in WVS Services Clubs till eventually there were no service men or women left in the neighbourhood. In 1948 there was a garden party at St James's Palace when the Queen, now the Queen Mother, received her guests. We lined up informally in the grounds and she passed among us

chatting, not only to members introduced by Lady Reading but to many others who captured her attention. Noticing, for example, Milly Beaty's overseas ribbon she stopped to chat about her service in Brussels and her work at home in Clothing Stores for which she received the British Empire Medal. The Queen strolled among us for close on two hours, wearing her WVS badge, and platform shoes which were then a very new fashion, and we marvelled at her endurance and unwearying interest in the variety of jobs that came our way.

I recall a meeting in one of the Savoy's elegant suites overlooking the river when Gerald Barry, Director-General of the South Bank Exhibition of the Festival of Britain gave us preliminary insight into something new in exhibitions, a series of things to look at, arranged to tell one continuous interwoven story. 1951 was the year of the Festival of Britain and in the midst of more onerous duties WVS members climbed on floats in parades, fed performers in pageants, staffed information bureaux and were, in general, dogsbodies to the Spirit of Carnival. There was a Thanksgiving Service in St Paul's Cathedral which Princess Mary attended in WVS uniform, and I had the first of several happy meetings with Lady Edwina Mountbatten.

When the WVS Roll of Honour, a memorial to members who were killed in the course of duty during the war, began a tour of the United Kingdom it was an honour to be entrusted with the care of this splendid book which now rests in Westminster Abbey. For a few days only it lay in Carlisle Cathedral, its illuminated pages turned by members wearing white gloves, and was displayed to over 200 people who were impressed by its significance, its beauty, and the high quality of its execution. One visitor from Australia described it as 'a fitting and beautiful record of loving work'; another wrote:

We marvelled at the fine workmanship which had gone into the making of such a memorial to the women of Britain who had died in the dark days. We read the Queen's message, we saw the pictures, each tiny leaf and

flower so perfectly drawn and painted, the people in the air-raid shelters, children playing outside an Anderson Shelter, all so vivid and alive. Slowly the pages turned . . . we read the names of the women, the towns and districts in which they lived and the variety of jobs they were doing, and at the top of one page was the name we had most wanted to see, that of my mother, a member of the Housewives' Service, just a home-loving soul, cheerful in spite of much suffering, doing her bit to help her country in the long struggle. She would never have thought of such honour as this, but I know how proud she would be to be included among those women who, like herself, answered the call.

I personally was touched to read the name of Myrtle Farquharson of Invercauld, with whom I had grown up. She was working in London in the distribution of clothing to people rendered homeless in the blitz when she was killed on duty.

In 1951 Carlisle staged a Historical Pageant in the open air for a whole week in August. We in the WVS were jointly responsible with the National Council of Women and the Women's Institutes for an Episode depicting a Fair of the eighteenth century, with side shows, a dancing bear, Punch and Judy, the arrival of a stage-coach and passengers, and a runaway wedding with an angry father in a post-chaise in hot pursuit. There were hundreds of performers and we had in our Episode the oldest and the youngest of them all. The oldest was Mrs Mapplebeck, aged seventy-five, who wore a wedding dress of grey silk, with a bride's bonnet, Paisley shawl, and shoe buckles, all of which were over a hundred years old and had belonged to her great-grandmother. She carried a reticule and a parasol trimmed with Spanish lace which were also very old. The youngest performer was Malcolm Fraser, aged seventeen months, who started his pageant career by riding on the coach all the way from Gretna Green to the scene of the Pageant, and thereafter never missed a performance. In his

embroidered pelisse, the exquisite needlework of his great-grandmother, he appeared daily, sometimes riding in a go-cart copied from a Kate Greenway picture, but more frequently as an outside passenger on the coach where he obviously enjoyed every minute of the proceedings.

It was in the following year that a deluge engulfed Lynmouth, one of Devon's loveliest villages, bringing terror. Before the storm had abated it had taken thirty-four lives. It seemed impossible that the stricken village could ever recover, but as refugees found billets in Lynton and Minehead the first of a fleet of bulldozers and excavators were already crossing Exmoor and combined emergency operations got under way. Gifts for the homeless poured in from every part of Britain, and in WVS Centres everywhere teams of workers for days on end packed bales of the best of our clothing stocks for the emergency relief of those who had lost everything they possessed in the disaster. Slowly a new Lynmouth took shape; with roads and bridges rebuilt and widened, river walls strengthened, the harbour restored. It took about two and a half years before the job was finished. Today the village shows no outward sign of its ordeal, and though a stranger may find it hard to visualise the horror of that August night twenty-three years ago there are many people still living in Lynmouth who can never forget.

My daughter, Elspeth, and I had seats in Hyde Park on the day of the Queen's Coronation in 1953. We shall never forget the splendour and colour of the Procession, the precision of the marching troops, men and women, who took part in it . . . nine thousand of them, not counting those who lined the route . . . the stirring music of the military bands and the pipers, the Life Guards trotting by with their scarlet cloaks and shining helmets, their coal-black horses catching at the jingle of their bits as if they knew that so splendid a sight must be accompanied by music. The great golden coach in which rode the Queen made all other carriages look like toys . . . to see it appear in the distance and slowly draw near, drawn by

eight greys with elaborate gold and scarlet trappings, accompanied by men on foot in the uniform of a bygone age, was like a page from a fairy story come to life.

The Queen sat rather high, well forward in her seat, her hands and every fold of her robes visible, the Sceptre and Orb glittering richly through the glass, and (womanly touch!) her little white purse lying on the opposite seat with the Duke of Edinburgh's cocked hat beside it. But before that momentous moment, when we had our first glimpse of the Queen, a long, long day had passed. We had been in our seats, by request, since 5.30 that morning, and in spite of the weather being cold and wet, there was never a dull moment throughout the day.

Nobody grumbled at the weather, the vast crowds standing in Hyde Park had been there all night and were still good-humoured. The more the rain pelted down the louder they sang, 'Land of Hope and Glory', 'It ain't gonna rain no more', 'Singin' in the rain' . . . anything to keep up their spirits while we in the open grandstand huddled under rugs and umbrellas, macintoshes and tarpaulins. In the early hours, before any of the real sights were to be seen, when foreign visitors appeared, of every colour of skin, black, brown, yellow, wearing colourful costumes and weird head-dresses, they all got a cheer . . . so did the LCC dust-cart which turned up at intervals to tidy up the road through the Park, and so did the elderly exhibitionist in vest and running shorts who insisted on running up and down the middle of the road till finally a good-natured policeman on a motor bicycle stopped him and evidently suggested that for that one day he might take his exercise elsewhere. He was seen to pat the policeman in a friendly way on the shoulder, and disappeared in the crowd. Now and again small bands of troops lining the route were withdrawn for a brief rest. During one of these sessions a lorry came round and packets of sandwiches were distributed to those men on duty.

One young soldier, on his return, protested to the man next to him, 'Here, mate, I've not got any!' The message was passed down the line. 'George hasn't any grub' till the crowd took it up and began chanting 'George hasn't any grub!

George hasn't any grub!' and presently there was thrust upon George, from all sides, more buns and fruit than he could eat!

Americans showered cigarettes upon our men, but, once the procession started, discipline was strict and behaviour rigidly formal. At intervals throughout the day, to stretch our legs, we went for a walk in Park Lane as far as the Dorchester Hotel, where we had been guests at a reception for Princess Margaret a few days before. On that occasion, in our best bib and tucker, clutching our gilt-edged invitation-cards, we had passed through the crowds at the entrance who were waiting to see the Princess; but on Coronation Day, wearing strong shoes, macintoshes, and head-scarves we mingled with the crowds that thronged the door, crowding round in spite of an imperturbable commissionaire in green livery, who tried to shoo us away and to prevent us seeing some of the celebrities who were staying at the hotel. However, we saw Humphrey Bogart; Alan Ladd stood on his balcony and waved, Hedda Hopper, the American columnist, consented to pose for her countrymen with cameras, who had shouted 'We want Hedda' till she came out wearing one of her striking hats (not the one made entirely of orchids which Shirley Maclaine sent her but one she had bought that very week in Paris). We saw two Arab sheikhs enter the hotel, clad in the flowing robes and headdresses of their country, and followed by an impressive entourage, and an irrepressible voice shouted, in the catchphrase of the day, 'Wot! No harem!' A Lancashire lady, a lone sightseer, asked us 'Is this Buckingham Palace?' When we told her it was the Dorchester Hotel, she turned away, saying in disappointed tones, 'Oh, a pub!' (What *would* the impassive and important commissionaire have said to that!) Wending our way back to our places we overheard an excited girl exclaim to a friend, 'Aren't you glad we haven't got seats . . . we wouldn't have seen Alan Ladd!'

When the Procession was over, the sun came out and Boy Scout programme-sellers shouted to the dispersing multitude, 'Buy your dry programmes now! All specially dehydrated!'

When the crowds had melted away, there was hardly an inch

of ground to be seen in Hyde Park. It was thickly covered with wet newspapers, sodden programmes, cartons, bottles, broken thermos flasks . . . it must have taken over a hundred men to clear that one corner of loyal London. When that night we returned to Hyde Park with the object of seeing the fireworks, the crowds were so dense that we could move neither forward nor backward. Women hung fainting where they stood in the tight-wedged mass, and while the pressure was so great they could not be moved to safety it also prevented them from being trampled underfoot. Elspeth and I, scared of being swept apart, eventually found ourselves within sight of the closed entrance of an underground station, through which police were permitting only four persons at a time to pass, lest the multitude surge in an uncontrollable mass down the stairs and on to the line. We saw no fireworks and thankfully boarded a train and returned to our base in Kensington. Next day we had great difficulty in finding a taxi to take us to Euston to begin our homeward journey. Practically every cab in London was engaged that day in conveying sight-seeing parties along the Coronation route.

When Lady Reading, lunching with the Mayor of Carlisle, suggested to him that WVS members should embroider in gros point and petit point a set of chairs for the Civic Centre, she promised to embroider the first one herself. This she did most beautifully and a group of talented needlewomen copied the design of the city's coat-of-arms. A dozen lovely chairs are now in the Library and are used on all special occasions.

Throughout the war the use of petrol was forbidden except for wartime duties. We cycled everywhere, through the streets and byways, laughingly quoting the poster which pointedly enquired, 'Is your journey really necessary?' Holidays were difficult, but the girls and I managed to enjoy a week under canvas one sunny July, propping our paraffin stove inside a disused chicken house, and spending long hours sunbathing in a secluded dell.

In 1954 my name appeared in the Queen's Birthday Honours

List and I found myself summoned to attend an investiture at Buckingham Palace. My two daughters, with hundreds of other guests, were ushered directly into the ballroom, while I joined the large number of men and women who were to be decorated that day. We passed through magnificent drawing-rooms, each more beautiful than the last, lingering a short while and then passing on, chatting as we went, and admiring the walls, covered with damask in shades of leaf-green, rose, and peacock blue, matching the upholstery of the gilded chairs. There were thick carpets everywhere, fine pictures, mirrors and glittering candelabra. At last we filed in alphabetical order into the vast ballroom where Yeomen of the Guard stood behind the Queen, and a Guards Band played soft music in the distant gallery. What a great experience it was to come into the presence of the Queen, to see her waiting there, so girlish and sweet, in a simple frock, to curtsey and then to hear her quiet voice speaking to me alone! While she pinned on my decoration she made me feel she was genuinely pleased to see me, conveying that impression to each and every one as they came forward.

Though the grandeur of the Palace and the dignity of the ceremony may eventually fade from my memory, I shall remember all my life the warmth of her handclasp and the friendliness of her smile. As I left the ballroom, one of the gentlemen in attendance deftly removed my medal, placed it in a case and presented it to me with a bow. When my daughters rejoined me we quietly slipped away.

It is a curious fact that, within living memory, peace and a settled existence seemed unable to attract a reigning monarch to Carlisle which during its long and vehement history has suffered much for its loyalty to the crown. Queen Victoria was known to break her journey from Balmoral for refreshment in a quiet siding at Carlisle but it took a war to get a formal Royal Visit.

In 1917, exactly 300 years after the visit of the last reigning monarch (James VI of Scotland and I of England) King

George V and Queen Mary were cheered in the streets of Carlisle. They had come to inspect the munition works at Gretna. Small wonder, then, that in 1958, when Carlisle folk were preparing to celebrate the City's Octo-Centenary Year, we were thrilled to hear that the Queen was coming to visit us, our love and loyalty sprouting from the seeds of that loyalty fought and suffered for, over the centuries . . . then, on the very morning of her visit, to learn that she was too ill to leave the Royal train! There was blank numbness in Carlisle hearts, and it was a great tribute to Prince Philip's personality that he, deputising for the Queen, turned such a damp beginning into the glorious day it was. As part of the proceedings, there was a historical procession depicting a number of episodes in the city's history. In spite of their acute disappointment at the absence of the Queen the city's pensioners had a wonderful day, having front seats on the route of the Procession and reserved seats in the Cathedral for the Service at which Prince Philip read the Lesson.

A very happy old lady was Jane Mann, whose name had been drawn 'out of the hat' and who therefore had the honour of representing all the pensioners at the Civic Luncheon given to the Prince. She looked charming in a dove grey suit with matching hat, white gloves and handbag. Seated between a High Court Judge and a Brigadier she got on famously with both, exchanging autographs and stories in Cumberland dialect. Seated opposite her were guests who had been detailed to see that she was quite happy. They afterwards declared that she had no need of special care; it was she who entertained everybody around her. Entertaining came naturally to her, for at Darby and Joan meetings she was often in demand to lead impromptu community singing in such favourites as 'A beautiful picture in a beautiful golden frame', 'Nellie Dean', 'A bird in a golden cage', 'The old rustic bridge by the mill' and the evergreen 'Love's Old Sweet Song'.

That year Carlisle women staged an Exhibition in the Gretna Hall, depicting Woman in her home from the time of the Roman Occupation to the Present Day. The script which

I prepared and used in a broadcast beforehand described the whole project:

> The idea was conceived a year ago when representatives of all the women's organisations in the city met to consider what our contribution should be to the Octo-Centenary celebrations. We felt that many stirring episodes in Carlisle's turbulent history would be recalled in pageantry, so we decided that our aim would be to bring to life the peaceful domestic scenes, to depict the ordinary housewife in her home environment through the centuries. Domestic scenes from the time of the Roman Occupation of Carlisle to the present day will be shown in a series of open-fronted rooms. In each room women will move about busying themselves with the appropriate tasks of their day. This is not a static exhibition . . . the people are real. A vast amount of reading has been done and authorities consulted, so that everything is authentic in colouring and design. We have been lent some fine pieces of period furniture and silver; other things have been made. Bowls and pots, for example, have been copied from Roman relics dug up in Carlisle, thrown at a local pottery, and baked in a school kiln. Costumes have been made at home.
>
> We have learned a great deal about the position of woman in her home in different eras. We show the comfort and efficiency of the Roman home where the matron was looked up to with respect. In Norman times the woman was used to hardship; in the absence of her husband she might be called upon to command the defence of the castle. In the times of the Crusades, when her man was away, her role was to sit at home and wait . . . it is from this period that many fine tapestries date. Contacts with foreign countries brought many comforts to the Elizabethan home . . . glass in windows, flock beds, pewter for kitchen and table use. Under the Georges, woman was expected to be wholly domestic and maternal.

In the Victorian Era she had not yet achieved emancipation, but she knew her power. The keynote today is Equality of the Sexes. It has been a delight to see how a large number of women, from over twenty organisations with widely different aims and objects, have pooled their ideas, and worked together with singleness of purpose. Everybody has worked very hard, and it has all been great fun!

The Exhibition was a great success and was visited by over 3,000 people. The seven rooms represented the Roman, Norman, Plantagenet, Elizabethan and Jacobean, Cottage and Victorian periods and Present Day.

In the Roman period, to take one example, from some fifty volunteers two-hourly rotas were arranged of four ladies—the Roman Matron, her daughter, maidservant and a guest. Sometimes there was a child, too. The size of the rooms did not permit of more actors. They were on view in the beautiful Roman room, attired in robes with lovely draperies, barbaric jewellery and sandals. The Matron reclined in an elegant attitude, toying with fan or needlework (with bone needles), the serving maid offered her a bowl of fruit or kneeling held up a mirror of polished bronze so that she might anoint herself from the unguent pot! The maid and the child played with knuckle bones, or an ancient form of draughts; the daughter played the cithera.

Later that year the Queen kept her promise to come to Carlisle; that was the happiest Royal Visit of all, 800 years after the granting of the First Charter, and 1,836 years after the Emperor Hadrian. Following their tremendous reception in the Market Hall, the Queen and Prince Philip moved to the quiet of the Cathedral, which had its dramatic moment. A few minutes before the Queen's arrival the Cathedral was plunged into darkness by a failure of the main fuse, but Dr Wadeley was master of the situation. He came down from his organ loft and, with the Queen sitting in one of the Canon's stalls, he conducted the choir in the singing of three anthems un-

accompanied. They had just reached the words, 'God is Light and in Him there is no darkness' when the lights came on again. Geoffrey Ellis, an electrician, vividly remembers how he spent the remainder of the Queen's visit to the Cathedral holding a fuse in position with a piece of wood!

Lady Reading, our much-loved Chairman, died 'in harness' and would have wished no other memorial than that the Women in Green, the army she had raised, should carry on with their mission wherever it should lead. In one of her last messages she said 'I believe that the richest and most worth-while wish I can send you today is that you may have the will to think deeply, to examine carefully, and to realise the example that is yours to live in order that it may generate in others not only confidence but the wish to do the same.' In this Year of Grace, 1977, the WRVS still soldiers on, wearing with pride the uniform, practical and hard-wearing, the colours more or less of spinach and beet. As older women retire younger women come forward to take their place. Training in tasks which are specially adapted to the needs of the community is widely recognised as a potential strength to the nation, so in their cheerful unregimented way, proud of their Yesterdays they build their Tomorrows, and in the words of Bishop King, 'go bravely on, doing the daily duties and trusting that as their day is, so will their strength be'.

J. M. Barrie declared that 'God gave us Memory so that we may have roses in December.' Olive Schreiner once said (and it could have been of my husband) 'A happy life consists of great love and much service.'

He and I kept right on to the end of the road together for nearly fifty-two years, with the sons and daughters and grandchildren with whom we have been greatly blessed, who were for us, over the long years, the source of inestimable joy and comfort, pride and thankfulness.

Those who depart loving us, love us still,
And we love them, always;

[296]

They are not really gone, those dear hearts and true,
They have only gone into the next room . . .
Presently we shall get up and follow them
And we shall all be re-united.

SOME BOOKS CONSULTED

CHAMBERS, ROBERT, LLD, *Traditions of Edinburgh*, W. R.
    Chambers, Edinburgh, 1868.
DOUGLAS, RONALD MACDONALD, *The Scots Book*, Alex,
    Maclehose, London, 1955.
DUNCAN, WALTER, 'Historical and Descriptive Notes on Parish
    Churches of Dumfries and Galloway', as yet unpublished,
    1974.
FARQUHARSON, DONALD ROBERT, *Tales and Memories of Cromar*,
    Planet Publishing House, Chatham, Ontario, 1930.
*First Fifty Years of St Cuthbert's Co-operative Association
    1869–1909* (edited William Maxwell, JP).
FRASER, DUNCAN, *Angus and the Mearns*, Standard Press,
    Montrose.
FRASER, KENNETH, MD, *A Doctor Remembers*, Robert Dinwiddie,
    Dumfries, 1961.
FRASER, MARK S., MD, DPH, FRCS.ED, *Englethwaite Industrial
    Colony*, James Beaty, Carlisle, 1925.
FRASER, W. R., *History of Laurencekirk*, Blackwood, Edinburgh,
    1880.
GIBSON, COLIN, *Bonnie Glenshee*, Culross, Coupar Angus.
HARPER, M. McL., *Crocket and Grey Galloway*, Hodder &
    Stoughton, London, 1907.
MESSENGER, ROSALIND, *The Doors of Opportunity*, Femina
    Books, 1967.

ORD, JOHN, FSA, *Bothy Songs and Ballads*, Alex. Gardner, Paisley, 1930.

SUTHERLAND, DOUGLAS, *The Yellow Earl*, Cassell, London, 1965.

YOUNG, DOUGLAS C. C., *Anthology of Scottish Verse 1851–1951*, Nelson, London and Edinburgh, 1952.

GLOSSARY

Adee, ado
Ahin, ahint, behind
Aits, oats
Aneath, beneath
Anent, with reference to
Anker, measure, varying in
 different countries, up to
 8½ Imperial gallons
Athole Brose, concoction of
 heather honey, oatmeal and
 whisky
Ava, at all
Averins, cloudberries
Back-end, autumn
Bade at hame, stayed at home
Barfit, barefoot
Bawbees, halfpennies, general
 term for money
Beadle, church officer
Be't tae, have to
Bidin', staying
Big, to build
Biggit, built
Biggin, building
Birl, spin, roll rapidly
Bittock, a little bit

Black Sugar, liquorice stick
Blin's, blinds
Bodach, old man
Boll, a measure about ten
 stones in weight
Bonnet laird, small landowner,
 cultivating his own ground
 and wearing a cap rather
 than a hat
Bothies, accommodation for
 farm-workers, where they
 cooked their own food
Bothy Ballads, songs popular
 among farm-workers
Bosie, bosom
Breeks, breeches, trousers
Breist, breast
Broust, a brewing
Bustle, a stuffed pad worn
 under the back of the skirt
 at waist-level, worn with the
 fashion's intention of
 improving the figure
But-an'-ben, two-roomed
 cottage
Butteries, morning rolls

Byre, cowshed

Caff, chaff

Cailleach, old woman

Caller, fresh

Canny, shrewd

Carle doddies, ribwort plantains used by children in duels

Carle, an old man

Carlin, a strong old woman

Cast (peats), to cut peats and expose them to dry

Catterans, reivers, freebooters

Caunnel, candle

Causey, causeway, main street

Chappit, knocked

Cheuch, tough

Clachan, small hamlet

Claes, clothes

Clash, gossip

Cleuch, cleugh, ravine

Clip cloots, cut cloth

Clockin' hen, broody hen

Coft, bought

Coles, haycocks

Cots, petticoats

Coorie, snuggle

Cooriss, Culross, Fife village where girdles (griddles) were made

Coorse, bad, rough

Corn-kisters, farm servants who sat drumming their heels on the wooden corn-bin in the bothy while they sang

Coulter, turf-cutter on the stem or beam of a plough

Crack, chat

Croft, small holding

Croon, crown

Cromach, shepherd's crook

Cushat doos, wood pigeons

Cut of wool, skein of about two ounces

Daunder, stroll

Dee, do, die

Deil, devil

Deil colic the wame o' ye, may the Devil give you a pain in your stomach

Dichts, wipes

Diddling, singing without words as an accompaniment to dancing

Dimity, stout white cotton, figured in the loom by weaving with two threads

Div, do (div ye ken, do you know)

Dockit, cut off

Doitet, confused in mind

Doos, doves, pigeons

Dormont Book, name probably indicated that book was left lying sleeping, or lying about to be referred to instantly, in case of emergency

Douce, quiet, well-mannered

Dour, stubborn

Drambuie, a Highland liqueur

Easterman Giants, Polygonum Bistorta

Eese, use

Etnach, juniper

Fa, who

Fa wad hae's, who would have us?

Fairly, expression equivalent to 'surely' or 'indeed'

Fan, fin, when

Far, where

Far past wi't, too old to work

Fat, fit, what

Faut, fault

Fee'd, Fee't, engaged for a term of work for a wage

Fegs, an exclamation of astonishment

Fermie, small farm

Fey, doomed, psychic, other-worldly

Fleggit, frightened

Fling, dancing or kicking motion

Fly cup, cup of tea served at short notice at any odd hour

Foo, how

Forebears, ancestors

Forenicht, evening

Forfochen, exhausted

Fouk, folk, people

Foul (*pronounced fool*), dirty, disgusting

Frien', friend

Freit, fret

Fulmar, a gull-like bird of the petrel family

Gang, go

Gang warily, move with discretion or caution

Gars, compels

Gauger, exciseman

Gaun, going

Gear, belongings

Gey, very

Girdle, griddle

Girds, hoops

Girnal, meal chest

Girss, grass

Glebe, land attached to a parish church

Goffered, plaited or crimped with hot tongs called goffering irons

Gomeril, fool

Goon, gown

Gowfin', golfing

Graip, agricultural fork

Greet, weep, shed tears

Grieve, farm overseer

Grumphie, pig

Gundy, toffee

Gweed, good

Haar, chill mist

Haigh, low-lying land

Hairm, harm

Hairst, harvest

Hake, hay rack

Hale, healthy

Halflin, half grown lad

Hap, cover warmly

Happin', warm wrapping, covering

Harl, rough cast

Haud thegither, hold together

Heid, head (of corn, the ears)

Hirple, to hobble or limp

Hogmanay, New Year's Eve

Howe, hollow or sheltered place

Hurl, hurll, a ride in any wheeled vehicle

Hurlled, wheeled

Ilk, kind (of that ilk, of that kind or clan)

Ilka, each, every

Inbye, inside, indoors

Jaiket, jacket

Jeel, jelly

Jings, an exclamation derived from a mild oath

Joukin', dodging, ducking

Kail, curly greens, colewort

Kailyard, cabbage-patch

Keepit, cared for, looked after

Kelpie, water-sprite said to haunt rivers at night, especially in storms

Kent faces, familiar faces

Kilmarnock bonnet, broad bonnet

Kirkin', a couple's first attendance together at a church service after their marriage

Kist, chest or trunk

Kist o' whistles, derogatory term for a church organ

Kitchen deem (dame), farm kitchen-maid

Knowes, hillocks

Kye, cows

Lade, channel leading water to a mill

Laird (*lord*), landowner

Lairt, sinking in mud

Laith, loth

Lallan, Lowland

Lane (*her*), by herself (his lane, by himself)

Langsyne, long ago

Larach, ruined foundation of a dwelling

Lauched, laughed, smiled

Lilt, a lively song

Linn, waterfall

Littlins, little ones, children

Loon, boy

Lug, ear

Luif, palm of hand

Maist, almost

Man (*her*), husband

Maun, must

Mercat Cross, a proclamation centre

Micht dae waur, might do worse

Moothies, mouth-organs

Moss, bog

Mounth, an expanse of mountain . . . applied to passes in the Grampians

Mutch, woman's cap

Nae eese, no use

Nae sae, not so

Neeps, turnips

Nevvy, nephew

Newsed, chatted

Nickums, mischievous children

Nowt, cattle

'oo', wool

Ootbye, outside, out-of-doors

Orra, odd

Orra man, orra loon, man for odd jobs

Oxter, armpit

Packman, travelling salesman

Pandrop, hard peppermint-flavoured sweet

Pented, painted

Penter, painter

Piece, open sandwich or packed lunch

Plaid (pronounced plaed, *never* plad), lightweight blanket or shawl

Port a Beul, mouth music

Preen, pin

Press, cupboard

Puckle, small quantity (also pickle)

Quaich, a drinking vessel

Queynes, quines, girls

Rantin', rollicking

Rashes, rushes

Reivin', thieving, destroying

Rive, tear apart

Rochest, roughest

Roup, sale by auction

Rowit, rolled, wrapped

Sair, sore

Sair sair, very sad

Scholars, school-children

Scraich o' day, at first light

Scunner, dislike, disgust

Shakky trummellies, quaking grass
Sheen, shoes
Skailed, emptied
Skelpin, spanking
Skirl, shriek
Snell, keen, sharp
Socht, sought
Soo, pig
Soomed, swam
Soree, soirée, social gathering
Sort, attend to
Soss, a mess
Soughin', sighing-like
Steekit, locked, bolted
Steenhive, Stonehaven
Stewartry, lands governed through a steward
Stilts, plough-handles
Stirks, steers or heifers, half-grown cattle
Stock, cattle, horses, etc, kept on a farm
Stooks, a shock of sheaves
Stot, an ox
Strae, straw
Sweir, unwilling
Swey, hinged or swivelled gantry over the fireplace
Tapôtement, percussion in massage
Tatties, potatoes
Tenty, careful, competent
Thackit, thatched
The day, today
The morn, tomorrow
The morn's morn, the day after tomorrow
Theevil, porridge-stick, spurtle
Thole, to bear pain, to endure
Thrashing (mill), threshing
Till'm, to him

Tinnies, small tin or enamel pails or mugs
Tirled at the pin, rang the door-bell
Toon, toun, farm buildings round farm-house
Tow, a string, rope
Traivelled, travelled on foot
Trauchled, weary by amount of work
Traviss, solid wooden partition between stalls in byre or stable
Trig, tidy
Troch, trough
Twa-three, a few
Twa-fa', lean-to, extension to cottage
Twae, two
Tyach (chach with a grimace!), expression of disgust or exasperation
Unco, unusually
Vasculum, botanist's collecting case
Verra, very
Vrocht, wrought, worked
Wame, stomach, belly
Want, lack
Weans, children
Whang, large piece, cut away
Wheesht, hush
Whins, gorse
Wifie, woman
Wincey, cloth, plain or twilled, a mixture of cotton and wool
Wir, our
Worsted, knitting wool
Wyse-like, sensible, suitable
Wyte, fault, blame
Yestreen, yesterday
Yowes, ewes

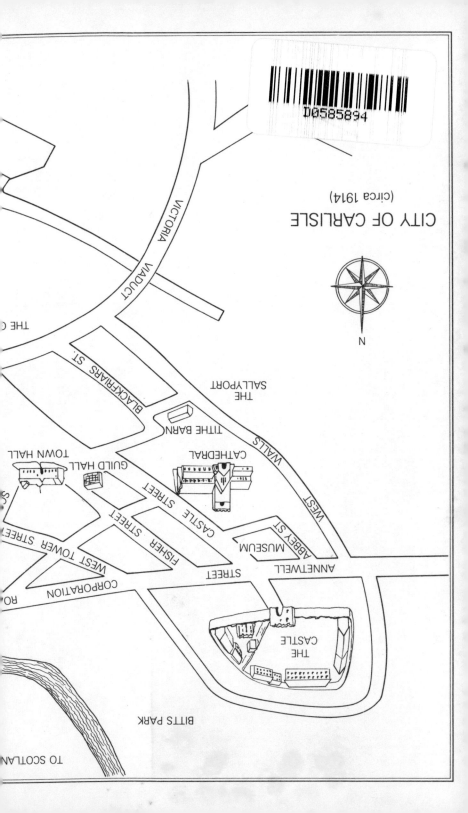

CITY OF CARLISLE
(circa 1914)

N

VICTORIA VIADUCT

THE SALLYPORT

THE C...

BLACKFRIARS ST.

THE BARN / TITHE BARN

CATHEDRAL

WEST WALLS

TOWN HALL

GUILD HALL

WEST TOWER STREET

CASTLE STREET

FISHER STREET

CORPORATION

MUSEUM

ABBEY ST

ANNETWELL

STREET

THE CASTLE

BITTS PARK

TO SCOTLAN...

RO...